Youth Unemployment and Health
A Comparison of Six European Countries

AF799710

Psychology of Social Inequality, vol. 9

Edited by Thomas Kieselbach, University of Bremen

YUSEDER Publications, no. 1

Thomas Kieselbach (Ed.)

in collaboration with
Kees van Heeringen, Michele La Rosa, Louis Lemkow,
Katerina Sokou und Bengt Starrin

Youth Unemployment and Health

A Comparison of Six European Countries

Springer Fachmedien Wiesbaden GmbH 2000

The editors:

Prof. Dr. Thomas Kieselbach is the international coordinator of the research project *"Youth Unemployment and Social Exclusion: Objective Dimensions, Subjective Experiences, and Innovative Institutional Responses in Six European Countries"* (YUSEDER). The project is supported by the Research Directorate General of the European Commission (DG XII) within the Targeted Socio-Economic Research Programme (TSER) of the 4th framework programme.

He is head of the Institute for Psychology of Work, Unemployment, and Health (IPG) at the University of Bremen (Germany) and teaches work and health psychology. From 2000-2003 he coordinates another European research project on *"Social Convoy and Sustainable Employability: Innovative Outplacement/Replacement Counselling"* (SOCOSE) in the European research programme „Improving the Socio-Economic Knowledge Base".

Prof. Dr. Kees van Heeringen is the Belgian partner of YUSEDER. He is professor of psychiatry and Chef de Clinique of the Department of Psychiatry in the University Hospital Gent and director of the Unit for Suicide Research at the University of Gent.

Prof. Dr. Michele La Rosa is the Italian partner of YUSEDER. He is professor of work and industrial sociology at the University of Bologna and director of the International Centre for Documentation and Sociological Studies on Labour Issues (C.I.Do.S.Pe.L.) in the Department of Sociology at the University of Bologna.

Prof. Dr. Louis Lemkow is the Spanish partner of YUSEDER. He is professor of sociology and vice-rector of the Autonomous University of Barcelona. He has worked in several European projects and cooperated closely with WHO/EURO in the areas of inequalities and health.

Katerina Sokou, M.A., is the Greek partner of YUSEDER. She is health sociologist, director of the Health Promoting School Sector at the Institute of Child Health in Athens, and president of the Greek Network of Health Promoting Schools.

Prof. Dr. Bengt Starrin is the Swedish partner of YUSEDER. He is professor of social work at Karlstad University in the Centre for Public Health Research. He cooperated closely with WHO/Euro on unemployment and health.

Die Deutsche Bibliothek – CIP-Einheitsaufnahme

ISBN 978-3-8100-2762-7 ISBN 978-3-663-11897-8 (eBook)
DOI 10.1007/978-3-663-11897-8

© 2000 Springer Fachmedien Wiesbaden
Ursprünglich erschienen bei Leske + Budrich, Opladen 2000
Das Werk einschließlich aller seiner Teile ist urheberrechtlich geschützt. Jede Verwendung außerhalb der engen Grenzen des Urheberrechtsgesetzes ist ohne Zustimmung des Verlages unzulässig und strafbar. Das gilt insbesondere für Vervielfältigungen, Übersetzungen, Mikroverfilmungen und die Einspeicherung und Verarbeitung in elektronischen Systemen.

Gedruckt auf säurefreiem und alterungsbeständigem Papier.

Contents

Figures

Tables

Introduction

Thomas Kieselbach

1 Object and organisation of the study

The present volume contains the first results of an international research project on youth unemployment and social exclusion describing the most up-to-date research of youth unemployment and health in six European countries. The project "Youth Unemployment and Social Exclusion: Objective Dimensions, Subjective Experiences, and Innovative Institutional Responses in Six European Countries" (YUSEDER) is supported by the Research Directorate General of the European Commission (DG XII) within the Targeted Socio-Economic Research Programme (TSER) of the 4th Framework Programme. The YUSEDER research project tries to answer some crucial questions with regard to the risk of social exclusion associated with long-term youth unemployment.

The European Commission launched a call for proposals looking for new knowledge of the key mechanisms linking the experience of long-term youth unemployment to various dimensions of social disintegration, conceived of in the theoretical framework of social exclusion. In this context, not only the mechanisms exacerbating the stress of unemployment (vulnerability factors) but also the protective mechanisms preventing or reducing the risk of social exclusion have to be taken into consideration. The second research question relates to new options of institutional and political intervention and counteraction in different national contexts. These analyses will be undertaken in three Northern European countries (Sweden, Belgium, Germany) and three Southern European countries (Spain, Italy, Greece).

The consortium of the research project is coordinated by Thomas Kieselbach (University of Bremen, Germany)[1] and is composed of the following national partners: Prof. Dr. Kees van Heeringen (University of Gent, Belgium)[2], Prof. Dr. Michele La Rosa (University of Bologna, Italy)[3], Prof. Dr. Louis Lemkow (Autonomous University of Barcelona, Spain)[4], Katerina Sokou, M.A. (Greek Network of Health Promoting

---

1 Members of the German research team: Thomas Kieselbach, Gert Beelmann, Andrea Stitzel, Ute Traiser, Ronald Meyer

2 Members of the Belgian research team: Kees van Heeringen, Wouter Vanderplasschen, Tine Willems, Gwendolyn Portzky

3 Members of the Italian research team: Michele La Rosa, Vando Borghi, Federico Chicchi, Roberto Rizza

4 Members of the Spanish research team: Louis Lemkow, Josep Espluga, Josep Baltierrez

Schools and Institute for Child Health Athens, Greece)[5] and Prof. Dr. Bengt Starrin (University of Karlstad, Sweden)[6].

The empirical research in the six countries is, on the one hand, dedicated to different national problems of youth unemployment, and on the other hand follows different scientific orientations and methodologies, namely sociological, psychological, psychiatric, and cultural.

The research project is organized around three work packages:

Workpackage 1:
- empirical evidence on youth unemployment and health in each country
- clarification of the concept of social exclusion
- description of social exclusion of different groups of young people at risk

Workpackage 2:
- qualitative analysis of 50 long-term unemployed young people in each country with regard to
  - antecedent variables facilitating long-term unemployment among young people,
  - the main factors contributing to social exclusion/inclusion (vulnerability factors and protective factors), and
  - the health effects associated with social exclusion.

Workpackage 3:
- innovative institutional responses on a local, regional and national level in various societal sectors to counteract the risk of social exclusion as a consequence of long-term unemployment.

The EU has developed a European Employment Strategy defined in the Presidency Conclusions at the European Council Meeting on Employment in Luxembourg in November 1997. As a result of this summit, the 1998 Employment Guidelines formulated recommendations to be followed by the Member States in which it is stated that "Member States will ensure that every unemployed young person is offered a new start before reaching six months of unemployment, in the form of training, retraining, work practice, a job or other employability measure." (European Commission, 1998).

The Employment Guidelines would nearly abolish the group of long-term unemployed young people when strictly put into practice. Nevertheless, at the time of the research study (1998-2000), the national research groups had generally no difficulties in finding members of the target group. The results of this research provides a relevant contribution to the formulation of a European as well as national employment policies by bringing together the experiences from different European countries that vary considerably with respect to
- the labour market conditions for young people,
- the transitions from school to work,
- and the support (economic and noneconomic) available for young people trying to find their entrance into the labour market,

---

5 Members of the Greek research team: Katerina Sokou, Demetra Bayetakou, Valentine Papantoniou, Katerina Christofi

6 Members of the Swedish research team: Bengt Starrin, Erik Forsberg, Marina Kalander-Blomqvist, Ulla Rantakeisu

- as well as the temporary or (continuous) alternative options of work in the submerged economy.

2 The social and scientific background of YUSEDER

Mass unemployment will clearly be an issue of major political relevance in the future, and European governments will be assessed in terms of how they propose and actually succeed in solving labour market problems. Since the beginning of the 80s, increases of unemployment rates have reached an even higher plateau after each economic recovery despite a general increase in the number of employees. On the other hand we find tendencies of deregulation and flexibilisation in many countries which lead to a widespread precarisation of the labour market (Kieselbach & Svensson, 1988). During the second half of the 90s we also find, however, a considerable reduction of unemployment rates in various European countries like the Netherlands, the United Kingdom, and Denmark. This can be explained partly by demographic changes, but also by innovative labour market policies, the creation of a low-income sector, the extension of part-time work, and last but not least, by a general economic recovery. Despite these trends which are slackening the labour market, the problem of long-term unemployment has not yet been resolved in most EU countries. This means that long-term unemployed people normally have not profited primarily from the amelioration of the economy.

The starting point of our research is the factual normalization of temporary exclusion from paid work for an increasing number of people capable and willing to work. Occupational transitions (passing from one occupational position to the other) have already increased and will do so even more in future. They tend to replace the normative perspective of a lifelong relationship to a certain company or profession against a patchwork biography of different phases within, between and out of employment. Many voices claim that we are at a time of change between a declining industrial society and something new. This new (or incipiently new) society has been variously referred to as the information society, the service society, the knowledge society, the risk society or simply the post-industrial society. Unfortunately, the difficulties of assigning a name to this "new" society arise from the fact that it is in an empirical vacuum of which we have no experience.

We cannot, of course, say much about what awaits us in the future. Opinions diverge, with some believing in a victory for common sense and the welfare society, with others forecasting the breakdown of societal links. It is common among debators and intellectuals to stress that we are on the threshold of a divided society. The kind of society they are talking about has got the name of the 2/3 society. The 2/3 society refers to a society consisting of two groups. A majority (two-thirds) will live in good financial, social and health conditions. Economic development will mean that their conditions will steadily improve. However, a minority (one-third) will be living under difficult conditions, with increasingly severe financial, social and health problems. In such a society, societal cohesion will have broken down.

The apprehensions of a coming 2/3 society will probably increase the forces leading to social exclusion. In such a society greater and greater numbers will encounter serious problems in meeting their needs. Furthermore a divided society increases polarisation and class differences between groups. In the scenario the welfare state will face severe tensions because in the scenario social security systems have been strongly weakened, and the safety nets that are supposed to catch those in need no longer break the falls of those in financial difficulty as well as they used to. In future, the social aspects will become increasingly serious, causing problems that will have to be solved.

Prognoses of the development of the European labour markets expect a further aggravation of the difficulties especially for the young generation. Therefore it seems to be important to find out

- the longer lasting effects of the exclusion from the labour market, that is, the exclusion from social participation within personal relationships, groups and social institutions,
- the key mechanisms which link labour market exclusion and social exclusion,
- the most vulnerable groups exposed to these processes,
- the contribution of social institutions to counteract tendencies of segregation and marginalization,
- the lessons to be learned from innovative interventions in other member states.

In many Western countries youth unemployment is presently characterized by a transition from unemployment of a predominantly temporary kind to consolidation and structuralization. In the member states of the European Community, there are more than five million unemployed young people betweeen 15 and 25 years of age. Of these, about one third must be counted among the long-term unemployed (i.e., those unemployed for longer than one year). The average rate of youth unemployment has been in recent years twice as high as the overall rate.

Significant research on youth unemployment comes mainly from Great Britain and Australia and, to a lesser degree, from Germany. Besides Italy and Spain, Australia and Great Britain were among those Western countries with an exceptionally high rate of youth unemployment. Astonishingly little research on the impact of youth unemployment has been done in the USA. This may possibly be explained by a different type of transition, as compared with other countries like Germany, between the educational system and employment, which leads to temporary unemployment (interrupted by several short-time, low-paid jobs) being regarded as quite ordinary for a young person's biography. That particular stage, which lasts up to the age of about 22, has been named "floundering period" (Hamilton, 1987).

A number of contributions have raised the question of a specific vulnerability of young people to the experience of unemployment (Roberts, 1984; Schwefel, 1986; Spruit & Svensson, 1987; Warr, 1984, Kieselbach, 1988). This means asking, on the one hand, which age group suffers more from psychosocial stress associated with unemployment and, on the other, whether there are age-dependent qualitative differences. A few arguments will, in the following, be put forward in order to elucidate the particular features of psychosocial stress with juveniles, emphasizing possible long-term effects (cf. Roberts, 1984):

Whether young people or adults suffer worse from the condition of unemployment cannot, considering the existing body of research, be stated unequivocally. Although there are indications that affliction with psychiatric symptoms is correlated with age in a nearly curvilinear way, that is, that affliction is strongest for the unemployed of medium age, weaker for the young and weakest for the older unemployed (Jackson & Warr, 1984), merely to ask for the most vulnerable group does not make sense. The purpose behind a question like this is to identify one group among the unemployed which is particularly vulnerable to psychosocial damage. By trying to grasp and to compare effects one-dimensionally only, however, the question is too short-sighted.

A lower vulnerability of young people with regard to psychiatric morbidity contrasts with higher ratings in other dimensions of stress. In a content analysis of qualitative data Viney (1983) found significantly higher rates for young unemployed below 20 years of age with regard to anxiousness, anger, helplessness, guilt and shame than for older ones. Schober (1978), concludes from a comparison of stress profiles that unemployed juveniles suffer considerably more from domestic tensions and attributions of blame, whereas adults more intensively perceive social isolation and stigmatization induced by unemployment. So we are obviously more precise in talking of age-dependent differential stress profiles.

Young people experience unemployment as a frustration of expectations which, in their previous educational career, they had been made to regard as crucial goals and orientations and which had been a major motivational basis for scholastic achievements. Being unemployed, to them, does not mean losing the positive concomitants of having a job. Furthermore, school leavers may indeed, initially, welcome unemployment as a relief from the exactions of the final stage of their school career (Winefield, Tiggemann, Winefield & Goldney, 1993).

One of the important results is that we find a widening developmental gap opening between unemployed and employed young people. This gap is determined, on the part of the unemployed, by stagnation and regression as a consequence of not being allowed to work as well as by the experience of unemployment as a cumulation of "daily hassles" and, on the other hand, by the effects of working (like greater independence, acquisition and utilization of skills, etc.) on employed juveniles.

When comparing the health hazards of unemployment for adults and young people we must take into account the good state of health of juveniles which may mitigate immediate negative health consequences of a critical life event such as unemployment. However, a riskier health behavior on the part of unemployed juveniles (with regard to eating and sleeping habits, alcohol and tobacco consumption, personal hygiene, and sporting activities) may well lead to delayed damage to their health, the extent of which cannot, at present, easily be estimated (Olafsson & Svensson, 1986). Finnish researchers who did find differences in the health behavior of unemployed and employed 19-year old males expressed the belief that the unemployed young people of today are likely to be the sick middle-aged men of tomorrow because they differ in precisely those health behavioral aspects that we already know to have a major impact on future health (Kannas & Hietarharju, 1979; quoted in Janlert, 1985).

Furthermore we are justified in assuming that empirical data on unemployed young people are somewhat marred by a conservative (under-)estimation of psychosocial stress because of a stronger selection of samples within that group (due to disappearance or refusal in cases of very bad affliction).

The proposed research aims at identifying central mechanisms linking unemployment and social exclusion. The recommendations derived from the results of the proposed research activities in every partner country of the consortium will allow policy makers to develop specific targeted measures to counteract social exclusion in order to harmonize the development of different countries within the EC. This can form a relevant contribution to facilitate the achievement of the goal of the European Commission of a simultaneous economic and social progress in all member states (Commission of the European Communities, 1994). The innovative policies necessary to cope with high rates of unemployment, especially of youth unemployment, require a deeper understanding of these processes of victimization and of higly vulnerable groups being driven out of the social fabric into the margins of society, thereby also weakening the resources to reenter the m ainstream of society. The development of a support framework for people in occupational transitions and outside the labour market will reduce the risk of being socially excluded by: concepts of social guidance and counselling for those being in occupational transitions, individualized concepts of facilitating the entrance into the labour market, innovative concepts of unemployment as a psychosocial moratorium related to the acquisition and exertion of qualifications, personality features and interests.

Comparative Report

Thomas Kieselbach, Gert Beelmann & Andrea Stitzel

1 Development of youth unemployment

1.1 Development of total unemployment figures

In the past 25 years, increasing numbers in total unemployment can be observed in all countries of the EU. This development was deeply influenced by the world-wide economic collapse in the mid-70s (the oil crisis) and the early 80s. At this time a considerable amount of basic unemployment had been reached in most European countries. In the meantime, also the increasing globalisation, flexibilisation, and world-wide economic competition are important factors influencing the rise of the unemployment rates. Furthermore, specific additional events have been named by the countries participating in this research project. In *Greece*, the fall of the dictatorship and the Turkish invasion in Northern Cyprus led to an increased instability of the economic system. In *Spain*, the growth of the active population caused by the baby boom in the 60s is seen as an additional reason for the spectacular increase in unemployment in the 80s. In *Germany*, the reunification process has especially influenced the labour market developments greatly.

In some countries (*Belgium, Spain*) the development of registered unemployment is characterised by an increase and decrease of rates. Following the Eurostat Data[1], in 1984, Belgium reached an estimated peak value of 11.1%, which then fell to 6.6% in 1991 and climbed to 10% in 1994. These numbers decreased again slightly – reaching 9.5% in 1997. In *Germany*, a continuous increase in unemployment from the mid-70s on can be determined. In 1997, the rate was at 9.7%. In comparison to the other partner countries, the development in *Sweden* was slightly better. After small variations on a low level in the 70s and 80s, the total unemployment figures rose from the early 90s to a value of about 10% in 1997. In *Greece*, numbers rose from a minimal 1.5% in 1975 to 9.6% in 1996 with the greatest rise in the early 80s. The development of the *Italian* unemployment figures is

---

1 Within the Comparative Report reference is made only to statistical data from Eurostat, due to comparability reasons, whereas within the different national reports specific national statistics are also taken into consideration. This means that the unemployment rates referred to in the Comparative Report are based upon the Eurostat employment surveys executed each year in the spring. These statistics can show considerable differences in comparison to the official national annual unemployment rates. For example, in Germany the official annual rate for 1997 amounts to 14% (adjusted to EU norms based upon all dependent and self-employed persons as denominators this number is 12.6%) as compared to the Eurostat unemployment rate of 9.7%.

comparable to the Greek ones. In 1975, the rate was a relatively low 4.8%. However, a continuous rise in the last 10 years has led to a figure of 12.1% in 1997. In *Spain*, peak figures were reached in the mid-80s (21.6%) and the mid-90s (24.1%).

Figure 1 demonstrates the developments of the overall unemployment figures for the period from 1983 until 1997.

Figure CR-1: General unemployment rates in six European countries, 1983-1997, seasonally nonadjusted

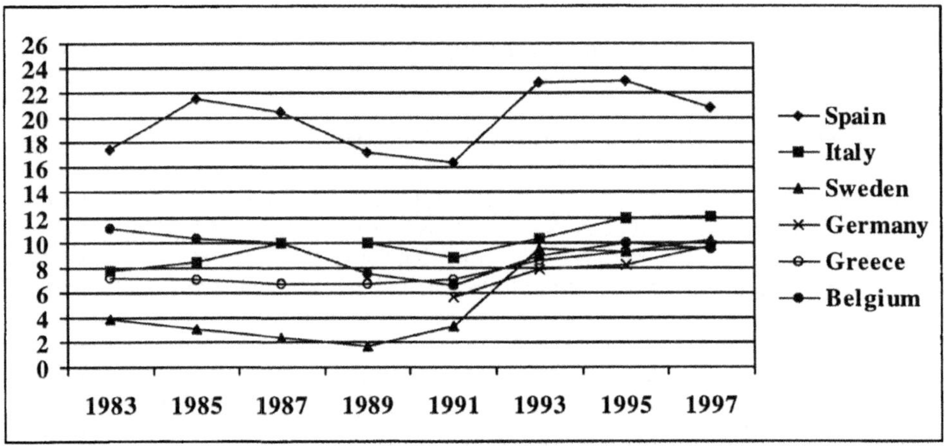

Source: Eurostat.

1.2 Development of youth unemployment

With the exception of Germany, the extent of youth unemployment in comparison to the total unemployment rates is significantly higher in all partner countries. Because of the dual education system and the associated longer periods of training in *Germany*, the rates of young unemployed people are about those of the adult unemployed. The lack of such an educational system in the partner countries is reflected especially in the unemployment rates among the 15- to 19-year-olds. Each partner country shows a considerably higher unemployment rate in this age group than in older young people. However, despite the similar developments of young and older unemployed persons, the German labour market is characterised by a high disparity between the West and East German youth. Especially the young unemployed between the ages of 20-24 years in East Germany are extremely affected by unemployment.

In *Belgium*, the development of youth unemployment rates has been similar to the total rates. At present, a stabilisation, or even a small improvement can be observed. However, the rates are still two to three times higher than the overall rates with female unemployment rates being especially high. An extreme situation can be found in the region Wallonia where over 40% of all females under 25 are unemployed. Parallel to the increase in total unemployment in the early 90s, in *Sweden*, youth unemployment increased rapidly and equally fast for the 16- to 19-year-olds and the 20- to 24-year-olds. After a slight decrease in the mid-90s, both age groups rates are at about 15% and thus twice as high as the overall unemployment rate. As opposed to the Belgian situation, the gender differences in Sweden are opposite: the rates are higher among men than among women (1995: 16.6% vs. 14.0%).

Youth unemployment figures in *Greece* are also considerably higher than those for adults. Well over a third of young people between 15 and 19 years of age were unemployed in 1995. Rates among young women are especially high. In 1995 the rate for young women between 15-24 years amounted to 37.7% as compared to that for men which was 19.4%. In big cities many affected young persons survive by working in the underground economy. In *Italy*, the proportion of young unemployed people constitutes two-thirds of the total number of unemployed people with lower numbers for young men (1997: 29%) than young women (1997: 37.7%). The number of young persons who have been looking for a job for more than 12 months is exceptionally high in this country (approximately two-thirds of the young unemployed). Among the partner countries, *Spain* shows the highest rate of youth unemployment. In addition to a continuous rise in the 70s, unemployment figures rose in the late 70s and early 80s to a peak value of nearly 40%. Especially among the 16- to 19-year-olds, the rate sometimes exceeded 50%.

A strongly sex-biased differentiation as in *Greece* can be seen in nearly all partner countries. Unemployment rates for young women are also significantly higher in *Belgium*, *Spain*, and *Southern Italy*.

Figure 2 (women) and Figure 3 (men) provide an overview of the youth unemployment rates for women versus men aged 15-24 years in the six countries participating in this project[2].

Figure CR-2: Youth unemployment rates for WOMEN age 15-24 years in six European countries, 1985-1995, seasonally nonadjusted (no data available for Spain in 1985)

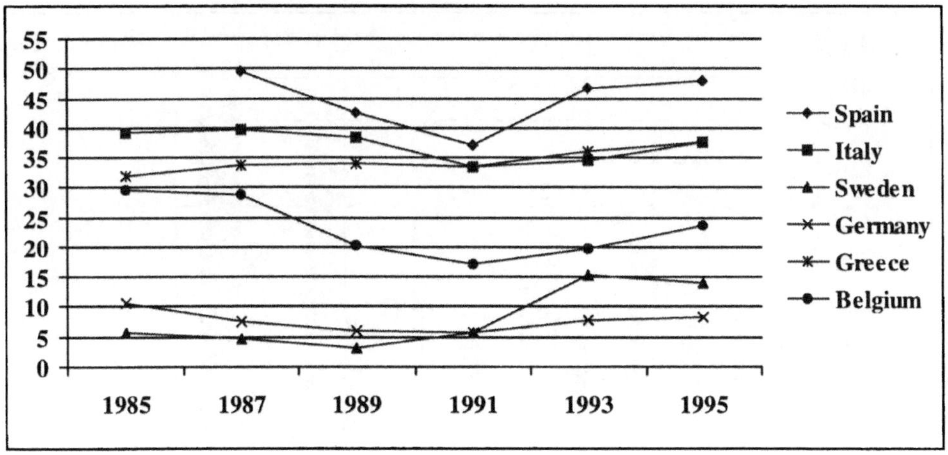

Source: Eurostat 1996.

2 The numbers of the total youth unemployment rates were not available in the Eurostat Yearbook 1996.

Figure CR-3: Youth unemployment rates for MEN age 15-24 years in six European countries, 1985-1995, seasonally nonadjusted (no data was available for Spain in 1985)

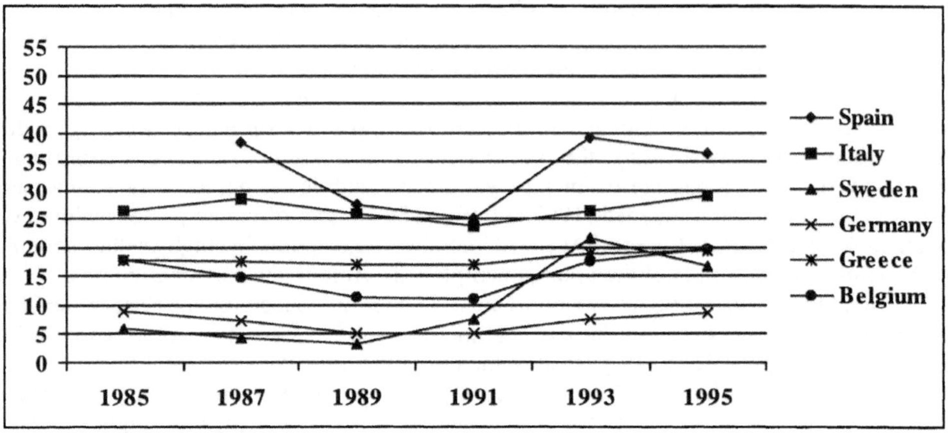

Source: Eurostat 1996.

To allow for an easy comparison of the overall unemployment rates with the youth unemployment rates for persons less than 25 years of age, the following figure provides an overview for the year 1997.

Figure CR-4: Overall unemployment rates vs. youth unemployment rates (>25 years of age) for six European countries in 1997

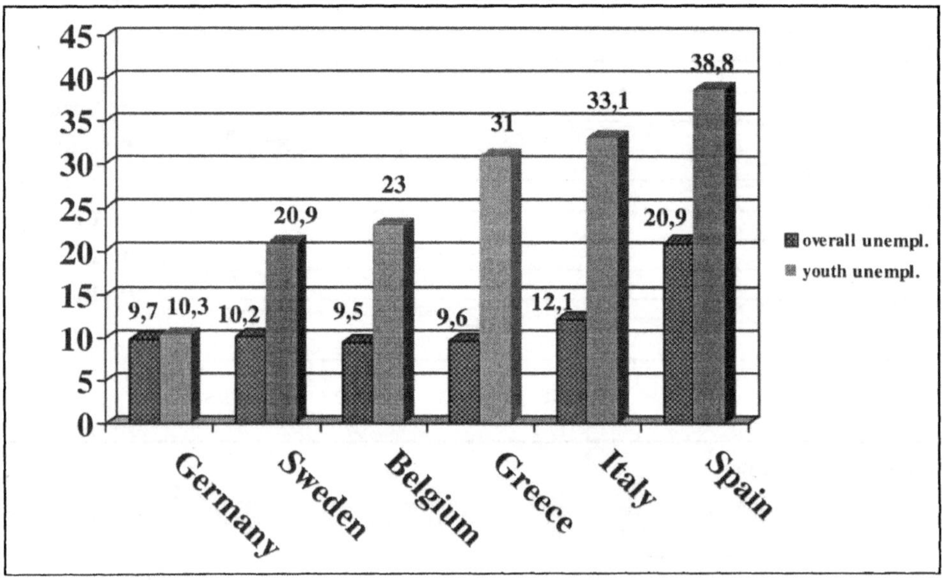

Source: Eurostat 1998.

1.3 Regional differences

Among the partner countries, regional disparities in terms of employment structure are highest in *Italy* with a territorial dualism splitting Southern and Northern Italy. In the 80s, the total figures in the South were twice as high as the figures in the North. Currently, they are three times higher in Southern Italy. This disparity is found also for the young unemployed. In *Belgium*, clear differences are apparent between the unemployment figures for Flanders, Wallonia, and Brussels. Whereas Wallonia and Brussels have a particularly high rate of youth unemployment, figures in Flanders are distinctly lower. In *Germany*, a clear disparity of economic growth has developed since the reunification. In East Germany, unemployment rates are twice as high as in the West. Especially youth unemployment in the East considerably exceeds that of the West. Since the beginning of the 90s the regional differences in *Sweden* are of less importance. In earlier times predominantly the forest regions of Sweden were affected by unemployment. In *Greece* regions with an agricultural structure are especially affected by unemployment. This pattern can also be found in *Spain* where the employment situation in the South is more tense than in the North. These agricultural regions have shown much higher unemployment rates than those areas where most people work in the service or industrial sectors (e.g., Madrid or Catalonia). Nevertheless, the labour market fluctuations in industrialised areas are much higher than in rural regions.

1.4 Specific qualities of the labour market (trends)

Specific qualities and developments of the labour market need to be reflected in conjunction with features of the structural situation and the welfare state. All countries stress the importance of reorganising the labour market. In *Germany*, discussions of the problematic labour market situation are characterised by the key words globalisation and flexibility. The new German government has promised to provide 100,000 jobs for young unemployed persons within the first year of their governmental period. Similarly, *Belgium* pursues a policy of lowering national insurance rates and the costs of labour as well as the control of illicit work. The integration of young people into the labour market has special priority. The labour market situation in *Sweden* is very dissimilar to that of the rest of Europe. For many years there were nearly no unemployed persons in Sweden. However, since the 90s unemployment has been on a steady rise, and industrial workers have been hit especially hard. Apart from a high rate of underemployment, full employment in *Greece* is very rare in comparison to the partner countries. The number of self-employed is very high, however, because many people work in agriculture. In the current period of massive unemployment problems, Greece is undergoing a transitional period leading to an increase in various employment initiatives and a more profound body of research on these issues. The employment situation in *Italy* is predominantly characterised by the socio-economic differences between the South and the North. Industrial mass production is not distributed equally across the country. Many people, especially in the Southern parts, work in the primary sector where underemployment and problems with employment are very apparent. In *Spain*, periods of economic upturn and recession have alternated regularly. Currently, after a policy of flexibilisation of employment relations, an active employment policy has been adopted. Education and training, opportunities for obtaining additional qualifications as well as the support of part-time employment are the central aims of the Spanish social policy. Last but not least, these are measures to prevent illicit work, which especially in the partner countries of *Southern Europe*, constitutes a fundamental economic problem.

2 International debate on youth unemployment and health

The international debate on youth unemployment and health has been led mainly by research studies from Australia, the UK, and the USA. Except for the British studies, the overall debate in Europe can be described as rather rudimentary. Since the middle of the 70s, in the above mentioned countries, extensive longitudinal studies have been conducted. Partially due to very differentiated methodological procedures, huge sample sizes (above 5,000 interviewees), and an unusually high return rate (above 95%), meaningful results could be obtained showing that an unwanted situation of unemployment during adolescence leads to a destabilisation of the health and well-being of the affected persons (*British studies*: Banks & Jackson, 1982; Jackson, Stafford, Banks & Warr, 1983; Ullah, Banks & Warr, 1985; Warr, Banks & Ullah, 1985; Banks & Ullah, 1988; *Australian studies*: Gurney, 1980a, 1980b, 1981; Tiggemann & Winefield, 1984; Patton & Noller, 1984, 1990; Winefield & Tiggemann, 1985; Feather & O'Brien, 1986; Winefield, Tiggemann & Goldney, 1988; O'Brien & Feather 1990; Winefield et al., 1993; *studies from the USA*: Dooley & Prause, 1995, 1997; Prause & Dooley, 1997; *Review of the literature*: see Kieselbach 1988; Spruit & Svensson, 1987; Olafsson & Svensson, 1986; Winefield, 1997).

Since the 90s, in most western industrialised countries, an increase in unemployment can be observed – with youth unemployment rates being two to three times higher than the general unemployment rates in most OECD countries. Among these countries, Spain has by far the highest youth unemployment rates (43.2%, 1993), whereas The Netherlands has comparatively low figures for young people (10.2%, 1993). Australia (18.6%) and Great Britain (17.3%) assume a middle position.

In general, health-related impairments due to unemployment during adolescence are usually seen as being less serious than for adults (Broomhall & Winefield, 1990; Rowley & Feather, 1987). As outlined by Jackson and Warr (1984), a curvilinear relationship can be found in the sense of the highest intensity of health impairment among unemployed middle aged persons when compared to older and young persons who display lower values (see Kieselbach, 1988). However, with regard to the social and economic development within a country, the importance of youth unemployment cannot be overestimated. According to Winefield (1997), unemployment among young persons has to be understood as a special problem when compared to the situation of adults (see also Kieselbach 1988; Spruit & Svensson, 1987), and it can be summarised that:

1. As outlined above, in most countries, youth unemployment rates are clearly above the level for adult unemployed persons.
2. Unemployment during adolescence has an enormous impact on the overall psychosocial development. At the same time, the affected persons are also denied all those aspects of work which stimulate personality development. Whereas employment provides the possibility to use their own experiences and abilities thus leading to an increase in independence, unemployed persons are often confronted

with more and more daily problems (so-called daily hassles) and an overall retardation of their own development. This has the consequence of an increasing developmental gap between unemployed and employed young persons.

3. In the international debate, alienation and increased deviant and anti-social behaviour are assumed to be one of the effects of unemployment.
4. In general, unemployed young persons are at increased risk for displaying suicidal behaviour.
5. The meaning of work is devalued due to unemployment (decreased work orientation of youth with length of unemployment, multiple spells of unemployment).

Despite the fact that the relation between unemployment and low levels of mental health and well-being has often been investigated and verified (see Winefield, 1995), different understandings exist with regard to the causation of the interrelation. Two explanations claim validity. On the one hand it is assumed that unemployment leads to mental impairments (causation hypothesis), and on the other hand, unemployment is seen as being a result of disadvantaged living conditions including lower health prerequisites (selection hypothesis).

From a methodological point of view, longitudinal studies are claimed to be necessary in order to assess causes and effects of health effects. One of the most useful study designs for adolescence are prospective longitudinal studies among school-leavers. In such a design, the first measurement is executed during the time the pupils are still in school. Further measurements take place at several times after they have left school. The main advantage of this design lies in the fact that the data obtained while still being in school is not influenced by an anticipated situation of unemployment. In addition, the mental impairments associated with unemployment are influenced by financial stress to a much lesser degree (Winefield, 1995).

In the following, three key longitudinal studies with different subgroups will be described on an exemplary basis. One of the first studies from 1978 was conducted in Leeds (UK) (Banks & Jackson, 1982). At three different times of measurement, all in all, 1,700 school-leavers were interviewed over a period of two years. Depending upon their employment status, significant differences in health status could be assessed. These differences were not detected during the time these persons were still in school. The General Health Questionnaire (GHQ-12) was used for the measurement of mental impairment. A developmental cleavage could be found in the way that symptoms of mental impairment increased among the unemployed youth, whereas they significantly decreased among those persons who went directly into work or a further qualification program after school. These results are also an important indicator for the stabilising effect of employment. All in all, this study revealed unambiguous causal effects of the influence of unemployment on mental health.

In an Australian study, 3,139 young persons were interviewed between 1980 and 1990 (Winefield, Tiggemann, Winefield & Goldney, 1993). The study incorporated a wide variety of psychosocial measurement instruments, and covered both differentiated cross-sectional and longitudinal evaluations of young persons with different occupational statuses. All in all, four groups were distinguished: 1) satisfied employed, 2) dissatisfied employed, 3) unemployed, and 4) students. Overall the central result of the study was that 'satisfied employed' persons and 'students' showed much better mental well-being when compared to 'unemployed' and 'dissatisfied employed' young persons. The distinction made between satisfied and dissatisfied reflects the assumption that work in general cannot have a protective influence per se. Instead, the subjective satisfaction with the respective job also has to be considered.

Likewise, Prause and Dooley (1997) stressed the quality and also the continuity of employment as one of the central aspects with regard to mental health. Within this study, 3,000 school-leavers were questioned in the USA between 1980 and 1987 with regard to central changes to their self-esteem after they had left school. The evaluation distinguished between employed and unemployed persons with the latter one being divided into the following subgroups: 1) unemployed, 2) intermittently unemployed, and 3) involuntarily part-time employed. When controlling for moderating factors it could be shown that the significantly lowest self-esteem values were among the group of underemployed young persons when compared to their employed peers. The authors stressed that it is important to also take into account the social and societal context upon which underemployment develops.

Despite further empirical evidence for these results from other longitudinal studies, differences could also be found with regard to different mental health constructions. According to Feather (1990), the inconsistent results within youth unemployment studies have to be related to three different aspects: First of all, the use of inconsistent instruments has to be criticised. Specific measurement scales are regarded as very sensitive to minimal changes, and provide differences between employed and unemployed persons. The GHQ (General Health Questionnaire) measures minor psychiatric symptoms (pre-clinical status) and is rather susceptible to changes in health status. Instead, the construct self-esteem is a relatively stable characteristic with which manifest psychiatric disorders can be measured. In this regard, Warr (1984) distinguishes between less constant (e.g., life satisfaction) and constant (self-esteem) characteristics of the person. A further criticism or explanation for variances within the available results is related to the low comparability of the sample structure of most longitudinal studies. In the British studies, mainly young persons with low school degrees were interviewed whereas Australian school-leavers were recruited from high school. Finally, different results have to be viewed in the light of cultural differences and also the work orientation within the different educational systems.

In sum, it can be said that according to international results that youth unemployment is leading to severe health impairments. Although Winefield (1995) refers to the highest health consequences for middle aged unemployed persons, the hypothesis that youth unemployment substantially leads to an intensification of health problems in later years due to effects of protraction is also supported (see Janlert, 1985; Kieselbach, 1988).

3 Youth unemployment and health in six countries of the EC

3.1 Available studies

When comparing the number of studies conducted within the countries participating in the YUSEDER project, it becomes obvious that most research on youth unemployment and health has been conducted in Germany with a total of 18 studies, followed by Sweden with nine different research studies (from the reported 15 publications, seven originate from one and the same research study conducted by Hammerström). In Belgium only five, and in Italy and Spain only six research studies each could be found on this matter which refers to young persons between 15-29 years of age. In Greece, no material dealing especially with youth unemployment and health exists. The results presented from Greece could only be extracted from general studies which were, in part, not even necessarily devoted to unemployment research.

In Sweden very few studies on unemployment and its effects on the health of the affected young persons were conducted in the 80s due to the relatively late rise of the general unemployment and youth unemployment rates not before 1990. The same is true for Italy despite the rather high youth unemployment rates in this country already at that time. Other factors such as the higher importance of the family as a support system for young persons, and also the buffering effect of the submerged economy might have been a reason why this issue did not start to be of concern until a few years ago on both a public and a scientific level. In Spain, the majority of studies were conducted at the end of the 80s – interestingly, this was a period of decreasing unemployment whereas the first five years of the 90s were years of rising unemployment rates. However, for this period of time no empirical research studies could be located. In Germany, the first study on the link between youth unemployment and health had been conducted as early as 1952 with most other articles being published in the 70s and the beginning of the 80s. One of the reasons for this situation might be that the remaining high youth unemployment rates in Germany led, after an initial interest, to a decline in the attention that was given to this subject in general. Belgium provides a more balanced picture with articles being published both in the 80s and 90s.

Considering how little well-known most research on youth unemployment and health from the six YUSEDER countries is within the international scientific community – an exception being only the Swedish studies from Hammarström – the question of level of empirical evidence comes into focus. Most studies have a quantitative, cross-sectional design and a sample size between 100 and 400 with some studies also including up to 1,000 persons and more. Specifically in this regard the Swedish studies from Hammarström (1986, 1991, 1994, 1996) with a sample size above 1,000, and the German IAB (Institut für Arbeitsmarkt- und Berufsforschung) study from 1987 with around 2,500 persons are worth mentioning. In Belgium, Germany, Spain, and Sweden the studies usually contain control groups. In Italy only two studies could be found with such a design. However, in several cases it has to be questioned whether the reported groupings were designed from a theoretical point of view before the respective study was conducted, or if they were "only" a more or less accidental result of the research project. Statistical analysis was done in all countries, both on a descriptive and analytical level, with more powerful statistical analyses being used in the 90s.

Sweden is the only country where, apart from cross-sectional research, a large longitudinal study has also been conducted which led to several publications by Hammarström et al. after 1986. This type of design is of central importance with regard to the meaningfulness of results on the health effects of unemployment (especially long-term effects). Due to the criticism in Germany that quantitative research does not allow for an explorative approach necessary to understand the wide variety of aspects related to psychosocial well-being and unemployment, a relatively large number of qualitative studies (8 out of 18 studies) exists. In most cases the sample size was between 13 and 80 persons with no control group being included. Only one of the earlier qualitative research studies from 1977 (Burger & Seidenspinner) had a sample of 314 young unemployed men and women from both urban and rural regions.

The regional foci within the sample selection has been handled quite differently. In Germany studies have focussed both on urban and rural regions alone and also on their comparison. From Sweden and Belgium no study dealing only with the rural population was reported. Spanish studies were conducted exclusively in metropolitan areas, and Italian research seems to distinguish mainly economically strong versus economically weak regions (instead of urban – rural) leading to a comparison of the situation in Southern versus Northern Italy.

3.2 Objective health indicators

In general, information on this subject with regard to youth unemployment has been rare within all countries – a result which could be expected because, in general, young people are much less affected by objective health effects than older people. Therefore, research on these indicators usually does not focus on the age bracket between 15-29 years. In addition, most available *mortality rates* of adolescents do not make any reference to unemployment. Only in the Italian report was one study mentioned (Costa & Segnan, 1988) which points out "an excess of mortality among unemployed persons of both sexes", and also "among the young unemployed seeking their first job" (see Italian report, p. 163). These higher mortality rates among the unemployed were mainly due to violent deaths. An interesting result could be revealed for the 15-30 years of age group within a Greek study: so-called "'people with undeclared occupation' ... (have) higher mortality rates caused by transport accidents, suicides, and self-inflicted injuries" (see Greek report, p. 145). Also the extrapolation of the results from *morbidity rates* to the target group of YUSEDER is questionable due to the fact that, usually, no breakdown of the official statistics with regard to the occupational position is made. An exception to this is Belgium which reported higher depression levels among unemployed youngsters when compared to students and workers. However, in another Belgian study it could be shown that unemployed adolescents with higher depression levels had more efficient job-searching strategies than those with lower levels.

The data on *suicidal behaviour* is slightly ambiguous due to missing studies focussing on the link to youth unemployment. In all countries it seems that a higher risk exists for attempted suicide among young unemployed persons with an even higher risk among the long-term unemployed. In Spain, most of the young people who committed suicide came from the sectors with the highest unemployment rates (respectively agriculture and industry), and in Greece, the suicide rates are higher in areas with high unemployment rates. In Germany and Italy unemployed persons are overrepresented in data on suicidal behaviour. In addition, one Belgian study (Van Heeringen & Jannes, 1993) reported that unemployment is a risk factor for suicidal behaviour among men but not among women for the 15-34 years age group. These results, however, are opposed by a missing correlation between suicide and youth unemployment rates in Germany and even a negative relationship between these two factors in Sweden. As outlined in the Belgian report, it might be that suicide among young persons is "less associated with socio-economic variables such as unemployment than with indicators of anomie and social disintegration..." (see Belgian report, p. 92; for a further debate see also Chapter 3 of this comparative report).

Specific data on the respective age bracket are also rather scarce regarding the frequency of *utilisation of health services*. Sweden could present one study which indicates an increase in the utilisation among unemployed young men whereas Greece stated that, at least with regard to preventive activities, young unemployed people avoid visiting the doctor. Belgium revealed contradictory results with one study showing a lower and another study a higher frequency of use of health services among young unemployed men when compared with older unemployed persons. In the latter study it was also noted that especially the unemployed with higher educational levels are more often registered in health centres. Data on the behaviour of unemployed people in general shows that unemployed persons seem to avoid professional help in order to protect their already threatened self-esteem (Germany). From Spain the observation was made that a positive correlation exists between the frequency of utilisation and the question of need in the sense that the frequency decreases with higher personal needs and lower personal resources. Interestingly, both an increase and a decrease in the utilisation of health services are reflected in the first German Health Survey (Kurella, 1992) which stresses that there are two different groups of unemployed persons: "those individuals who seldom visit a doctor and those who visit a doctor considerably more often than employed individuals" (see German report, p. 120). Despite the fact that an extrapolation of this general data to young unemployed persons is possible only with reservations, the question of frequency of utilisation seems to be influenced by additional variables among which educational and socio-economic level might play a decisive role. In addition, it seems to be important to stress that the utilisation depends also upon the availability of health facilities in their own neighbourhood, and also upon the question of whether a person can afford health insurance (see Greek report Health behaviour).

In sum, the lack of available data on objective health indicators for young unemployed persons makes it rather impossible to make a final statement. However, the results already provide a first impression of the increased vulnerability of young persons depending upon their employment status – especially when considering the higher suicide rates among the respective unemployed groupings outlined in the Belgian report. In addition, as the results on the utilisation of health services specifically point out, the link between objective health indicators and unemployment can only be understood when other variables such as, for example, educational level, economic difficulties, and spatial segregation are also taken into account.

3.3 Subjective health indicators

All in all, the results from data on subjective health indicators seems to be relatively homogeneous within all countries. Due to the limited number of studies which, in addition, are usually coming only from one or two research teams, it is quite likely that different results occur only due to the specific foci of research taken within the respective country.

One of the most important *psychosocial strains* of unemployment for young persons in all countries seems to be the financial limitation which affects not only consumption and leisure time activity patterns (e.g., savings for clothes, holidays, transport charges, etc.), but also social relationships (for more details see also Chapter 4.4. under financial strain/stress). In addition, the financial dependency can easily lead to frustrations and feelings of uselessness (Greece). Apart from these aspects, the results from the German IAB study (Schober, 1987) revealed that boredom and the inability to structure their own time are also very stressful experiences for most of the interviewed persons (see also Greece). Young unemployed people show a great fear of not only a continuous exclusion from the labour market (Germany) with an even greater deterioration among those who do not expect to find a job again (Spain), but also with regard to their future in general (Germany, Italy, Sweden). In the Italian report it was stressed that the heightened feelings of hopelessness and uneasiness among the young unemployed can lead to a passive adaptation to their own situation and, in the long run, to social apathy. A strong focus with regard to factors counterbalancing this type of "self-fulfilling prophecy" was placed on the importance of personal (qualification) and social resources (social support from family and friends). In addition, in the German studies it was found that young unemployed persons feel stigmatised due to their situation and are afraid of not belonging anymore. Spain even reported that when compared to employed young persons, young unemployed people suffer twice as much from mild (non psychotic) psychological disorders.

These aspects are also reflected in the data summarised under *subjective well-being.* Although no clear association between youth unemployment and psychosomatic problems exists (for a further discussion see the reports from Belgium and Germany), young unemployed persons reported more subjective health problems such as headaches, stomach aches, sleeplessness, anxiousness, pessimism, etc. (Spain, Sweden, Germany). In the Swedish longitudinal study from Hammarström (1991), the mental health among the unemployed persons decreased over time, and as compared to employed persons, unemployed youngsters were the least happy group (Hammarström, 1986). Especially persons with a high work orientation and a tendency to blame themselves for their own inability to find a job were those who had the highest levels of depression or psychological disturbances (Spain, see also Belgium under Morbidity rates). Also the length of unemployment seems to influence the relation between unemployment and depression level (Greece). In a Greek study among chronic unemployed young persons between ages 25-30 years there was even a "tendency to associate the consequences of unemployment with the consequences of AIDS: 'no joy of life', 'unable to live decently', 'stigmatised by society', 'injustice', and 'death' " (see Greek report, p. 147). In Italy, no correlation between unemployment and depression level could be found. Instead, higher depression levels were detected among those persons in unstable and also stable but high risk working conditions when compared to young unemployed persons whose depression levels remained the same over time. These results mirror the effect of an adaptation of unemployed persons to their own situation mentioned in the previous paragraph. Interestingly, data on relief scheme participants do not seem to be consistent with Belgium reporting that – as compared to the short-term unemployed youth – young people within schemes suffer more from their unemployment situation whereas, in Sweden, an improvement of the mental health status among the latter grouping was found.

The question of psychosocial strains and subjective well-being is also strongly related to the *self-esteem* of young unemployed persons. The results from the different countries can be summarised in the way that the affected persons have a tendency to feel more often vulnerable, inferior, worthless and useless, and even depressive (Belgium, Germany, Greece, Spain) – with feelings of inferiority being especially strong among the long-term unemployed young persons and young unemployed women (Germany, Greece). In addition in a broad Spanish research study, "two out of five young unemployed people (even) agree that unemployed people give a certain impression of being parasites and lazy'" (see Spanish report, p. 189). This type of self-devaluation can have enormous consequences for the self-esteem of the affected youth and shows the potential for an internalisation of prejudices and also stigmatisation in respect to the social environment. As opposed to unemployed persons in general, these developments do not seem to have an effect on sociability among the youth. Only one German study reported lower values for young unemployed persons whereas, for example Belgium could not find evidence of a social withdrawal among unemployed young men. Surprisingly, although a high value given to work is related to higher depression levels among unemployed persons – a serious obstacle to well-being in the context of labour crisis – Spanish data could also show that a high work orientation seems to be a protective factor for their own self-esteem. In Greece, the level of education also seems to be important due to the fact that, independent of the labour market status, a university qualification is highly valued in this society.

With regard to *political alienation* the results are heading in two different directions. Belgium, Greece, and Spain found data that unemployed persons have the tendency to become apathetic and resigned and through this also less active politically. These results were opposed by Sweden which reported that "a greater proportion of the unemployed increase their political activity during unemployment as compared to those unemployed persons who decrease their political activity" (see Swedish report, p. 63). The dissatisfaction with their living situation can lead to a higher criticism of the democratic system with the consequence of a higher demand and an increased tendency for (spontaneous) political activities (Germany, Spain). However, it can also result in the development of groups outside the political system (Greece). Although no link between political extremism among young persons and unemployment could be found (Germany), Spanish data demonstrated that traditional values and norms are often rejected among unemployed young persons. In light of these results, the assessment made by Spain that unemployment has to be seen as an indicator for the fragility of the current political system seems to be justifiable.

These results are mirrored in the studies dealing with *social deviation*. Except for Italy where the link between the rising numbers for criminal behaviour among young persons have been strongly discussed on a general level with regard to unemployment and poverty (especially for Southern Italy), none of the other countries could prove a direct relation between unemployment and delinquent behaviour. However, due to a higher availability of recreational drugs among non-working persons, in Belgium drug-related behaviour could be found more often among young unemployed persons (and students) than among the employed youth. In sum, it has to be assumed that unemployment is only one risk factor leading to delinquency. Other factors – such as social support on the part of family and peers – seem to be of much higher importance especially when considering the prevention of social deviation (Germany, see also Greece under Subjective well-being). Belgium stressed that instead of a link "between employment status and delinquency, a causal relation between the lack of financial resources and delinquent behaviour was demonstrated" (see Belgian report, p. 95). The same might be true for the situation outlined for Southern Italy where an increasing number of young persons are living below the poverty level.

Research on *health behaviour* among young persons is directed mainly toward smoking and alcohol consumption. Also with regard to these issues, unemployment has to be understood as only one risk factor among others (Germany). Only in the longitudinal studies from Hammarström (1996, 1991) could it be shown that young unemployed men increased their alcohol consumption while unemployed young women increased their cigarette smoking. However, this link between alcohol consumption and unemployment could not be revealed by two other Swedish studies. The importance of taking part in a further qualification programme or of getting a job on health behaviour is indicated by additional Swedish results which found that "the transition from unemployment to youth trainee decreased alcohol consumption" (see Swedish report, p. 63). Interestingly, in this study, an increase in physical activity among the unemployed youth could also be detected. This positive effect of unemployment in Sweden is opposed by the Greek results which point out a deterioration in hygienic, dietary, and sleeping behaviour among the young unemployed.

To sum up, it can be said that unemployment has to be considered as one of the central risk factors for the subjective well-being of young persons with length of unemployment and gender being important mediators for this relation (see also Chapter 4.4). This becomes especially true in light of the effects unemployment has with regard to the drifting apart of the developmental processes of young unemployed versus young employed persons. With reference to the research done by Hahn (1996) in a study focussing on East Germany, the German report concludes that "on a long-term basis, substantial exclusion mechanisms for unemployed adolescents could develop" (see German report, p. 121). However, other factors such as the economic and the relational dimension are also of a similar or maybe even higher importance than the situation of unemployment per se. Both personal and institutional support systems have to be considered with regard to their possible counterbalancing or even preventive measures, especially when thinking about the long-term effects of unemployment.

3.4 Mediators (demographic variables)

The data from the different countries show that *age* is an important mediator for the manner in which people experience their unemployment. First of all, the greatest troubles with regard to mental health seem to exist among middle-aged persons and the lowest among older unemployed people (Belgium, Germany, Spain). In addition, in the German report it was outlined that "young unemployed constitute a very heterogeneous grouping of individuals" with very different labour market related difficulties depending on the respective age bracket (see German report, p. 125). For those below 20 years of age the main problem is the difficulty to find a place within a training or qualification scheme, whereas between 20-25 years of age the respective persons face problems with entering the labour market itself. The group between 26-30 years of age consists mainly of either long-term unemployed persons or academics trying to find a job. It can be assumed that rather different health-related problems occur within these three groupings. Except for Greece, which reports more psychological disturbances among the latter grouping, no corresponding data exists in any of the other countries participating in this project.

From the available research studies it could be concluded that with regard to *gender*, women seem to be able to adapt more easily to unemployment – especially in the long run – although the general situation of young unemployed women on the labour market in all countries participating in this project can be described as being more difficult than that of men. Despite the tendency of women to report more health problems

(Italy, Sweden) – a result matched by most general health studies for women independent of their employment status – and a higher occurrence of short-term depressive symptomatology, these differences could not be observed for depressive symptoms of long duration (Belgium). Spanish data could show that, as opposed to employed persons, young unemployed men have higher depression levels than women, and in Greece "unemployed women present (even) an overall better health state than men" (see Greek report, p. 148). These results are matched by the Belgian study from van Heeringen & Jannes (1993) who found out that "unemployment was a greater risk factor for attempted suicide among young men" (see Belgian report, p. 95). The seemingly better adaptability of women might be due to their stronger orientation towards the family and the traditional role as a mother or housewife (Germany, Greece) – a solution paid with a high price because early marriage and pregnancies easily interfere with the developmental processes of the affected young women. Therefore, it must also be questioned if this adaptability happens in a constructive or rather resigned way. In addition, when considering that most of the studies referred to in this context were conducted in the 80s, it is quite likely that such results on the higher adaptability of women are context-related. At the end of the 20th century work has also become a more central aspect in the life of women in all European countries, and it is only reasonable to assume that an increasing participation in the labour market will diminish their satisfaction with and therefore, their adaptability to, alternative roles.

Differences in coping with unemployment can also be observed when considering the *educational level* of young persons. In all countries, data demonstrated that a higher education is an advantage when dealing with daily problems related to unemployment. Persons with lower school-leaving exams have not only more limited possibilities for further qualifications leading to a higher risk for unemployment (Germany), but are also more vulnerable to health problems (Greece, Spain). Young persons with higher educational levels show lower levels of depression (Spain) and higher levels of self-esteem (Greece), have fewer difficulties for coping with financial strains, and are better able to deal with the necessary institutions (Germany). Italy stated that "the school variable has been shown to act as a reinforcement of other factors – especially with regard to the availability of psychosocial resources" (see Italian report, p. 168) which seem to be lower among the less educated young unemployed (see also Greece). As already outlined above, this has enormous consequences for their health and well-being, and also their overall social integration. Therefore, education can be considered as an essential personal resource of young people to deal with their living situation.

Data on *social class* are rare. In Belgium and Sweden the reason for this can be found in a missing classification system for social class. However, when considering social class in a wider perspective, the results in all countries can be interpreted as rather homogeneous: A less favourable family situation with regard to income level, living standard, unemployment within the family (in Italy and Spain especially the unemployment of the father), low educational level, and a single parent household increases the risk not only of becoming unemployed but also of developing psychosomatic and other health-related problems (Belgium, Germany, Greece, Italy, Spain). As outlined especially in the Spanish report, unemployment affects most of all persons with few personal – physical, mental, social, and professional – resources. These people are "often associated with or derived from prior deficits in the family social situation" (see Spanish report, p. 192).

One of the most important mediators with regard to the health effects of unemployment is the *length of unemployment,* with an increasing duration leading to an increase in health-related problems (Belgium, Germany, Greece, Sweden). In the longitudinal study from Hammarström & Olofsson (1997) it could be shown that the length of unemployment is directly related to nervous problems and depression (Sweden). Similar results were outlined in the German report, which refers not only to a general increase in depressive symptoms and resignation, but also to an increase in passive behaviour (decrease in completing applications), economic deprivation, and general sickness-related symptoms (see also Greece). However, as a result of the adaptation process, the negative effects on health seem to decrease after an unemployment duration of more than two years (Spain). In addition, a study from Italy and one from Spain each reported a missing correlation between the duration of unemployment and the well-being of the respective young persons (Alvaro, 1989b; Sarchielli, Depolo, Fraccaroli & Colasanto, 1991).

All in all, the influence of the demographic variables on youth unemployment and health reflect the general understanding of high risk groups: Persons from lower social classes with lower educational levels are mainly affected by health related problems especially with an increasing length of unemployment. Among these, men suffer more from their situation than women. Despite the fact that this result must be interpreted carefully because the respective data were ascertained mainly in the early 80s, it reflects the traditional value system which puts more pressure on men than on women with regard to the responsibility for the family income. Although age has to be considered as a central criterion for dealing with unemployment in general, no relevant distinctions can be made about differences in health-related problems within the age bracket between 15-29 years of age.

3.5 Moderators (psychological variables)

The three moderators 'work and job orientation', 'financial strain/stress', and 'social support' have an important influence in all countries on the experiences and the coping abilities with unemployment and its health consequences for the affected person.

As opposed to the public debate on the deterioration of work values among young persons, youth studies from Germany and Spain, for example, could verify that most young persons have a high *work orientation* including a strong identification with and a high value given to work in general. In one of the leading youth studies conducted in Germany among 2,000 young people between 13-29 years of age (Shell-Study, 1997) "every second adolescent viewed the topic of unemployment as the current greatest problem" (see German report, p. 126). In Spain the importance given to the 'social representation of work' for the health and well-being of young persons is reflected in the centrality given to this subject in all Spanish studies on youth unemployment and health. Although work orientation can also be a protective factor for the respective person, as outlined for the variable self-esteem most data highlight that a high value given to work is negatively related to psychological well-being (Belgium, Greece) especially among persons aged 17-19 years (Italy) and positively related to a deterioration of mental health (Spain) of young persons. Greece outlined that minimising the expectations towards work and their lives in general (as a defensive coping mechanism) seems to heighten the coping abilities with the own unemployment situation. Interestingly, in a qualitative German study with a rather large sample size (Burger & Seidenspinner, 1977), a higher activity level with regard to further applications could also be found among those young persons who did not have primarily an economic-instrumental, but rather an expressive orientation towards work. This leads to the hypothesis that the type of work orientation could be a central mechanism for its protective versus reinforcing effect also on health-related problems due to unemployment.

As the most obvious effect of unemployment, *financial strain/stress* (respectively, the problem of poverty) has already been directly and indirectly discussed under several other variables (e.g., psychosocial strain, self-esteem, gender, social class, length of unemployment, work orientation, etc.). This issue is not only of such immense importance for young persons because of the general limitations this implies for their daily living, consumption, and leisure time activities, but also because of increasing family problems and tensions due to the economic dependency of young persons on additional family support (Germany, Greece). When considering that persons who do not receive any unemployment benefits have even worse mental health levels than those who are entitled to those benefits (Spain), it has to be assumed that insufficient or even missing state support given to young persons has enormous consequences for their health and well-being in all countries. An important buffer, especially in the Southern European countries, seems to be the submerged economy which provides the young unemployed "with some kind of financial and emotional relief" (see Greek report, p. 149). Surprisingly, none of the available Italian studies has taken up the subject of financial dependency. The reason for this might be found in the missing state support for young persons, the general centrality of family bonds, and therefore, the rather usual state of affairs in Italy that youth unemployment is linked with family dependence (not only on an economic level).

An interesting, additional moderator for the link between family income and/or financial strain on the one hand and psychological well-being on the other hand was outlined in the Swedish report. Rantakeisu, Starrin, and Hagquist (to be submitted) found that especially among those persons who experienced very high levels of both *financial strain and experiences of being shamed*, "the extent of ill-health, mental problems, and feelings of powerlessness were considerably greater" than among those groups who did not show this combination of factors (see Swedish report, pp. 64-65). This result leads not only to the question of acceptance of the unemployment situation by the young persons themselves (see also paragraph on work orientation) but also by their social surroundings as outlined in the following paragraph.

As the data from all YUSEDER countries highlight, *social support* from side of the *family* and friends is one of the most powerful buffers against all types of stressful (critical) life events including unemployment. In a Spanish study, unemployed persons who "feel barely or not at all cushioned by family and/or friends score significantly higher in the General Health Questionnaire (GHQ) than those who say they feel cushioned" (see Spanish report, p. 194). In Greece, the family plays a central role in the social and financial support of their children (due to low state support), but the high pressure often exerted from the family can also have negative consequences for the unemployed youth. In Germany, results on both the missing interest and understanding from the side of the family including a devaluation of the young unemployed person (especially of women), and on the importance of the family as a safe social retreat were described. The same is true for Belgium which found that unemployment can lead to an increase and a decrease in time spent with the family. With regard to *social support* from *friends*, the results seem to also depend on the gender perspective: In Belgium and Germany, young unemployed persons diminish their external contacts in general with men intensifying and women decreasing their remaining contacts to peers (Germany). Social support also depends in Spain on regional aspects: Persons coming from rural areas with high unemployment rates feel much more supported by family, neighbours, and friends than people from urban areas. In this country the aspect of sameness obviously leads to a higher acceptance and understanding for the situation of a young unemployed person and, therefore, to lower stigmatisation processes. Although no data on this issue were given within the other reports, it can be assumed that similar mechanisms are coming to fruition in those countries also. These results are summarised in the Italian report which states that "lower psychological costs with regard to the condition of unemployment (are paid) in case of a sustaining person giving support in moments of difficulties; a good family atmosphere...; a group of friends...; (and) an absence of pressure both by parents and friends in finding a job" (see Italian report, p. 169).

From the three above mentioned variables, financial strain/stress is obviously one of the most essential moderators for the effect of unemployment on the health of young persons. However, this aspect is also strongly dependent on social support, respectively, social acceptance of the young person and his or her situation by social environment. In this regard preventive mechanisms are coming into focus. Peer and family support are important buffers in times of unemployment, and also their own work orientation – especially an intrinsic value given to work – seems to have a protective effect on the health of the unemployed youth.

3.6 Conclusions

Despite the criticism from most countries with regard to the limited number of studies and also their level of empirical evidence (mainly cross-sectional data), the analysis of the national reports revealed rather homogenous results on the link between youth unemployment and ill health. In general, it was reported that as compared to their employed peers, young unemployed persons have a higher risk for health-related problems. This is especially true for mental health and psychosocial problems leading to an increase in depression and a poorer quality of life, but also for objective health indicators especially when considering the higher risk for suicidal behaviour among the unemployed youth. This is also reflected in the health behaviour of young unemployed persons especially with regard to the finding referring to the amount of alcohol and cigarette consumption depending on the employment status.

Both in the Northern and Southern European countries work plays a central role in the developmental process of young people. The denial of an access to the labour market implies foremost financial limitations meaning that for young persons the dependency on the family and because of this, the overall juvenile phase becomes prolonged. Although family support is an important buffer, this protection might also hinder the development of the young person to become an independent adult. In this regard it is important to note that research increasingly focusses not only on monetary aspects, but also on the psychosocial consequences of a high work orientation. The lack of work is not only linked with economic strains but also with limitations in central living dimensions caused by economic strains. Work also has an important intrinsic value which, when missing, can have detrimental effects for the personality of the unemployed young person. Feelings of general vulnerability, inferiority, worthlessness and uselessness, and depression among this group could be found which lead in the long run to a decrease in self-esteem and a higher dissatisfaction with their lives. Stigmatisation processes from the social environment add to this situation. This interaction between financial and social conditions is reflected specifically in the Swedish research dealing with financial hardship and shaming experiences. Unemployed persons who felt devalued and belittled exhibited more ill health than their employed peers.

Due to the higher expectations on men to fulfill the role of the breadwinner in the family, young men seem to be under more pressure than women when being unemployed. This is reflected not only in the higher depression levels among young unemployed men, but also in the strong influence that the unemployment of the father has on young persons in general especially in the Southern European countries. Although women seem to adapt more easily to their situation – due to lack of pressuring expectations, but also to marriage and early pregnancy – this solution has to be seen rather critically because it gives way to a further discrimination of women on the labour market and a re-traditionalisation of gender roles. In addition to this gender perspective, the length of unemployment is an important mediator for the health effects of unemployment at least in the Northern European countries. It can be assumed that for these countries, the statement that unemployment is only *one risk factor for ill health among others* is only true as long as the duration of unemployment is not considered. With the increasing length of time, the unemployed person suffers more and more from his or her situation – an aspect which implies that both the possible positive and negative influence of other factors diminishes over time.

The aspects mentioned in the previous paragraph indicate slight differences for the Northern versus the Southern European countries – especially with regard to the importance of the family, the expected role of men to provide financial support for the family, and also the effects of long-term unemployment. Although it might be assumed that the central importance of the family in Southern Europe cushions a further reinforcement of the effects of unemployment in case of a longer duration of this situation, the low number of studies calls for further research on these issues in Southern Europe before making any final statements about this interrelationship. In addition, as already outlined above, it can be expected that the changing family structures in the Southern European countries (decreasing birth rates, increasing number of single parents) will also diminish the positive influence of the family in the future.

Preventive aspects were also highlighted within the reports from all countries. Especially social support – both on the part of family and friends – is an important social resource for the affected youth. In this regard, the general family situation (income, missing father or mother, unemployment within the family, etc.) also has an enormous influence. In addition, a very powerful personal resource has to be seen in the level of education of young people. Not only is the employability increased with a better qualification, but also persons from higher educational levels are more capable of dealing with institutions and also with their own financial situation. Considering this, it becomes obvious that the different institutions – especially the school but also those offering training and further qualification measures – play an essential role with regard to the health status of young persons.

Despite the fact that from a scientific point of view, the available data from the six countries participating in this project do not allow for definite answers, it becomes obvious that the strong and complex interlinkage between youth unemployment and different health-related aspects calls for innovative and multifaceted answers to the emerging problems of today. As outlined in the Spanish report, youth unemployment cannot be tackled only by employment policies anymore. Also a strong focus on financial aspects does not seem to be the sole solution – especially when considering the general lowering of unemployment and social aid in most countries of the European Community. To deal with the large amount of low qualified unemployed youngsters, institutions of all kinds are called to support the affected youth and also their families and the wider social surroundings. However, the general understanding of and attitude towards work in the industrialised countries seems to also be in need of a reconceptualisation.

Annex 1: Understanding the health consequences of unemployment – the finance/shame model

Bengt Starrin, Ulla Rantakeisu, Erik Forsberg & Marina Kalander-Blomqvist

Modern research into unemployment has shown that unemployment can result in social and health-related problems (see e.g. Hammarström, 1996; Janlert, 1991; Janlert, 1992; Brenner, Petterson, Levi & Arnetz, 1988). A considerable portion of the research that has been conducted to study the link between unemployment on one hand and social problems and ill health on the other hand has been, to a great degree, focussed on surveying the problem and was not based upon a theoretical concept. Still, interesting theoretical attempts can be found. Among the better known are Jahoda's theory of the manifest and latent functions of employment (Jahoda, 1982), Warr's theory of vitamins (Warr, 1987), Fryer's agency theory (Fryer, 1986), Ezzy's status passage theory (Ezzy, 1993), the theory of locus of control (O'Brien, 1986), the classical theory of stress (Janlert, 1991) as well as the theory of economic deprivation (Janlert, 1991). Among these, stress theory, in its more or less developed form, serves as the basis for an interpretation of the link between unemployment and ill health.

1 The finance/shame model: Some general aspects

The finance/shame model was developed to better understand the question of why unemployment becomes a torment for some while for others it does not involve any negative health effects (Starrin, Rantakeisu & Hagquist, 1996). The model consists of a combination or synthesis of two theoretical 'traditions' which have been developed separately from each other: the economic portion of the model is tied to research on economic stress and economic deprivation (Horwitz, 1984). The social portion is tied to the micro-sociological research on social relations (Scheff, 1990) and social networks (Berkman & Syme, 1979).

The finance/shame model postulates the importance of two conditions for understanding the link between unemployment and ill health and social problems – namely, the degree of financial hardship and the degree of shaming experiences. The working assumption can be formulated as follows: The higher the degree of financial hardship during unemployment and the more experiences of being shamed, the more serious ill health and social consequences of unemployment are. Conversely, the less one experiences financial hardship and the less experiences of being shamed, the milder the health and social consequences are for the individual. The finance/shame model is illustrated in Figure CR-5.

It has been noted that research on unemployment has only paid attention to an insufficient degree to what is lost because of unemployment, namely income and social prestige, status and respect. The finance/shame model considers both of these aspects. The economic portion of the model recognises the importance of lost income due to employment, which for many people provides the only real reward for hard work (Willis, 1986). Besides, income also facilitates important social and cultural activities. A person needs money to stabilise and maintain an established lifestyle, and money is also important for social interaction. Moreover, money can convey a feeling of control and power (Underlid, 1992). The fact that economic aspects of unemployment have not been recognised to any degree by modern unemployment research until now is somewhat surprising because it concerns a central and classic research area.

Figure CR-5: Finance/shame model and the consequences of unemployment

		experiences of being shamed	
		more experiences	***less experiences***
financial hardship	***higher degree***	more ill health and unemployment-related health deterioration	
	lesser degree		less ill health and unemployment-related health deterioration

In general it can be said that research illuminating the link between economic conditions on the one hand and ill health and social problems on the other hand has found, above all, that low economic status, economic stress, and poverty all relate to an increased risk for health and social problems. These factors also have a strong effect on well-being (Horwitz, 1984). The research on unemployment which has addressed the economic side of unemployment has shown that the more difficult the economic situation during unemployment is, the greater the risk is that the person is also afflicted by ill health in some form (see, e.g., Starrin, Rantakeisu & Hagquist, 1996).

The other aspect that is recognised in the finance/shame model is the potential for feeling shame due to being out of work. In addition to the fact that paid work provides income, it can also be socially fulfilling. To varying degrees it provides status, prestige, and respect. Viewed historically, there is clear evidence that the lower social classes – which encompass the unemployed – are looked down upon and are disparaged. The suggestion that unemployment depends on the personal qualities and attitudes towards work of the unemployed has been widespread (Gallie, 1994).

The ways in which other people regard the unemployed person is important for his/her identity. Studies show that many unemployed people are aware of feelings of being judged and valued by others (Hayes & Nutman, 1981). When they meet other people, authorities, and institutions, the self-esteem of the unemployed person is subject to a test. The feelings can sometimes be strong and involve anger, rage, shame, and depression. Wadel (1973) notes in his classic study that for many unemployed people, rage and aggressive argumentation are ways to protect their own dignity and self-esteem.

Studies have also found out that the unemployed risk being devalued and disparaged. Some research studies refer explicitly to stigma, shame, or status perspectives. Stigma can be seen as an aspect of status. A person that becomes stigmatised is ascribed a low status. Status, according to Max Weber, concerns the presence or absence of social dignity. The status that some groups enjoy is based presumably on a specific positive or negative social judgement of honour and credit. There is also a close relationship between status and stigma (Spicker, 1984). People that are stigmatised run the risk of losing their social position through either the stigma limiting their possibilities to assume a certain role or the stigma defining lower or subordinate roles. With stigma, the risk of experiencing economic difficulty and poverty is increased; therefore, stigma can be regarded as limiting the possibilities to obtain employment and to earn an income.

Stigma can also be seen as an aspect of social disgrace – as a sign of degradation, loss of worth, or loss of good reputation. Low status implying inferiority and an imputation of subordinate position is an aspect of stigmatisation. Shame can be defined as the emotion of having less worth and of subordination. It is the emotion that is awakened when the individual suddenly becomes aware of a defect or weakness with one's own self, a goal that is not attained or an expectation that cannot be met. Shame and its related emotions of humiliation and degradation refer to a painful feeling caused by one's own self, when one's pride or self-image is reduced. Shame is involved when a person is placed and regarded in a painfully depreciating way. Shame reveals the inner part of one's self and places it on view for others. No other feeling appears to be so central for the development of identity and self-image than shame; therefore, the experience of shame can be painful (Kaufman, 1993).

As an expression of the quality of social relations, shame proceeds from the assumption that when the bonds between people are threatened, negative feelings arise. The quality of the social bonds is understood not only through the interpretation of what is said but how it is said, that is to say, through people's behaviour. Shame and its opposite, pride, are indications of the quality of the social bonds connecting people – if they are insecure or secure. Shame and pride are, in addition, emotions that are pushed to the outskirts in the modern, increasingly individualistic society. Shame is suppressed and a person is ashamed of being ashamed. For Scheff, shame and pride are feelings of a social nature. However, the way we experience shame and pride is overall culturally conditioned (Scheff, 1990).

Eales (1989) found that feelings of shame are common among adult unemployed men. In this study shame was also related to psychological problems such as depression and anxiety. Studies have also shown that the more the unemployed person perceives that others look down on them or feel shame as a result of unemployment, the greater the likelihood that they will experience ill health (Rantakeisu, Starrin & Hagquist, 1997).

2 Empirical support for the finance/shame model

The finance/shame model has been examined in a number of different studies. Some of the studies are summarised below.

2.1 Young unemployed women and men

The finance/shame model was tested in a questionnaire study of 502 unemployed women and men aged 16-25 years. The results from this study show that the extent of ill health, depression, and feelings of powerlessness were considerably higher within the 'Higher/ More' group than within the 'Lower/Less' group (Rantakeisu, Starrin & Hagquist, 1999). From Figure CR-6 it can be seen that the incidence of serious psychosomatic problems, powerlessness, and depression is considerably greater among those exposed to a higher degree of financial hardship and more shaming experiences. This applies both for men and women. The differences found between men and women included a considerably greater extent of problems, powerlessness, and depression among the women than among men.

Figure CR-6: Finance/shame model, serious psychosomatic disorders, powerlessness, and depression during unemployment

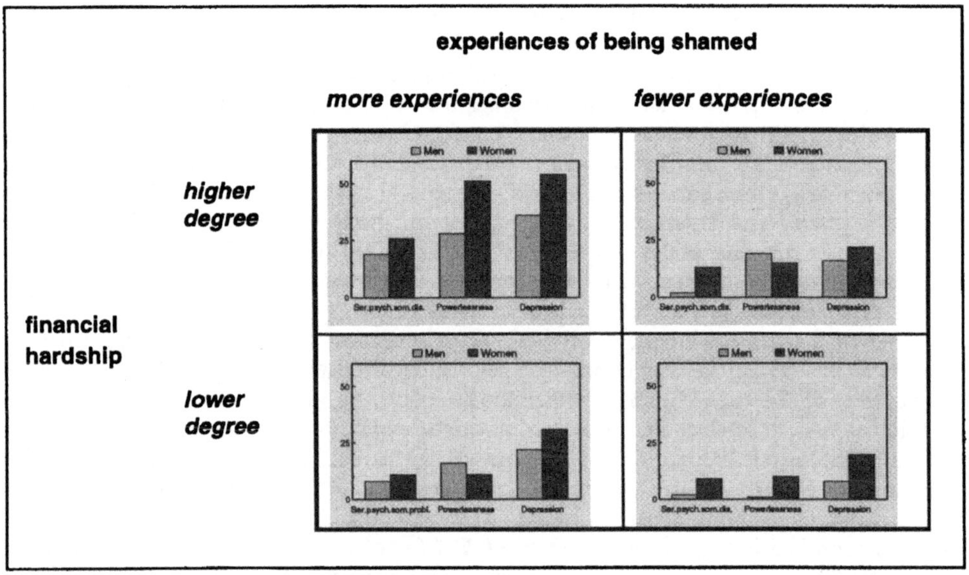

Source: Rantakeisu, Starrin & Hagquist, 1999.

2.2 Long-term unemployed women and men

The finance/shame model has also been tested in a study among long-term unemployed persons (Starrin & Jönsson, 1998). As Figure CR-7 illustrates, the distribution of unemployment-related health failings is concentrated in the group 'Higher/More'. 64% of the women and 46% of the men in this group have suffered from unemployment-related health deterioration. The comparable number for women and men in the group 'Lower/ Less' is 5%.

Figure CR-7: Finance/shame model and unemployment-related health problems

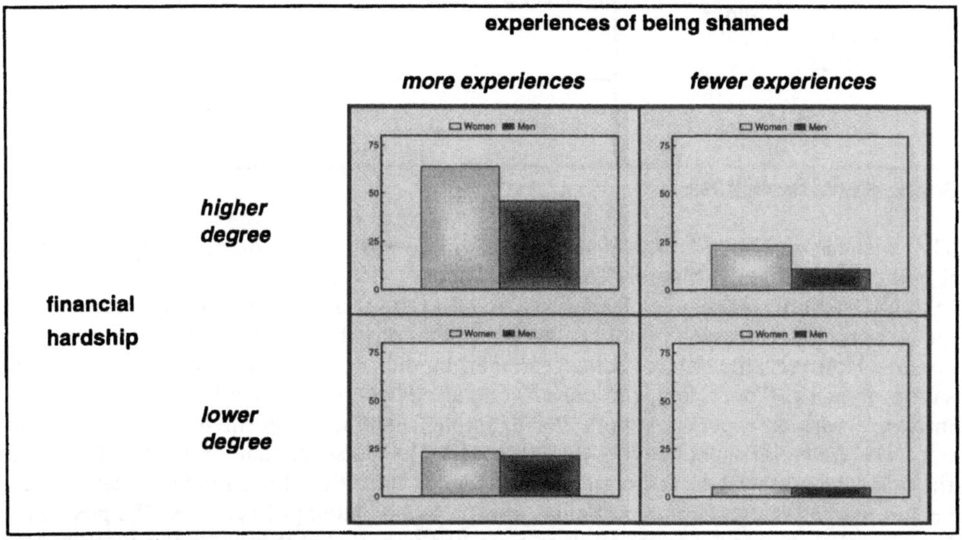

Source: Starrin & Jönsson, 1998.

3 The finance/social bonds model

The finance/shame model can be regarded as a specific case of a more general model that we wish to designate the finance/social bonds model (Starrin, Rantakeisu & Hagquist, 1996; Pihl & Starrin, 1998). Factors such as social bonds that call attention to social relations are included in the model. Shame and pride can be regarded as the most primary of the social emotions because they are, in different ways, expressions of social bonds (Scheff, 1990). As noted above, shame expresses tense relations – broken off or facing the prospect of a break – while pride expresses relaxed and well functioning relationships. The finance/social bonds model also includes both shame and pride and, therefore, may have a more general value in explaining and understanding social and health-related problems.

A hypothesis that can be formulated from the finance/social bonds model is that the combination of 'fewer economic resources' and 'more shame-filled social bonds' increases the risk for 'ill health' and reduces well-being. Another hypothesis that can be formulated is that the combination of 'more economic resources' and 'social bonds that are characterised by pride' increase the chance of well-being and good health (see fig. CR-8).

Figure CR-8: Finance/social bonds model

		social bond	
		more shame	***more pride***
financial resources	***more***	ill health and social problems	
	less		health and social well-being

Source: Pihl & Starrin, 1998.

The finance/social bonds model has aspects in common with the currently well established control-demand theory (Karasek & Theorell, 1990). The control aspect in Karasek and Theorell's theory is clearly connected to the economic conditions because adequate personal financial resources increase the possibilities for influence and self-control. However, the control concept in their model is even related to the social organisation of work. Concretely, the control concept concerns the available possibilities to influence various aspects of work, for example, planning, implementation and evaluation. The financial aspect covers this only partly in the sense that a very good personal financial situation leads to greater independence and, therefore, makes it easier for a person to even resign from a particular job if a second attempt to increase the possibility for control in the work has failed. It is quite likely that what is regarded as work-related stress has, to a considerable extent, to do with financial stress. One study shows that the reported stress experienced in employment could be reduced by half when controlling for the degree of economic difficulty (Pearlin & Lieberman, 1979).

The other part of Karasek and Theorell's model – the demand – comes into the picture when the demands or expectations from the social environment are small or large. These demands or expectations indicate the quality of the social bonds in our model, and can be more filled with shame or more characterised by pride. The sources of stress researchers have identified through the concept of control-demand should as well – if our assumptions are valid – be covered to a considerable degree by the finance/social bonds model.

The finance/social bonds model has been tested and confirmed in a large population study encompassing 9,970 people in the age group 20-64 years (Pihl & Starrin, 1998). As illustrated in Figure CR-9, the extent of depression and suicidal ideation is concentrated in the 'frequent economic hardship/weak social support' quadrant. Of the people covered by this combination of factors, 35% of women and 14% of men suffer from depression.

When controlling for underlying conditions such as age, status of employment, ethnicity, drinking habits, and chronic health problems it could be shown that the connection still remained, and in some instances became even stronger.

Figure CR-9: The finance/social bonds model, depression, and suicidal ideation among women and men

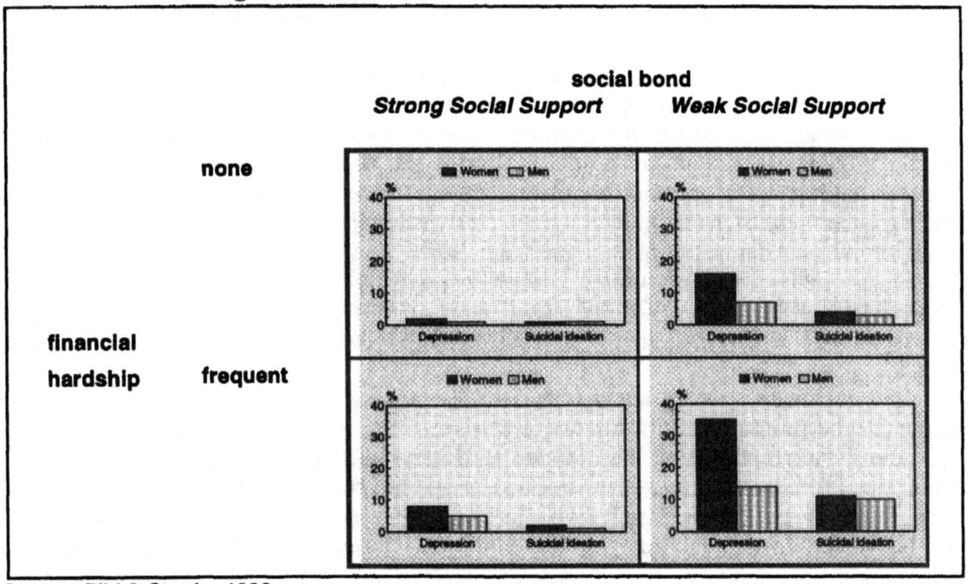

Source: Pihl & Starrin, 1998.

4 Finance/shame model – A concluding discussion

As suggested by our empirical data, many ill health effects are found among the groups which live under a higher degree of economic hardship and which, at the same time, have greater experiences of the shame-causing effects of the surroundings. The difference in the onset of serious ill health in either the form of daily headaches, stomach aches, or sleeping disorders and the onset of depression is considerable among those that are simultaneously exposed to higher degrees of economic stress and more shame-causing experiences and those exposed to a lesser degree.

The first question that arises is which emotions are associated with serious economic problems. To live under a high degree of economic stress means living under a considerable threat that there will not be enough funds for the most basic necessities. Economic hardship is an expression of a danger, a threat. A person is, for example, concerned about not being able to pay bills, worried that the funds quite simply will not be enough, and is asking her-/himself what will happen when the funds run out.

The other important emotions are shame and humiliation which arise partly as a consequence of how a person believes she/he is regarded by others, and of experiences of how a person actually is encountered by others. In this connection, both the quality of the horizontal relationships as well as that of the vertical relationships may play an important role.

Scheff (1992) regards shame as a master emotion in the sense that emotions such as fear, grief, anger and even shame itself can give rise to pathological processes only when they occur in connection with shame, that is to say, when shame gives rise to further emotional reactions, for example, shame-fear, shame-shame, shame-anger. However, not all forms of shame are injurious to the individual. It is only, according to Scheff, the non-acknowledged feeling of shame (the residual and suppressed) that leads to pathological processes.

The emotion of shame is basically an expression of a threatened social bond. It essentially concerns a feeling of lack of respect and regard from others – regardless of whether this absence is real or imagined – leading to a negative self-evaluation and to shame. If shame is recognised it can be short-lived. If shame is not recognised it can possibly lead to open and undifferentiated shame (re-coded words, gestures, blushing, among others) or bypassed shame (hyperactive thoughts and/or actions). With open undifferentiated shame the person feels emotional pain to a degree that thought and speech are delayed or interrupted. People try to forget the painful episode both for themselves and for others. With bypassed shame people try to avoid emotion as means of preventing the onset of shame. It manifests itself through hyperactive thought and speech.

In conclusion, our argument is based upon an assumption that an important, but not sufficient, prerequisite for distress or illnesses of a psychological or psychosomatic character is the combination of emotional activation and emotional suppression, that is, when one emotion is activated to suppress another. The principle cause of this is the disruption of social bonds. Much evidence exists to support the idea that the mediating link between the social environment's conditions – characterised both by economic exposure and a social-relational exposure (financial-shame) – and psychosomatic reactions is mainly the activation of two emotions, namely, fear and shame. Furthermore, the health consequences due to these exposures are even more serious when these emotions are bound together in such a way that an activation of the one causes a suppression of the other.

Annex 2: Youth unemployment and suicidal behaviour: A review of the literature

Kees van Heeringen & Wouter Vanderplasschen

1 Introduction

Suicidal behaviour is a major public health problem in a majority of European Community member states, and the costs of suicidal behaviour at human and socio-economic levels are enormous. For example, based upon the results from the WHO/EURO Multicentre Study on Parasuicide, the annual rate of attempted suicide in Europe is estimated at approximately 160 per 100,000 inhabitants (Bille-Brahe & Crepet, 1996) indicating that more than one million people attempt suicide in Europe each year.

The prevention of suicidal behaviour still poses a major challenge to policy-makers, clinicians, and researchers due to its unpredictable character and multifactorial etiology. The known causes of suicidal behaviour can be categorised into five groups. A first group consists of genetic and biological factors, including mainly dysfunctional serotonergic neurotransmission in the central nervous system. A second group of risk factors includes psychiatric disorders, as suicidal behaviour is clearly associated with depressive disorders, schizophrenia, alcoholism, and personality disorders mainly of the borderline type. The third group of causes of suicidal behaviour includes personality characteristics, such as impulsivity, hostility, and sensitivity to social stressors. Fourthly, detrimental socio-economic conditions among which *unemployment plays a major role* are associated. The association between youth unemployment and suicidal behaviour will be discussed in this review. A fifth and heterogeneous group of risk factors includes the availability of means to attempt or commit suicide, and the presence of models of suicidal behaviour, such as suicidal behaviour by peers, friends, relatives, or in mass media reports. Figure CR-10 shows a stressdiathesis model to explain the pathogenesis of suicidal behaviour in which the risk factors are grouped according to trait- and state-related characteristics. The trait-related characteristics include the biological and personality characteristics while the state-related factors mainly refer to the depression-like psychiatric problems which are commonly induced by psychosocial stressors including detrimental relational or professional conditions.

Figure CR-10: Stress diathesis model of pathogenetic factors in suicidal behaviour

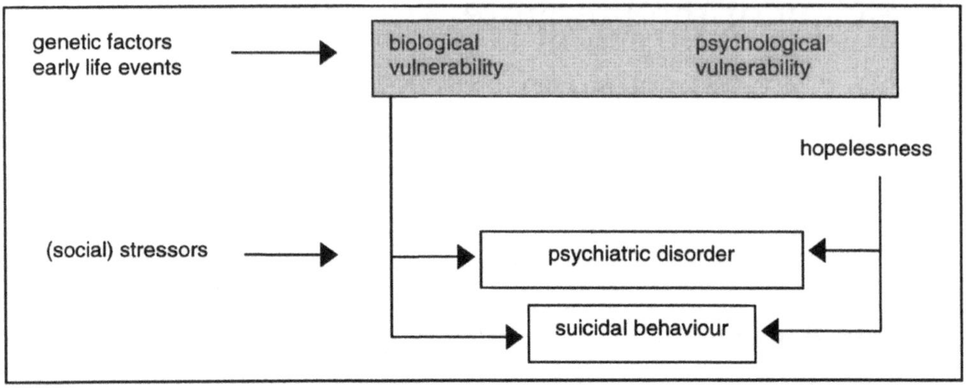

In view of the continuously increasing rates of unemployment and suicide in many European countries, especially among the young, the association between unemployment and suicidal behaviour is a major focus of concern for developing efficient strategies to prevent suicidal behaviour. Although there is little doubt about a significant association between unemployment and suicidal behaviour, the meaning of this association is still a matter of debate. Three possible explanations have been proposed including a vulnerability model, an indirect causation model, and a non-causal model (Jones, Forster & Hassanyeh 1991). In brief, the vulnerability model states that unemployment may increase the impact of stressful life events while according to the indirect causation model, unemployment may increase the risk of occurrence of events (such as relationship difficulties or financial problems) and thus precipitate suicidal behaviour. Finally, the non-causal model states that the association between unemployment and suicidal behaviour is – wholly or partially – spurious and arises because both unemployment and suicidal behaviour are influenced by common or correlated causal factors that are antecedent to both outcomes and are related to both suicide and unemployment. Based on a review of recent studies, Jones et al. (1991) concluded that there was no firm evidence that unemployment acts as an indirect causal variable or as a vulnerability factor in the way to self-poisoning (one method to attempt suicide), and that the non-causal interpretation remains a viable hypothesis.

In this review, studies are included that approach the potential association between unemployment and suicidal behaviour among young people from different points of view. The studies are first grouped according to the form of suicidal behaviour that was examined, that is attempted suicide versus completed suicide. Secondly and as far as data were available, studies were subgrouped according to patient characteristics, that is unemployed persons versus individuals who showed suicidal behaviour. Finally, the studies were grouped according to the use of individual versus aggregate data.

2 Methodological considerations

Part of the studies that are included in this review were found in the library of the Unit for Suicide Research at the University Gent. References of these publications were searched for in additional studies. Moreover, a literature search was performed by means of MEDLINE and PSYCLIT, first using 'unemployment' and 'suicide' and 'youth' as key words. This search revealed 11 records. Second, the key words 'unemployment' and 'suicide' were used for an additional search which resulted in 179 records. As far as these studies were available for review they were checked for age-specific data on the association between unemployment and suicidal behaviour.

A review of studies on the association between youth unemployment and suicidal behaviour, however, is hampered by several problems. First, the applied definitions of youth, unemployment, and of suicidal behaviour differ between studies. Second, while a substantial part of the studies have been published about the effect of unemployment on the occurrence of suicidal behaviour, the number of studies dealing with youth is limited. Third, mental health is regarded as the main outcome variable in a number of studies, sometimes without mentioning suicidal behaviour but including characteristics that are strongly related to suicidal behaviour such as hopelessness. These studies, however, were not included in this review which aims to focus specifically on studies using suicidal behaviour as an outcome variable.

3 Youth unemployment and attempted suicide

Due to the fact that nationwide data on the occurrence of attempted suicide are not available, the study of the association between youth unemployment and attempted suicide has been limited to research using individual data – as far as it is known to the authors. However, the subject has been addressed from two points of view: by studying attempted suicide patients and by studying young unemployed individuals.

3.1 Studies of young unemployed individuals

Only one study was found which included suicidal behaviour as an outcome variable among young unemployed individuals. In their longitudinal study, Fergusson, Horwood & Lynskey (1997) assessed 1,025 young adults at 18 years of age about the long duration of their exposure to unemployment from age 16 onwards and psychiatric problems including attempted suicide. They found that 3.6% made a suicide attempt between the ages of 16 to 18 years. The rate of attempted suicide increased significantly with *duration of unemployment* to 9.9% among those who were unemployed *for 6 months or longer*. However, when family and individual characteristics prior to exposure to unemployment were taken into account in a multivariate analysis, the association between unemployment and attempted suicide became insignificant. Based on these results the authors conclude that unemployment probably does not make a strong contribution to the risk of attempted suicide in young people. Thus, the results suggest that an apparent association between unemployment and attempted suicide has arisen from selection processes in which those predisposed to adjustment problems were at greater risk of becoming unemployed.

3.2 Studies of attempted suicide patients

In their study of 50 adolescents aged 13-18 years who were admitted to hospital following deliberate self-poisoning, Hawton, O'Grady, Osborn and Cole (1982) found that *problems with school or work including unemployment* commonly preceded the overdose.

Hawton et al. (1982) studied the employment status among female attempted suicide patients of all ages. The highest annual rate of attempted suicide was found in *unemployed females* in the age group 30-49 years, followed by age group 16-29 years. Irrespective of age, many more unemployed females, when compared with employed females, suffered from psychiatric problems such as *alcoholism.* Repeated suicidal behaviour was far more common among the unemployed. Furthermore, unemployed women appear to share with men the increasing risk of attempted suicide the longer the *duration of unemployment*, with a very marked increase in risk in those unemployed more than a year. Finally, the results demonstrated an increase in the proportion of unemployed females attempting suicide during the study period (1976-1985) although this increase was less than expected on the basis of the general population unemployment statistics.

As described in the introduction, attempted suicide is a strong predictor of completed suicide. In order to determine factors associated with completed suicide in young attempted suicide patients, Hawton, Fagg, Platt & Hawkins (1993) conducted a case-control study in which the cases were young attempted suicide patients (aged 15-24 years) who died from suicide or possible suicide. Controls were attempted suicide patients matched by gender, age, and length of follow-up. Univariate logistic regression analyses demonstrated an association between (possible) suicide and *low social class, unemployment* (odds ratio 2.8, 95% confidence interval 1.4 to 5.8), *previous in-patient psychiatric treatment, substance misuse* (alcohol and/or drugs), *personality disorder, and previous attempted suicide.* Multivariate analysis identified previous in-patient psychiatric treatment (adjusted odds ratio 3.7) and substance abuse (adjusted odds ratio 3.9) as risk factors. The authors conclude that suicide after attempted suicide among young people is associated with substance abuse.

In their report of the results monitoring the characteristics of attempted suicide patients in the context of the WHO/EURO Multicentre Study on Parasuicide for five years (1988-1993), Hjelmeland and Bjerke (1996) described that young male and female patients were *unemployed* and *abusing drugs* significant more often than older patients who attempted suicide.

By comparing patients who attempted suicide by means of self-poisoning to those who injured themselves, Robinson and Duffy (1989) showed that *male youth unemployment* is associated with self-injury. Shepherd, Robinson and Levers (1990), on the other hand, could not demonstrate an association between youth unemployment and self-injury.

The association between employment status and the occurrence of attempted suicide was investigated by Van Heeringen and Jannes (1993) by means of a case-control study. Cases were attempted suicide patients of all ages while data on controls were extracted from the Population Census Records. Employment status was categorised as economically inactive, unemployed (seeking a job), and employed. Odds ratios were computed following stratification by gender and age. While simultaneously adjusting for marital status and living situation, the odds ratio of attempted suicide in young unemployed males was 5.7 (95% confidence interval 2.7-11.8), whereas in young unemployed females the adjusted odds ratio was 2.0 (95% confidence interval 1.0-4.0) indicating an insignificant increased risk. Thus, a significant association between *unemployment* and the occurrence of attempted suicide was found in *young males.*

4 Youth unemployment and completed suicide

The studies on the association between unemployment and completed suicide can be categorised according to the type of data that were used. In contrast with the reviewed studies focussing on attempted suicide, 11 aggregate data studies, including those with data on young people, regarding the association between unemployment and completed suicide were found.

To determine the trends in youth suicide in Victoria and Australia as a whole and their relation to youth unemployment, Krupinski et al. (1994) analysed aggregated data on the occurrence of suicide between 1907 and 1990 in young people aged 15-24 years. Moreover, an in-depth study of youth suicides between 1980 and 1990 was conducted. A steady increase in youth suicide could be demonstrated since 1960 in males but not females. The increase in youth suicide was not associated with the rise in unemployment. Male (not female) suicide rates were higher in areas of high youth unemployment.

Brenner (1980) studied societal consequences of youth unemployment in the USA during the period from 1947 to 1976 by calculating percent changes in measures of pathology for a 1% rise in youth unemployment rate, while assuming that the total unemployment rate does not change. It was shown that a 1% rise in youth unemployment is associated with a 4% increase *in mortality due to suicide among 15-24 year old non-white males.*

Rates of birth, divorce, marriage, and unemployment were analysed and compared to rates of suicide from 1965 to 1985 in Canada and the United States by Leenaars and Lester (1995). In Canada, measures of *domestic integration* (as measured by divorce and birth rates) and the *economy* (as measured by unemployment rates) predicted youth suicide rates more successfully than they did adult suicide rates. In the United States, for the same period, there was less variation in the predictors of suicide by age. The authors concluded that the results of studies on the association between suicide rates and social variables should not be generalised without taking account of *age or region.*

The relationship between the extent of social integration and the occurrence of completed suicide in young Canadians (aged 15-29 years) was investigated by Trovato (1992), using family integration (as measured by divorce rates), religious integration (as measured by the percent of the population reporting no religious affiliation), and economic anomie (as measured by unemployment rates) in 1971 and 1981 as indicators of social integration. The results provide confirmation for the hypothesis that *religious detachment* among the young is associated with increased proneness to commit suicide. The effect of *family dissolution* was significantly positive in 1981 but not in 1971, giving partial confirmation for the family integration explanation of suicide. No effect of unemployment on the occurrence of suicide among young Canadians could be demonstrated.

Lester (1991) found significant associations between the 1980 suicide rate of youth and the variables social integration, age structure, and race/region in the United States. These associations were also found for older groups, thus suggesting similarities in the impact of social variables on regional suicide rates.

Snyder (1992) studied associations between age- and gender-specific yearly mean percentages of *unemployment* and suicide rates in Northern Ireland over a 19-year period. Significant associations were found for only two age *groups of males (15-24* and 45-54 years) and none for females.

In his time series analysis study on the effect of religiosity on suicide among young people (aged 15 to 29 years), Stack (1991) found an association between religious trends and youth suicide rates. However, changes in religion were too closely related to changes in divorce to ascertain whether religious change or a more general trend towards social individualism was responsible for increases in youth suicide. Changes in the rate of youth unemployment were not related to suicide.

Pritchard (1992) studied the extent to which suicide rates were statistically associated with unemployment (as defined by being jobless) among males. The study was based on general and youth suicide rates and aggregate data on general unemployment rates in 13 European Community member states between 1977 and 1988. It was found that in almost all European countries (except West Germany and Denmark), youth suicide rates rose more than the general rates. Moreover, there were statistically significant associations between unemployment and general and youth suicide in all countries except Denmark, West Germany, and Portugal, with the link being weaker in respect to youth suicide rates than to general suicide rates. The latter finding, however, may be an artifact due to the lack of age-specific levels of unemployment. A more detailed analysis of UK data indicated that youth suicide rates were more strongly associated with general rather than young adult levels of unemployment. Based on this finding the author suggests that having an *unemployed father at home* actually compounds the burden for young men.

Based on their review of studies on the association between unemployment and psychological and physical ill health in young people aged 15-24 years using aggregate data, Morell et al. (1998) found a strong association between *youth unemployment* and *suicide*, *depression*, and *loss of confidence*. Moreover, the use of *cannabis* and, less consistently, *tobacco* and *alcohol* was found to be more prevalent among unemployed than among employed young people.

A comparative time series analysis of the connection between per capita *alcohol consumption* and suicide mortality based on Finnish data from 1950-1991 showed a significant association in men in the age groups 15-34 and 35-49 years. In this study, indications for a confounding role of real income, divorce rate, and unemployment rate were found.

Besides these aggregate data studies, two studies using individual data on young people have been published. Both studies used data that were collected by means of the psychological autopsy method following the suicide of a young individual. Runeson (1992) studied the extent to which young suicide victims consulted psychiatric care providers before committing suicide. Moreover, characteristics of young suicide victims (aged up to 25 years) who did not consult psychiatric care providers before their suicide were compared to those of suicide victims who did seek help. It appeared that 27.6% were not known in psychiatric care, and that unemployment, substance abuse disorder, and a history of previous suicide attempts were significantly less common among non-patients.

As described above in the section on the association between attempted suicide and unemployment, Hawton et al. (1993) performed a case-control study in which the cases were young attempted suicides who committed suicide. The univariate finding of an association between unemployment and suicide following attempted suicide disappeared after controlling for social and psychiatric characteristics.

5 Discussion

The findings from this review of studies on the association between youth unemployment and suicidal behaviour can be summarised as follows: First, it is clear that the number of studies is limited despite the fact that rates of suicidal behaviour, and more specifically suicide, are increasing among young people in a majority of countries in the Western World, and that the association between unemployment and suicidal behaviour, in general, is well-documented. Second, while there is a relatively substantial number of studies on completed suicide using aggregated data, no such studies are available on its most robust predictor, that is, attempted suicide. Although studies on aggregated data cannot be used to attribute any causal meaning to demonstrated associations, their results can act as generators of hypotheses to be tested in individual research.

Third, relatively few studies in young individuals are based on such a hypothesis or a theoretical framework. Thus, this review of studies of young people may add little to our understanding of the association that has been demonstrated and interpreted in adults, the more so due to the apparent lack of longitudinal studies of young people. Although the results from studies using aggregated data were rather inconsistent which may be due to intercultural differences in the effect of unemployment, this review appears to confirm the existence of an association between unemployment and suicidal behaviour in young people. Based on the results from the only longitudinal study in young unemployed individuals, it can be concluded that the apparent association between unemployment and suicidal behaviour arises mainly from selection processes in which those predisposed to adjustment problems are at greater risk of becoming unemployed. An important finding concerns the potential role of substance abuse in the pathogenesis of both attempted and completed suicide among unemployed individuals. A recent study among young people (Metha, Chen, Mulvenon & Dode, 1998) clearly supported findings from earlier studies on substance use as an important predictor of suicide.

Rates of suicide are increasing among young people, thus leading to very substantial premature loss of life. This review suggests that young unemployed individuals constitute a group with increased risks of suicidal behaviour. However, this review also demonstrates the need for further research in the mechanisms by means of which unemployment and suicidal behaviour are associated. Several types of studies may be appropriate to reach this goal. First, a large scale quantitative study on the occurrence of suicidal behaviour among unemployed individuals may be useful, provided that personal, psychiatric (including substance abuse), and social characteristics are included in the assessment, and that careful temporal sequencing of employment status and behavioural problems is made possible. In view of potential intercultural differences in the effect of unemployment on the occurrence of suicidal behaviour as described above, such a study should preferably be designed as a multinational study, thus including the assessment of international and intercultural effects. Second, psychological autopsy studies of young suicide victims may help to elucidate these mechanisms. However, a large group of suicide victims needs to be studied and a carefully chosen methodology will be required, particularly with regard to the identification of factors such as psychiatric disorder (including substance abuse), current problems, personality disorder, relevant social factors (including unemployment), and contacts with helping agencies (Hawton & Morgan, 1994). Thirdly, research might be directed towards more qualitative studies in order to search for deeper mechanisms and explanatory theories (Hammarström, 1994) of the association between unemployment and suicidal behaviour.

National Reports on Youth Unemployment and Health

Youth Unemployment and Health in Sweden

Bengt Starrin, Marina Kalander-Blomqvist, Erik Forsberg & Ulla Rantakeisu

1 Introduction to youth unemployment and health

1.1 National development of youth unemployment

For many years, full employment was a feature of the Swedish labour market, with unemployment rates having been very low since the end of the Second World War (Janlert, 1991). However, this situation changed drastically during the 90s. During the first three years of this decade almost half a million jobs disappeared. In 1990, the national figure for total unemployment was about 3% (open unemployment, including those in special relief projects provided by the authorities to tackle local unemployment) and proceeded to rise very rapidly reaching about 12% in 1993.

Figure S-1 shows the growth of unemployment in Sweden between 1976 and 1996. The data indicates open unemployment. It can be seen that unemployment among young persons has been considerably higher than for the entire population (16-64 years age group). This gap widened during the first three years of the 90s. Up to the beginning of the 80s, unemployment for the 16-19 years age group was considerably higher than for the 20-24 years age group, after which it fell sharply, largely as a result of various educational policy and labour market policy measures. It can also be seen from the diagram that youth unemployment in the two younger age groups increased very substantially during the first three years of the 90s. There are certain noteworthy differences between the sexes, although these are not shown in the diagram. In 1991, unemployment among men in the 20-24 years age group was 7.2%, while that for women was 5.1%. In 1993, the corresponding figures were 21.7% and 14.2%, respectively. The figure also shows how unemployment in both age groups has fallen since 1993, while remaining essentially the same for the overall 16-64 years age group.

Figure S-1: Unemployment in Sweden, 1976-1996, by age groups

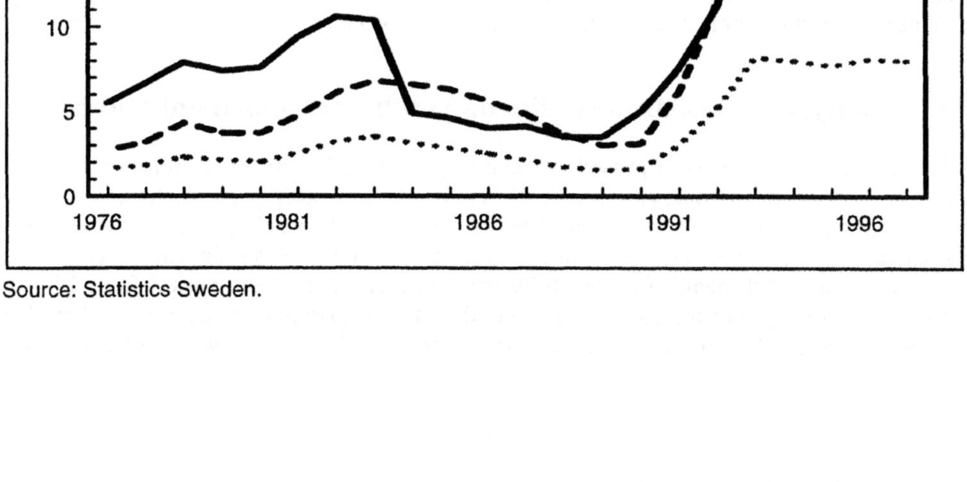

Source: Statistics Sweden.

1.1.1 Various regional differences

A characteristic feature of the economic recession of the 90s is that the regional pattern of unemployment has changed: Despite regional and labour market policy measures, the employment situation varies from region to region. Earlier recessions in Sweden had primarily afflicted the forest counties: thinly populated areas and traditional industrial areas. However, since the beginning of the 90s the recession has hit all regions hard so that there are only relatively minor differences today in the proportions of those in work from one region to another. The highest proportion of those in work is found in Stockholm with 78%. Other regions lie between 73% and 76% (Davidsson, 1997).

Although the regional differences in employment intensity are not particularly great, youth unemployment varies considerably from one area of the country to another. A comparison between the forest counties, the areas around the major urban centres, and other counties shows that youth unemployment is considerably higher in the forest counties than in (particularly) the areas around the major urban centres. Unemployment in the forest counties during the recession of 1992-95 has varied between about 15-24% for young persons in the 20-24 years age group, which can be compared with about 8-15% in the areas around the major urban centres (Ungdomsstyrelsen, 1996).

1.2 Unemployment and health – some theoretical considerations

The post-war years in Sweden were marked by a long period of full employment. This past situation might be the reason that there has been only little Swedish research into the relationship between unemployment and ill health. One of the first surveys that was carried out looked at what happened in the wake of closing a factory (Backlund, 1973). During the early 80s, this working area was picked up again (primarily) by Janlert, a worker in the social medicine field, and acquired contemporaneous interest through the acceptance by the National Board of Health and Welfare of the discoveries concerning the relationship between unemployment and ill health that had been made internationally (Janlert, 1981).

With a few exceptions, the Swedish research into youth unemployment and health has not been theory-driven, meaning guided by existing theories. However, links have been made to existing theories in the field such as stress theory, gender theory, and deprivation theory. In addition, most Swedish research into youth unemployment has not attempted to combine theories of unemployment with theories of youth and youth culture. The implicit assumption in many studies seems to have been that unemployment may lead to improved health rather than the reverse.

2 Analyses of research studies on youth unemployment and health

The aim of this report is to provide a general picture of Swedish research into the relationship between unemployment and ill health among young persons. In this context, young persons are those in the 16-29 years age group. In writing this review we have selected Swedish investigations that are known to us into the relationship between unemployment and ill health for the 16-29 years age group over the period from 1973 to 1998. The selection of the surveys was based on the following criteria. *Firstly,* there had to be a detailed description of the method. *Secondly,* the surveys were not carried out earlier than 1973, while *thirdly,* it had to be possible to identify the age group within the 16-29 years age range to which the investigation relates. Only one exception to these criteria was made. We have employed various methods in order to obtain information on the Swedish studies that have been performed of the relationship between youth unemployment and ill health. We searched in a number of international databases: Medline, Psychological Abstracts, and Current Contents. We also searched the Swedish LIBRIS library database which covers all literature available in the Swedish university and university colleges sector. We employed a very wide definition of ill health including not only illness as such but also self-reported mental and psychological troubles as well as indicators of alienation. In our review, we also have included what is sometimes referred to as health-related lifestyle and sometimes as health-related habits.

2.1 Description of the available data

2.1.1 Longitudinal studies

2.1.1.1 Individual studies

One of the first and more comprehensive surveys of the situation for young unemployed persons was carried out by Anne Hammarström in the middle of the 80s. Hammarström described the results from a longitudinal survey in a series of articles. The surveys started in 1981 when all the pupils in the ninth school year of an area of Northern Sweden completed a questionnaire. The survey was followed up in 1983 and 1986. The original population was comprised of 1,083 individuals. The loss of subjects in the 1983 follow-up was very low, less than 2%. The pupils were divided into groups depending on what they were doing after the ninth school year. Those who were 'studying and motivated for studies' made up about 40%; 'studying but not motivated' made up 48%; while those 'working' made up 5% and consisted of pupils who had been employed for 12 weeks or more. The fourth group, 'unemployed', accounted for 7% and consisted of those pupils who had been openly unemployed for 12 weeks or more. The parameters that were investigated included health, social background, free time, school, work life experience, plans for the future, school qualifications, school health records, and the results of various tests including personality tests.

The results of a two-year tracking survey were presented in 1986 (Hammarström, 1986). At the first follow-up it was found that the study-motivated group was happiest and the unemployed group the least happy. As far as the presence of psychosomatic problems was concerned, considerably greater numbers of the unemployed group cited psychosomatic problems than did the control groups. Girls quoted more psychosomatic problems than boys. The mental health of the working group (the unemployed in labour market relief schemes) improved between one survey and the next, but not for the unemployed group. As far as alcohol was concerned, consumption increased primarily among boys. Young men in the unemployed group had the highest consumption. Over the two-year period smoking increased substantially among girls: Among boys snuff usage increased more than smoking. As far as narcotics were concerned, cannabis abuse increased among the unemployed group. Concerning the utilisation of health services there was an increase among the unemployed young men. Hammarström's conclusions were that unemployment results in more mental problems, greater consumption of alcohol, greater abuse of cannabis, more psychosomatic problems (among girls), and reduced activity in associations or societies (among girls).

Hammarström (1991) presented the results of the 1986 follow-up in a summarising article. She noted that during the five-year period covered by the survey, over half of the cohort had been unemployed at some time or another. 17% of the girls and 15% of the boys had been unemployed for a total of more than a year. A slight increase in blood pressure could be noted among the unemployed relative to those who were not unemployed (in the 5-year follow-up study an increase in blood pressure was found only among the young unemployed men). Mental problems increased among the unemployed in comparison with those who were not unemployed, with a greater increase among girls than among boys. A strong relationship could also be noted between unemployment and the consumption of alcohol among those for whom no special measures were being applied.

Janlert and Hammarström also looked more closely at the relationship between the consumption of alcohol and youth unemployment. In an article in the 'British Journal of Addiction' Janlert and Hammarström (1992) showed that, particularly among men, the consumption of alcohol increased substantially between the two survey occasions of 1981 and 1986. Among women, consumption increased for about the first 20 weeks of unemployment, after which it fell back to more normal levels. Among men, consumption tended to increase in step with the length of unemployment. The survey thus shows a clear relationship between unemployment and the consumption of alcohol. Consumption, however, decreased among new mothers within the unemployed group.

In a separate article Hammarström and Janlert (1994) also described results concerning the relationship between smoking and unemployment. The survey showed that the use of tobacco was more common among 16-year-old girls than among boys, but that the situation had equalised five years later. However, women still smoked more while men took more snuff. At the start of the survey there were no noticeable links between men, smoking, and unemployment, but this situation changed after a longer period of unemployment when the tobacco consumption increased among men. The tendency to start or to increase smoking was higher among those with long-term unemployment as compared to those with no or a short length of unemployment.

In an article in 'The Journal of Adolescence', Hammarström and Janlert (1997) took up the relationship between unemployment and young persons' mental ill health. The material on which this was based was the same as that for the previous articles. The total frequency of symptoms did not alter significantly over the observation period. Nervous symptoms increased among women but decreased among men over the period. Depressive symptoms occurred only to a lesser extent, although it could be seen that the length of unemployment was linked to increasing problems among both men and women. Nervous problems appeared earlier than depressive problems, which manifested themselves only after a longer period of unemployment, such as a year or more. Young women displayed more depressive symptoms the longer their unemployment lasted.

Ståhl (1987) compared, in a follow-up study from 1986, a group of young persons (n = 221) born in 1965 who were without a firm link to the labour market (unemployed) after they left school in 1981 with a control group consisting of 43 young persons who had been accepted for continuing studies in upper secondary school (not unemployed). He investigated the occurrence of psychosomatic problems such as headaches and stomach aches, together with other problems that he defined as anxiety about the future, a tendency to be discouraged, scepticism about a reasonable job, despondency, and a feeling of failure. Ståhl found that more persons had suffered from headaches and stomach aches in the unemployed group. They were more anxious about their future, more pessimistic about the chances of getting a decent job, and generally felt more despondent, disconsolate, and unsuccessful. However, no relationships were found between alcohol consumption and being unemployed.

2.1.1.2 Aggregated studies

In an aggregated study Hagquist (in print) examined the relationship between unemployment and suicide rate among young people in the age group 20-25 years. The study covers the years 1980-1996. The results show a tendency towards a negative relationship between the unemployment rate and the suicide rate in the way that when the unemployment rate increases the suicide rate decreases.[1]

In an official report published by the Swedish Welfare Board (Social Rapport, 1997), it could be shown that for unemployed persons the risk of dying from suicide has doubled since the beginning of 1960s up to the end of 70s. The risk was found to be higher among long-term unemployed young men.

2.1.2 Cross-sectional surveys – with control groups

2.1.2.1 Comparison between a group of unemployed persons and a control group

In a survey that was carried out in 1981, Fredlund and Tomth (1985) compared two groups of young persons in the 16-24 years age group. The unemployed group consisted of 70 young persons with extensive, current unemployment. All had been out of work for at least the previous six months before they were interviewed. At the time of the interview, the 137 members of the control group were either in permanent employment, on a labour market relief scheme, or studying. The results revealed considerable differences in the occurrence of symptoms of ill health. A larger proportion of the unemployed group had suffered more from sleeplessness or stomach ache in the recent past than the control group. Again, a considerably larger proportion of the unemployed group had felt worried/restless, and also more depressed than the control group. Over a third of the unemployed group felt that unemployment had damaged their health. As far as the consumption of alcohol (wine, beer or spirits) was concerned, no significant differences were found between the two groups. A majority within both groups said that they seldom or never drink any alcohol.

2.1.2.2 Comparison between a group of open unemployed persons and a group participating in work experience programmes

Hagquist and Starrin (1996) compared two groups of young persons. One group consisted of 81 openly unemployed youngsters while the other group consisted of 143 youngsters participating in work experience courses. Various indicators of ill health were investigated: stomach problems, headaches, sleeping difficulties, depression, powerlessness, nervousness/restlessness. Questions concerning the extent to which unemployment or work experience had caused health changes were also included. The results showed a clear link between unemployment and mental ill health among young persons. In the group of openly unemployed over 25% of the men and 50% of the women stated that their mental well-being had deteriorated during unemployment. None of the men and only 4% of the

---

1 In the article, a short analysis is also presented which shows a clear link between economic deprivation on the one hand and suicide on the other. The probability of those on social allowance committing suicide was more than two times higher than those in the control group.

women stated that their mental well-being had improved. In the work experience group, 25% of the men and 40% of the women stated that their mental well-being had improved after they had obtained their work experience position while only 4% and 5%, respectively, stated that it had deteriorated. The survey asked whether unemployment or work experience had resulted in an increase or decrease in alcohol consumption. Significant differences could be noted between the sexes and between the unemployed and those in work experience. Almost 30% of the young unemployed men stated that unemployment had resulted in an increase in alcohol consumption. The corresponding figure for young women was only about 4%. Alcohol consumption appeared to have fallen for the work experience group, and this applied both for men and women. Hagquist and Starrin also found that the transition to unemployment tends to increase smoking among women. The study showed that changes in health-related habits appear, above all, at the transition to unemployment. However the patterns for men and women are different. While men increase their alcohol consumption, women increase their smoking. The study also showed that among men and women, a comparatively large proportion exercise more while a small proportion diminish their exercising. Also, a link between financial problems and a deterioration in mental health could be detected. Those in a poorer financial situation were more worried about the future than the group in a better situation. The financial situation also varied reflecting the general state of mental health in the way that the poorer the financial situation is, the more mental problems occur.

Data on political participation and political activity is presented in the Official Government Report Series (SOU, 1994). Two groups were compared, unemployed and not unemployed. It was found that the participation rate in elections was lower within the unemployed group as compared to the non-unemployed group. Political activities were also lower within the unemployed group.

2.1.2.3 Comparison between open unemployment, unemployed persons on welfare schemes, students, and those in work

Health data for various groups – open unemployed, unemployed on welfare schemes, students, and young persons in work – were described in a recently published project ‚Unemployment conditions – On young persons, unemployment, and marginalisation in the Nordic countries in the 90s' (Hammarström & Olofsson, 1997). The survey has made comparisons between Finland, Iceland, Norway, Sweden, and Denmark. Here we shall describe only the results of the analyses for Sweden. The Swedish material covered 1,247 men and 1,287 women between the ages of 18 and 24 years. The investigation found that there were significant differences between the subjective health of the different groups. The proportion reporting that their health was average or poor was greatest among the open unemployed, and this applied for both men and women. The investigation also found that the proportion of unemployed youngsters reporting average or poor health increased with the length of unemployment. The survey also asked the respondents whether they had been drunk at least once a week during the last 12 months. No significant differences between the unemployed group and the working group could be found. However the number of men who had been drunk was twice as high as that of women. The investigation also noted that the proportion of open unemployed persons suffering from mental problems increased stepwise with the length of unemployment. Another important factor was the financial situation: the poorer the respondents' finances, the poorer was their health.

2.1.3 Cross-sectional surveys without a control group

A study carried out by Rantakeisu, Starrin, and Hagquist (1997) looked at the question of whether the individual's experience of being belittled and looked down upon as unemployed could affect the relationship between unemployment and ill health. The umbrella term that was used for this was 'shaming experience'. The survey included 502 unemployed persons in the 16-25 years age group. It looked at the occurrence of psychosomatic problems, depression, nervousness/restlessness, frustration, etc. Changes in health and well-being reported by the sample were also considered, as were changes in living habits and changes in their social networks. Questions as to whether the respondents had been regarded as lazy or ignorant because they were unemployed or whether they had ever kept out of the way because they were unemployed were used as quantifiers for shaming experience. The study showed that those who had experienced more shame as a result of unemployment were also more troubled by psychosomatic and mental problems. These persons also reported a higher extent of health deterioration as a result of their unemployment. In addition, those who had experienced more shame had a higher tendency to report an increase in alcohol consumption and a reduction in exercise. The study also revealed reduced contact with parents, relatives, and friends among the unemployed, particularly among those who had experienced more shame.

Another study performed by Rantakeisu, Starrin, and Hagquist (1997) concentrated on the development and testing of a model – the Finances/Shame model – for understanding the relationship between unemployment and ill health. The sample consisted of 502 unemployed persons in the 16-25 years age group. The health indicators and the shaming quantities were the same as in the Rantakeisu et al. study (1997, see above). A composite measure of financial pressure was used based on questions as to whether the interviewees had been forced to pawn property, sell property, borrow money during their unemployment, or had difficulties in paying bills on time. The results from this study revealed that the extent of ill health, mental problems, and feelings of powerlessness were considerably higher within the 'Higher degree of financial hardship/More shaming experiences' group than within the 'Lower degree of financial hardship/Less shaming experiences' group. It was shown that the extent of serious psychosomatic problems, powerlessness, and depression is considerably wider among those exposed to a higher degree of financial hardship and having a greater experience of feeling shamed by their surroundings. This applies to both men and women. The differences between men and women were that there was a considerably greater extent of problems, powerlessness, and depression among women than among men.

2.2 Summary evaluation of the presented studies

2.2.1 Objective health indicators

2.2.1.1 Mortality rates
No data is available.

2.2.1.2 Morbidity rates
No data is available except for blood pressure. *Blood pressure* was used in two longitudinal studies. Hammarström (1986) noted a slight increase in blood pressure among the unemployed relative to those who were not unemployed. In a 5-year follow-up study she found an increase in blood pressure among young unemployed men (Hammarström 1996).

2.2.1.3 Suicidal behaviour

Swedish aggregate studies show no consistent pattern regarding the link between unemployment and suicide rates. In an aggregated study Hagquist (in print) has examined the relationship between the unemployment rate and the suicide rate among young people in the age group 20-25 years. The study covers the years 1980-1996. The results show a tendency towards a negative relationship between the unemployment and the suicide rate in the way that when the unemployment rate increases the suicide rate decreases. In an official report published by the Swedish Welfare Board (Social Rapport, 1997), it was shown that for unemployed persons the risk for death by suicide has doubled since the beginning of 1960s up to the end of 1970s. This risk was found to be higher among long-term unemployed young men.

2.2.1.4 Utilisation of health services

Hammarström (1986) found in her 2-year tracking survey an increase in the use of health services among unemployed young men.

2.2.2 Subjective health indicators

2.2.2.1 Psychosocial strains

Hagquist and Starrin (1996) compared two groups of young persons. One group consisted of 81 openly unemployed youngsters while the other group consisted of 143 youngsters participating in work experience courses. They showed that the *view of life* became darker and that the belief in the future diminished among a very large proportion of men and women who were at the transition to unemployment, whereas at the transition to youth training programs, the view of life became brighter and the belief in the future increased.

2.2.2.2 Subjective well-being

There seems to be a consistent pattern between unemployment and different indications of subjective well-being. Unemployment is associated with more negative self-reported *well-being*. Hammarström (1986) found in a longitudinal study, at the first follow-up, that the unemployed group were the least *happy* among the studied groups. She also found that a considerably greater number of the unemployed group cited *psychosomatic problems* than did the control groups. The mental health of the working group (the unemployed in labour market relief schemes) improved between one survey and the next. However, this was not true for the unemployed group. Hammarström (1991) noted that *mental health problems* increased among the unemployed in comparison with those who were not unemployed, with a greater increase among girls than among boys.

In a follow-up study from 1986 Ståhl (1987) compared a group of young unemployed with a group of not unemployed persons. He found that more persons had suffered from *headaches* and *stomach aches* in the unemployed group. They were more *anxious about their future*, more *pessimistic* about their chances to get a decent job, and generally felt more despondent, disconsolate and unsuccessful. Fredlund and Tomth (1985) compared two groups of young persons in the 16-24 years age group. They found considerable differences in the occurrence of symptoms of ill health. A larger proportion of the unemployed group had suffered from *sleeplessness* or *stomach aches* in the recent past than had the control group. Again, a considerably larger proportion of the unemployed group had also felt *worried/restless*, and had felt more *depressed* than the control group. Over a third of the unemployed group felt that unemployment had damaged their health.

Hagquist and Starrin (1996) compared two groups of young persons. One group consisted of openly unemployed youngsters while the other group consisted of youngsters participating in work experience courses. The results showed a clear link between unemployment and *mental ill health* among young persons. Among the group of openly unemployed, over 25% of the men and 50% of the women stated that their mental well-being had deteriorated. None of the men and only 4% of the women stated that their mental well-being had improved. Among the work experience group, 25% of the men and 40% of the women stated that their mental well-being had improved after they had obtained their work experience position, while only 4% and 5%, respectively, stated that it had deteriorated.

Hammarström and Olofsson (1997) found, in a comparative study, that there were significant differences between the *subjective health* of the different groups of young people. The proportion reporting that their health was average or poor was greatest among the openly unemployed, and this applied for both men and women.

2.2.2.3 Self-esteem

No data is available.

2.2.2.4 Alienation (political orientation)

The relation between unemployment and possible indications of alienation, such as political activity, is contradictory in Sweden. On one hand, it has been shown that the unemployed are less politically active as compared to nonunemployed individuals (SOU, 1994). It was found that the participation rate during elections was lower within the unemployed group as compared to the nonunemployed group. On the other hand it was shown that a greater proportion of the unemployed increase their political activity during unemployment as compared to those unemployed persons who decrease their political activity (Hagquist & Starrin, 1996).

2.2.2.5 Social deviation

No data is available.

2.2.2.6 Health behaviour

Swedish studies regarding the relationship between unemployment and *alcohol* consumption is somewhat ambiguous. Some studies show a positive relation, others do not. On one hand Hammarström (1986) found in her follow-up comparative study that the young men in the unemployed group had the highest consumption of alcohol. She noted that, over the 5-year period, a strong relationship could be noted between unemployment and the consumption of alcohol (Hammarström, 1991). Hagquist and Starrin (1996) found that the transition from unemployment to youth training programmes decreased alcohol consumption. On the other hand, no significant differences in alcohol consumption between unemployed and not unemployed persons were found in two studies (Ståhl, 1987; Fredlund & Tomth, 1985).

Smoking has been shown to be related to unemployment among young women. Hammarström (1986) found, in her longitudinal study, that over the 2-year period smoking increased substantially among girls. Among boys, snuff usage increased more than smoking. Hagquist and Starrin (1996) also found that the transition to unemployment tended to increase smoking among women. In her follow-up study Hammarström (1986) found that the use of *cannabis* increased among the unemployed group. Regarding *physical activity,* one study showed that a comparatively large proportion of the unemployed increased their amount of physical exercise (Hagquist & Starrin 1996).

2.2.3 Mediators

2.2.3.1 Age
No data is available.

2.2.3.2 Gender
In two studies gender was important for the relation between unemployment and indications of *subjective well-being*. Women showed a tendency for reporting more health problems as compared to men (Hammarström & Olofsson, 1997; Hagquist & Starrin, 1996). The increase in the consumption of *alcohol* during unemployment seems to be valid only for men (Hagquist & Starrin, 1996), and the increase in *tobacco smoking* only for women (Hagquist & Starrin, 1996). With regard to alienation the importance of gender is not consistent. One study showed that a greater proportion of women increased their political activities during unemployment as compared to men (Hagquist & Starrin, 1996). Another study showed that young unemployed women decreased their social activities in clubs (Hammarström, 1986).

2.2.3.3 Education
No data is available.

2.2.3.4 Social class
No data is available.

2.2.3.5 Length of unemployment
Studies on the length of unemployment display a consistent pattern. The increase in the length of unemployment was always related to an increase in *nervous problems* and *depression* (Hammarström & Janlert, 1997). Hammarström and Olofsson (1997) found that the proportion of unemployed youngsters reporting average or poor health and mental health problems increased with the length of unemployment. Some indications point to an increase in *alcohol consumption* the longer the period of unemployment lasts. Janlert and Hammarström (1992) showed that, among men, alcohol consumption tended to increase stepwise with the length of unemployment.

2.2.4 Moderators

2.2.4.1 Work and job orientation
No data is available.

2.2.4.2 Financial strain
Studies on the role of financial strain showed consistent patterns in relation to subjective well-being: The greater the financial strain the greater the intensity of *self-reported ill health* (Hammarström & Olofsson, 1997; Hagquist & Starrin, 1996).

2.2.4.3 Social support/shaming
One study examined the role of experiences of being shamed during unemployment. It showed that the more the unemployed persons experienced being shamed, the more ill health and negative changes in living habits (*increase in alcohol consumption* and *reduced exercise*) could be found (Rantakeisu, Starrin & Hagquist, 1997).

2.2.4.4 Financial strain and experiences of being shamed
One study demonstrated that the extent of *ill health*, *mental health problems*, and feelings of *powerlessness* were considerably greater among those who had more experiences of fi-

nancial strain and more experiences of being shamed as compared to the other combinations of financial strain and experiences of being shamed (Rantakeisu, Starrin & Hagquist, 1997).

3 Summary of results

A review of the studies that have compared young unemployed persons with other groups of young people shows that, on the whole, the former group tends to report poorer health than the latter group. Young unemployed persons also tend to report more mental and psychosomatic problems than those who are not unemployed. Some studies indicate that young unemployed women tend to report more health problems (both mental and psychosomatic) than young unemployed men. A few studies also report that the length of unemployment tends to be a significant factor. As far as the relationship between alcohol consumption and unemployment is concerned, the results from the Swedish surveys are not entirely consistent. Some studies lean towards alcohol consumption among men tending to increase during unemployment, while a few studies have not been able to find any such relationships. It is known that unemployment affects young persons in different ways. For some, unemployment is a torment while for others it has no noticeable adverse effects. One study that looks at both financial and social conditions found that those young persons suffering from both a higher degree of financial hardship and having more experience of being devalued and belittled (shamed) exhibit noticeably more symptoms of ill health and, to a considerably greater extent, state that their health has deteriorated during unemployment than those living under less financial hardship and having less experience of being devalued and belittled (shamed).

There are some features that characterise the Swedish research on youth unemployment. First, it is mainly quantitatively oriented. We have not been able to find any study that fulfills the criteria that we apply for a qualitative orientation. The lack of qualitatively oriented studies is a weakness in Swedish research on youth unemployment because such studies would make it possible to achieve a better understanding of what unemployment actually can involve. In addition, qualitatively orientated studies would inspire new approaches because they are open to surprises. Second, the characteristic feature of most quantitative studies is that they have been exploratory in their nature. In only very few cases have they started from an explicit theory that was to be tested, and again only in very few cases has any attempt been made to construct models or theories on the basis of existing sets of variables. Links have been made to existing theories such as general stress theory, gender theory, deprivation theory, and so on. However, our impression is that the distance between empirical results and theoretical presentations is, if not remote, then at least very considerable. With only a few exceptions Swedish research on youth unemployment has not attempted to combine theories of unemployment with theories of youth and youth culture. Third, it has become apparent that the health effects of youth unemployment have not interested Swedish researchers to any greater extent. In particular, there are few established researchers working in this area. A possible explanation for this might be that youth unemployment has not been a problem prior to the 90s in those areas where most Swedish researchers are active, that is, in the larger towns. It is noteable that the group of researchers having the longest experience in this particular field (Hammarström & Janlert, 1994; 1997), and whose work has attracted the greatest national and international attention, are active in the northernmost parts of Sweden which, over many years, has had a relatively high level of youth unemployment.

Youth unemployment and health: Swedish studies – an overview

Author	Sample	Instruments/ Methods	Population	Dependent variables	Results
Fredlund/ Tomth 1985	N= 207 unemployed: n= 70, not unemployed: n= 137	cross-sectional studies with control-group interview	– 16-24 years, – urban /rural	psychosomatic problems alcohol consumption social network economic difficulties	unemployed persons: – more psychosomatic problems – less contact with relatives – higher alcohol consumption – more of economic difficulties
Hammarström 1986	N= 1,073 unemployed: n= 78 employed: n= 55 motivated to study: n= 424 not motivated to study: (n= 506)	indiv. longitudinal studies with control group (3 years follow-up study) survey	– 1981: 16 years 1983: 19 years – urban population	psychosomatic problems mental ill-health alcohol consumption, smoking habits, narcotics utilisation of health services activites in clubs	unemployed group compared to the other groups: 1. women: – decrease in alcohol consumption – increase in abuse of narcotics – increase in psychosomatic symptoms – increase in tobacco consumption – decrease in social activities in clubs 2. men – increase in psychological symptoms, dyspepsia – increase in utilisation of health care services – alcohol consumption higher than women – slight increase in abuse of narcotics
Ståhl 1987	N= 264 – unemployed: n=221 – employed: n=43	indiv. longitudinal studies with control group (3 years follow-up study) survey registered data	– 21 years	psychosomatic/psychological problems alcohol consumption	– more psychosomatic/psychological problems among the unemployed compared to nonunemployed – no relations between the groups with respect to alcohol consumption
Hammarström 1991	N= 1,062 – unemployed: n= 92 – employed: n= 968	indiv. longitudinal studies with control group (3 years follow-up study) survey	– 1981: 16 years 1983: 19 years 1986: 21 years – urban population	psychosomatic problems mental ill-health alcohol consumption blood pressure	– increase in blood-pressure, psychosomatic problems, mental health problems among the unemployed relative to those not unemployed – greater increase in mental problems among women than among men – increase in alcohol consumption among men, and among long-term unemployed women

Author	Sample	Instruments/ Methods	Population	Dependent variables	Results
Janlert & Hammarström 1992	N= 1,062 (individuals can belong to several categories): no unemployment: n= 311 short unemployment: n= 147) long unemployment: n= 102	indiv. longitudinal studies with control group (5 years follow-up study)	–16-21 years –urban population	alcohol consumption	–higher alcohol consumption among the unemployed as compared to those not unemployed *Changes in alcohol consumption* –increase among men with long unemployment –decrease among women with long unemployment. –negative correlation among women: a) in the beginning of the study, b) during motherhood
Hammarström/ Janlert 1994	N= 1,062 (individuals can belong to several categories): no unemployment: n= 439 short unemployment: n= 442 long unemployment: n= 140	indiv. longitudinal studies with control group (5 years follow-up study) survey	–16-21 years –urban population	smoking habits	–unemployed women smoked more than unemployed men
SOU 1994	N= 33,000	cross-sectional studies with control-group of statistical data	–16-29 years urban/rural	participation in election political activity	unemployed: –less politically active in the election –fewer political activities

Author	Sample	Instruments/ Methods	Population	Dependent variables	Results
Hagquist/ Starrin 1996	N= 224 unemployed: n= 81 trainees: n= 143	cross-sectional studies with control-group survey	– under 25 years – urban/rural	mental ill-health psychosomatic problems political activity alcohol consumption tobacco habits physical activity	– more sleeping problems, headache, restlessness, worries, among unemployed men compared to male trainees – more stomach ache, headache, powerlessness, depression, restlessness, worries, tiredness and difficulties to relax among unemployed women compared to female trainees – more of psychosomatic problems and mental ill-health among unemployed women than men – more psychosomatic problems and mental ill-health among people who are in a worse economic situation – political activity higher among unemployed men/women – higher alcohol consumption among men, – higher tobacco consumption among unemployed women than men
Hammar-ström 1996	N= 1,062 –unemployed: n= 165 –employed: n= 409 –studying: n= 250 –youth trainee: n= 239	individual longitudinal studies with control group (5 years follow-up study) survey medical record	– 16-21 years – urban population	blood pressure	– increase in blood-pressure among long term-unemployed young men
Hammar-ström & Janlert 1997	N= 1,062 (individuals can belong to sev. categories): never unemployed: n= 439 unemployed during last 3 years: n= 190 unemployed during last year: n= 160 unemployed now: n= 92 long-term unemployment: n= 140	individual longitudinal studies with control group (5 years follow-up study) survey	– 16-21 years – urban population	psychological ill health	– increase in nervous symptoms among both women and men – increases in depressive symptoms as the length of unemployment increase with women showing more depressive symptoms

Author	Sample	Instruments/ Methods	Population	Dependent variables	Results
Hammarström & Olofsson 1997	N= 2,534	cross-sectional studies with control-group survey some items from Hopkins symptom list	– 18-24 years – urban/rural – open unemployed, unemployed on welfare schemes, students, persons in work	self-reported health alcohol consumption mental problems cannabis	– more often health problems among open unemployed persons (increase of problems with length of unemployment) – higher alcohol consumption among open unemployed women as compared to the other groups; no significant links among men. – increase in mental problems among unemployed group with length of unemployment – the poorer the finances the poorer health
Ranta-keisu, Starrin & Hagquist 1997	N= 502	cross-sectional studies without control-group survey	– 16-25 years – urban, rural population	psychosomatic disorders, changes of living habits (smoking, alcohol consumption)	– more shaming leading to: – more ill-health – deteriorated state of mental well-being – negative changes in living habits
Ranta-keisu, Starrin & Hagquist 1997	N= 502	cross-sectional studies without control-group survey	– 16-25 years – urban, rural population	psychosomatic disorders change of living habits (smoking, alcohol consumption) changes in health and mental well-being	– greater degree of financial hardship and more shaming experiences leading to: – more psychosomatic disorders – deteriorated state of health and mental well-being – negative living habits
Social Rapport 1997	N= 962,409	aggregated longitudinal studies statistical data	– 15-24 years	suicide	– risk of dying in suicide has doubled among non-employed men since the beginning of 1960 up to the end of 1970 – increased risk among young long-term unemployed
Hagquist 1998	N= 1,166,164	aggregated longitudinal studies aggregated data	– 20-25 years	suicide	– no positive links over time at the aggregated level among the data – there seem to be tendencies towards a negative relationship

Youth Unemployment and Health in Belgium

Kees van Heeringen & Wouter Vanderplasschen

1 Introduction to youth unemployment and health

Although a substantial amount of literature on causes, figures, trends, and consequences of unemployment in Belgium is available, relatively little has been written about unemployment among specific groups, such as youth. As opposed to the Dutch situation, a considerable lack of knowledge about objective health indicators is apparent in Belgium and inequities in health according to socio-economic variables have rarely been studied. This report provides the most up-to-date review of the Belgian debate concerning youth unemployment and health. The analysis of two different unemployment rates in Belgium and the analysis of data at different national and regional levels (Belgium and its regions Flanders, Wallonia, and Brussels) causes overlapping and sometimes incomplete information and may interfere with a clear presentation of the statistical information on youth unemployment. Due to the fact that only a very limited number of studies on youth unemployment and health is available, this report includes several studies on unemployment in general and on divergent health-related topics. Moreover, no central database on (youth) unemployment and health is available in Belgium, and information is spread across a number of institutions and departments. It appears that especially scientific information on the Wallonian situation is difficult to obtain. Therefore, this report cannot be regarded as an exhaustive summary of all available information. Nevertheless, information from all major scientific institutions is included in the report so that it can be regarded as a thorough evaluation of the Belgian debate on youth unemployment and health.

1.1 National development of youth unemployment

1.1.1 Unemployment in general

Like most European countries, Belgium has faced increasing rates of unemployment since the first oil crisis in 1973. Before 1973, unemployment was only a marginal phenomenon. However, between 1973 and 1985 the number of unemployed persons has gradually increased, reaching peak values in 1984 with 512,400 unemployed persons entitled to unemployment benefits (Federaal Ministerie, 1997). Since the mid-80s, the unemployment figures, although decreasing, have constantly remained at a high level. The 90s can be characterised as a new period of high unemployment rates, and in 1994 the psychologically important threshold of 500,000 unemployed persons was reached again. Recently, unemployment figures appear to decrease slowly. Vranken, Geldof and Van Menxel (1997) suggest that this decrease is due to statistical interventions such as the fact that some groups of unemployed persons (e.g., older unemployed persons) are not included anymore and also due to specific governmental measures (e.g., employment initiatives and suspensions of unemployed persons from the entitlement to employment benefits) rather than to a real improvement of the economic situation.

One of the most obvious reasons for the huge unemployment problem during the last two decades has been the reduced demand for employees which, among others, has been induced by the enormous technological evolution (e.g., automatisation, increased productivity) and the high labour costs causing delocalisation and outsourcing (Traisnel, 1997). Other causes of unemployment can be found in the growing participation of women on the labour market, the development of the information era and the knowledge-society, globalisation, flexibilisation, and the strong competition (Stuurgroep, 1997).

Absolute numbers accurately indicate the total number of unemployed persons, but the use of unemployment rates is preferable to compare the problem of unemployment in a European perspective. Overall unemployment rates have increased from a nearly 'zero-unemployment' to over 10%, reaching its peak in 1983-1984 (Federaal Ministerie, 1997). During the second half of the 80s unemployment rates clearly decreased, but have increased again in the 90s. As opposed to the absolute unemployment figures, the relative unemployment rates appear to decrease only slowly and remain at an extremely high level (13%). This unemployment rate indicates that one in seven persons in the active population is unemployed (Vranken et al., 1997).

The majority of unemployed individuals are women, and nearly two in three unemployed persons have been unemployed for more than one year (Vranken et al., 1997). Although the educational level of the population has increased, almost 60% of all unemployed persons have only achieved primary or lower secondary education. A more in-depth analysis of the Belgian unemployment rates shows substantial regional differences (Rijksdienst, 1998). Flanders has a comparatively low unemployment rate (10.3%), while rates in Brussels (23.6%) and Wallonia (23.8%) are considerably higher. Within Flanders, the former mining region of Limburg (13.1%) and the cities Gent (12.0%) and Ostend (14.7%) have the highest unemployment rates. In Wallonia, Charleroi (29.8%) and Mons (33.0%), in the former mining area, as well as Liège have the highest unemployment rates.

1.1.2 Youth unemployment

The analysis of youth unemployment rates is hampered by the fact that official youth unemployment rates are available only at a regional level (see Table 1). This official unemployment describes the proportion of unemployed persons entitled to employment benefits in comparison with persons insured against unemployment. Therefore, because this is probably an overestimation of the actual situation, the use of the data from the Belgian active population questionnaire collected in the context of an extensive EUROSTAT study (Nationaal Instituut voor de Statistiek, 1997) seems to be preferable. Although these data are based only on an extrapolation of an original sample of approximately 24,500 Belgian families, they seem to be comparable because of the use of the same unemployment concept as in several European countries. Moreover, this study is the only one which distinguishes age-specific unemployment rates for Belgium and its different regions (Flanders, Wallonia, and Brussels).

Youth unemployment figures have evolved in a similar way as global unemployment figures. Starting from the mid-70s, youth unemployment figures increased sharply and reached a historical peak of over 150,000 unemployed youngsters in the early 80s. Due to a more prosperous economic situation, decreasing birth rates, the increasing proportion of youngsters who continued studying, and the growth of part-time employment, the youth unemployment figures decreased during the late 80s and the beginning of the 90s (Hoger Instituut voor de Arbeid, 1988). In 1993 and 1994, Belgian youth unemployment reached new peaks, but the situation clearly improved afterwards (Federaal Ministerie, 1997). However, youth unemployment rates are found to still be two or three times higher than the overall unemployment rates.

As shown in Table 1 and Figure 1, a clear effect of age can be observed in young unemployed persons. Youth unemployment rates are especially high among the very young (aged 14 to 19 years) and among the 20-to 24-year-olds, with unemployment rates of respectively 30% and 20%. It is predicted that unemployment will further increase especially among the very young (Stuurgroep, 1997). Moreover, clear differences according to gender can be demonstrated (see Figures 2a-c) since the unemployment rates are obviously higher among females in all age groups and in all regions. Again the differences between the Belgian regions are striking. The youth unemployment rates in Wallonia and Brussels are more than twice as high as in Flanders, e.g., 35% and 30% versus 12% among the 20-to 24-year-olds. Also youth unemployment rates are remarkably higher in Wallonia and Brussels among the other age groups as well (Rijksdienst, 1997). The most alarming fact appears to be the extremely high female unemployment rate in Wallonia, where over 40% of all females under 25 are unemployed (Tegenbos, 1998).

Table B-1: Total unemployment rate (proportion of unemployed persons entitled to employment benefits compared with all persons insured against unemployment), February 1998

		Flanders	Wallonia	Brussels	Belgium
less than 20 years	M	8.6	23.5	19.9	99.9
	F	11.4	26.9	23.0	99.9
	T	9.9	25.1	21.5	99.9
20-25 years	M	9.1	29.7	27.4	99.9
	F	14.0	38.3	30.1	99.9
	T	11.5	33.9	28.8	99.9
25-30 years	M	6.3	21.8	23.6	99.9
	F	11.6	33.5	27.3	99.9
	T	8.8	27.5	25.5	99.9
Total	M	7.1	19.4	22.2	11.5
	F	14.5	29.4	25.1	18.8
	T	10.3	23.8	23.6	14.7

Source: RVA, 1998.

Based on these findings it can be concluded that the labour market position of youngsters in Belgium is extremely precarious and that youngsters are clearly overrepresented in the unemployment statistics, but underrepresented in the employment statistics (Hoger Instituut voor de Arbeid, 1988; De Witte, 1989; Degimbe, 1996; Stuurgroep, 1997). Youngsters, and especially the very young, are confronted with unemployment twice as much as other persons. This is especially true for females, youngsters who leave school with minimal qualifications, and youngsters living in Brussels or Wallonia. Moreover, youth unemployment is apparently only the tip of the iceberg, since the part-time employment rate among youngsters (15-to 24-year-olds) is permanently three to four times higher than among persons over 25 years of age and since many youngsters work as temporary employees (Bellens, 1996). On the other hand, the Ministry of Employment and Labour states that many youngsters can find a job once they are 25 years old (Ministerie, 1995). The employment situation appears to improve beyond the age of 30 years, but the inclusion of youngsters into active working life remains a huge problem with no direct solutions (Bellens, 1996).

Figure B-1: Total yearly youth unemployment rates according to age[1]

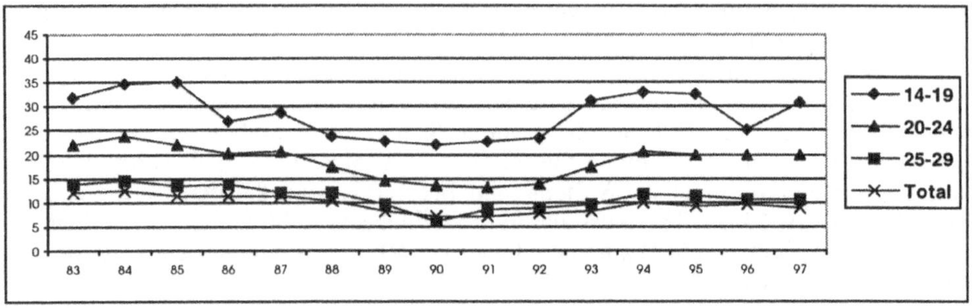

Figure B-2a: Yearly youth unemployment rate for age 14-19 years according to gender[1]

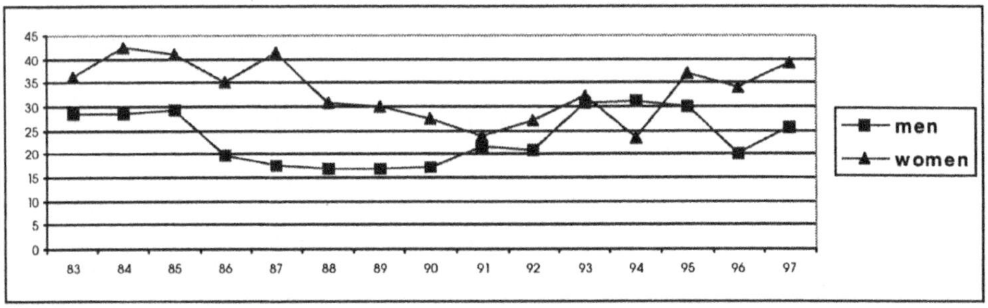

Figure B-2b: Yearly youth unemployment rate for age 20-24 years according to gender[1]

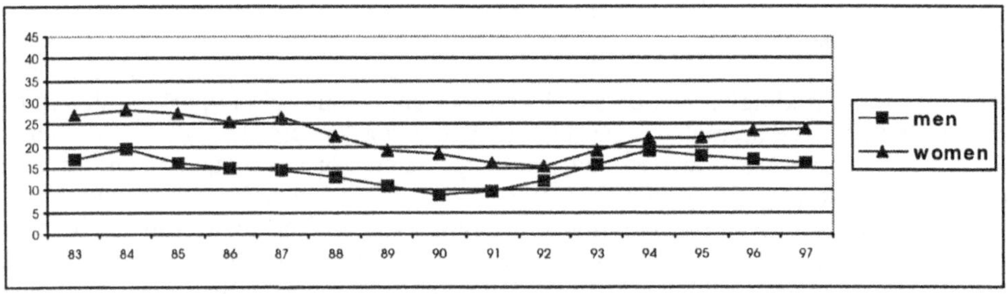

1 In percentage of the unemployed persons compared with total active population; Source: Nationaal Instituut voor de Statistiek, 1997

Figure B-2c: Yearly youth unemployment rate for age 25-29 years according to gender[1]

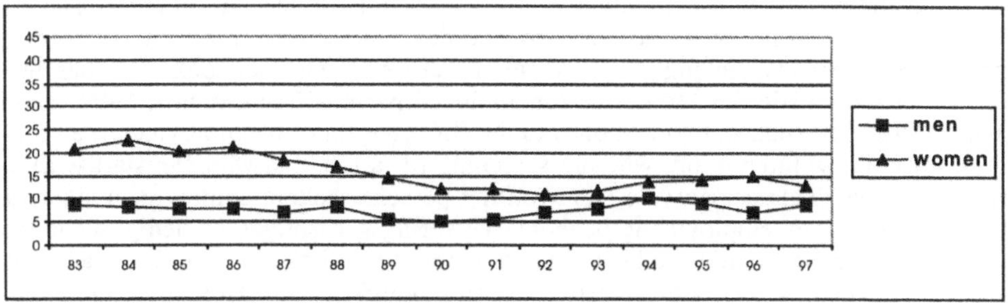

1.2 Unemployment and health – some theoretical considerations

Before we discuss the theoretical context of unemployment and health, the applied terminology regarding 'unemployment' and 'health' has to be clarified. Following an overview of theories concerning unemployment and health with a specific focus on the consequences of unemployment, causal and selective interpretations of the demonstrated association 'unemployment and health' will be addressed.

1.2.1 Some considerations concerning unemployment

Sigmund Freud, the founder of psychoanalysis, thought of labour as a crucial prerequisite for an untroubled life (De Pauw, 1988). The prominent Belgian philosopher Kruithof describes five essential functions of employment: develop all abilities, satisfy several needs, develop creativity, strengthen the willpower, and develop morality and responsibility. The ability to work is the underpinning of a satisfactory transition into adulthood, since it provides the financial means necessary for these changes and it gives the individual an identification that is recognised in the adult world (Verhaegen, Deykin & Sand, 1994). Professional integration can be regarded as the most significant element in the psychosocial structure of the individual, since it interfaces with a large number of complex emotions, opinions, feelings, motivations, and values (Born & Gavray, s.d.). Glorieux (1995) has studied the role of labour for unemployed and employed persons and concludes that work is of central significance for individuals, especially if they are unemployed. Labour mainly has an instrumental function for employed persons, while it has an irreplaceable social function for unemployed persons. A small devaluation of the importance of labour over time has been observed by Glorieux among employed persons, but not among unemployed persons. Labour appears to be still indispensable for life and psychological well-being (Elchardus & Glorieux, 1995). Moreover, unemployment forces unemployed persons to get involved in other job-replacing activities (Glorieux, 1995). Elchardus and Glorieux (1995) have presented two theoretical approaches to unemployment, both belonging to the 'cognitive dissonance reduction' approach. This approach is based on the 'status inconsistence' and 'mental incongruence' theories. While the 'status inconsistence' theory describes an imbalance between the highest and the lowest status ('employed person' vs. 'unemployed person'), the 'mental incongruence' theory focuses on the incongruence between cognition and values. This incongruence causes shame which may lead to a decrease of social contacts. These considerations of Belgian theoretician show that Freud's viewpoints may still be applicable today and that work is of crucial importance.

The definition of 'unemployment' is a matter of debate in Belgium and has changed several times over the last two decades. For several years the concept of 'nonworking persons seeking employment' (Niet-werkende werkzoekende) has been used by official institutions to define 'unemployed persons' (Rijksdienst, 1997; Stuurgroep, 1997). This concept corresponds to the ILO concept of unemployment i.e., it describes persons without a job, who are searching for a job, and who can start working within 15 days. This category of 'nonworking persons seeking employment' includes persons entitled to employment benefits (Uitkeringsgerechtigde volledig werklozen [UVW]), youngsters waiting to be entitled to employment benefits, and freely and obligatorily enrolled nonworking persons seeking employment. However, the media (newspapers, magazines, news, etc.) still use the old and more limited definition of unemployed persons as being 'unemployed persons entitled to employment benefits' (Uitkeringsgerechtigde volledig werklozen [UVW]).

Youth unemployment figures based on this 'UVW' concept can be misleading as the relatively large category of 'youngsters waiting to be entitled to employment benefits' (10% of all unemployed persons) is not included. This waiting period can last up to one year and depends on the age of the unemployed person. For young individuals up to 25 years of age it takes approximately nine months before being entitled to employment benefits, while for people older than 25, this period takes approximately one year.

The definition of 'non working person seeking employment' can still be contested as, among others, older unemployed persons, part-time unemployed persons, pre-pensioners, and persons who planned a career break are not included. Therefore, a more subjective definition of unemployment has recently been used in some studies (Stuurgroep, 1997). According to this definition, people are considered as unemployed in cases where they define themselves as unemployed.

An additional problem resulting from this inconsistent definition is the processing of unemployment rates. Two different unemployment rates are computed based on two different definitions of unemployed persons, but neither of these rates appear to be exact. The first unemployment rate is the number of unemployed persons ('non working persons seeking employment') compared to the active population (all persons 14 years of age and older who are working or unemployed). The second unemployment rate is the number of unemployed persons ('unemployed persons entitled to employment benefits') compared to the number of individuals who are insured against unemployment. These two different conceptualisations lead, of course, to two different unemployment rates.

1.2.2 Some considerations concerning health

Though commonly seen as individual characteristics, health, disease, and mortality might rather be considered as characteristics of social groups, as health appears to be unequally distributed among different social groups (Polus & Louckx, 1991). Without any doubt health is related to variables like age, gender, heredity, environment, health care, and education. Although some Belgian studies have focussed on the association between socio-economic status and health (Vuylsteek, 1984; Lagasse, Humblet, Lenaerts, Godin & Moens, 1990), no study has been found in which the category 'unemployed persons' is included. These studies have mainly focussed on differences between classes (e.g., workers vs. employees vs. executives) rather than on differences within classes (e.g., employed workers vs. unemployed workers). Nevertheless, as unemployment is an important variable related to socio-economic status which appears to affect health, these studies have resulted in some interesting findings (Polus & Louckx, 1991).

This (albeit limited) overview of Belgian publications concerning health-related topics may obscure the complete lack of health indicators in Belgium. Due to the fact, among others, that several departments and administrations are in charge of health care, the federalisation of the state, wrong and incomplete registrations, and a lack of a research tradition concerning health, health indicators have been (and still are) rather scarce in Belgium (Aiach & Carr-Hill, 1989; Van Oyen & Tafforeau, 1993). Consequently, health indicators cover mostly only recent years, and a delay of some years can be observed in comparison with other European countries (see, e.g., the Eurostat data). This situation has improved substantially by the yearly publication of health indicators by the Ministry of the Flemish Community (Aelvoet, Capet & Vanoverloop, 1998) and by the organisation of the first Belgian Health Questionnaire. However, in comparison to other countries, health indicators are still clearly lacking.

1.2.3 Unemployment and health

During a period of continuously increasing unemployment rates in Belgium, Lagrou (1982) has been the first to discuss unemployment and health by introducing the classic 'Marienthal' study of Jahoda and by warning of the devastating consequences of unemployment. Lagrou has outlined the different manifest (pay and working conditions) and latent (time structuring, social contacts, a higher goal, status and identity, activity and creativity) functions of labour as observed by Jahoda. A year later, Vilrokx (1983) has noted that only a few new insights concerning the experience of unemployment were gained since 1930. Indeed, at that time the discussion concerning the consequences of unemployment had mainly been inspired by the work of Jahoda. Though criticised for its mechanistic approach, the theory of Jahoda is still playing a crucial role in the Belgian debate (Hoger Instituut voor de Arbeid, 1988; Glorieux, 1995; Masschelein & De Witte, 1997).

De Witte (1993) has contributed to the theoretical discussion by reviewing the international literature on the (psychological) consequences of long-term unemployment, merely based on foreign (longitudinal) studies. He has presented three theoretical viewpoints concerning the consequences of unemployment which are all relevant for a discussion of the Belgian debate on this topic:

- The "cumulative stress" hypothesis states that the longer unemployment lasts the worse people feel. According to this theory, very long-term unemployment (i.e., more than 2 years of unemployment) is associated with devastating consequences.
- The "adaptation" hypothesis is more optimistic by predicting an amelioration over time.
- The "phases" theory describes unemployment as a process, consisting of different phases.

Based on his overview De Witte (1993) concludes that psychological well-being decreases shortly after becoming unemployed mainly due to financial loss, but stabilises later at a lower level. After some months or years, the psychological state will slightly improve or fluctuate around the same level, but the original level is not reached again. However, re-employment can induce total recovery of psychological well-being, mainly thanks to an improvement of the financial situation. Thus, De Witte provides evidence in favour of the "adaptation" theory, including an adaptation to the role of 'unemployed person' and to the removal from the labour market. The role of 'unemployed person' is a totally new role containing several stressful aspects such as signing the unemployment register. The involvement of unemployed persons in the labour market also diminishes in order to, for example, avoid confrontations with unemployment, mitigate the importance of paid work, and decrease the frequency of job applications. After some time, unemployed persons adapt to this new role by gradually withdrawing from the labour market and by not applying for any new jobs, thus making unemployment more tolerable. However, this resignation may well extend the duration of unemployment and diminish chances of re-employment. De Witte (1994) and other authors call this the 'adaptation trap', which means that by adapting to their unemployment people become trapped in unemployment. Thus, long-term unemployment may lead to a vicious circle and thus to a decrease in psychological well-being. Psychological well-being may improve if one resigns oneself to the unemployment state, but only through re-employment can this evolution be changed.

De Witte and colleagues later found empirical evidence for this theoretical viewpoint and have refined it by researching the psychosocial profile of short- and long-term unemployed persons (De Witte, 1992b; De Witte & Hooge, 1995; Hooge, 1995; De Witte & Hooge, 1997). In these studies the typology of unemployed persons is based on subjective characteristics such as job-seeking behaviour, wishes and expectations concerning work (work involvement), and experience of unemployment. As shown in Table 2, De Witte (1992b) has created a psychosocial typology of long-term unemployed persons.

Table B-2: Psychosocial typology of long-term unemployed persons

	Percentage	Work involvement	Job-seeking behaviour	Experience of unemployment
Optimists	28.3%	±	+	±
Desperate persons	11.2%	+	+	– –
Discouraged persons	13.6%	+	±	–
Adapted persons	16.9%	+	–	+
Withdrawn persons	29.9%	–	– –	+

Source: De Witte, 1992b.

He describes 28.3% of all long-term unemployed persons (irrespective of age) as being 'optimists'. These 'optimists' are moderately involved in work, search intensively for a job, have a quite neutral experience of unemployment, and show an 'average' psychological well-being. 'Desperate' and 'discouraged' persons show a comparable profile. 'Desperate' persons are clearly involved in the labour market, as they are intensively seeking for a job and experience their unemployment as extremely negative. 'Desperate' persons are usually older unemployed persons who have few qualifications and who lack financial resources. 'Discouraged' persons experience their unemployment as less negative and are not seeking a job intensively. The 'adapted' and 'withdrawn' categories include individuals who have adapted to being unemployed. They are not searching any longer and experience their unemployment as rather positive. Withdrawn persons usually are unemployed women with children and the discussion remains whether these persons even see themselves as unemployed.

Hooge (1995) has conducted a comparable study among short-term unemployed persons aged up to 46 years. As shown in Table 3, four types of short-term unemployed persons are described due to the fact that no 'adapted persons' were found in this group who have been unemployed for up to ten months.

Table B-3: Psychosocial typology of short-term unemployed persons

	Percentage	Workinvolvement	Job-seeking behaviour	Experience of unemployment
Optimists	28.5%	±	+	±
Desperate persons	23.1%	+	+	– –
Discouraged persons	20.8%	+	±	–
Withdrawn persons	27.6%	–	– –	+

Source: Hooge, 1995

In a subsequent publication De Witte and Hooge (1995) have reported this typology of unemployed persons to be valid and reliable. Moreover, it is hypothesised that 'desperate' persons become 'discouraged' after some time and further evolve towards the category of 'adapted' persons.

Masschelein and De Witte (1997) have recently completed the 'deprivation' theory of Jahoda with three dimensions, based on Warr's 'vitamins' model (1987). They state that well-being also depends on the possibility to influence the situation, on a clear and transparent environment, and on the degree of physical security. Challenges act as 'vitamins' for psychological well-being, and can stimulate persons, while a lack of vitamins causes distress.

1.2.4 The potential influence of unemployment

The association between youth unemployment and health is poorly documented in Belgium. As described in Chapter 2, a limited number of studies has been conducted and a majority of publications are based on foreign research findings (e.g., Lagrou, 1982; Vettenburg, Walgrave & Van Kerckvoorde, 1984; De Witte, 1993, 1994). The few publications on (youth) unemployment date from the mid-80s and the beginning of the 90s. Recent research focusses more on the effects of long-term unemployment.

Shortly after the peak in unemployment rates during the early 80s, for the first time Belgian researchers warned of the devastating consequences of youth unemployment (HIVA-stuurgroep, 1986). When entering adulthood, youngsters face three developmental tasks: leaving the parental family, completing their identity development, and integrating into society. Employment can help to achieve these tasks, but unemployment keeps these youngsters in a dependent position. Therefore, unemployment might be associated with a number of problems such as unstructured life, social isolation, loss of prestige, boredom, lack of self-reliance, and political apathy. De Witte (1989) has later stated that youth unemployment affects psychosocial development. Therefore, the generation of young unemployed individuals can be described as a 'broken generation' (De Witte in: HIVA-stuurgroep, 1986).

In general, youngsters appear to be affected by unemployment to a lesser extent than older unemployed individuals (Hoger Instituut voor de Arbeid, 1988; De Witte, 1989, 1994). They usually have better perspectives regarding jobs and less financial responsibility, there is no loss of status and less social isolation in spite of being unemployed. As the group of unemployed youngsters is very heterogeneous, age-specific differences may be relative (De Witte, 1994). Moreover, consequences of unemployment can hardly be generalised as to the whole group since unemployment does not equally affect all unemployed young persons.

Unemployment can cause divergent psychological, physical, and social problems (Vettenburg et al., 1984; De Witte, 1994; Masschelein & De Witte, 1997). Van Loon, Pauwels & Van Humskerke (1982) have reported long-term youth unemployment to cause feelings of dependency and insecurity and to affect self-esteem. Unemployed persons often feel bored and inferior. Feelings of shame and inferiority can lead to passivity and withdrawal (Vettenburg et al., 1984). Although passivity and apathy can be observed, unemployed youngsters are more commonly tired than idle, and intensively seek for a job (De Witte, 1989). Also the ethical aspects of work appear not to be affected among young unemployed persons who are prepared to make substantial concessions in order to find a job (Opvoeding, s.d.; HIVA-stuurgroep, 1986; De Witte, 1989). However, based on her study on short-term unemployment, Degimbe (1996) warns that youngsters may become discouraged and demotivated because of their limited professional perspectives. Due to lack of control unemployment may also induce a kind of 'learned helplessness'.

Based on a meta-analysis of early studies on the health consequences of unemployment, De Pauw (1985) concluded that 25-30% of unemployed adults report serious health problems at the moment of referral to a community mental health centre, including depression, insomnia, apathy, nervousness, and lack of concentration. Unemployed persons are generally more anxious, depressive, and pessimistic (De Pauw, 1988; Masschelein & De Witte, 1997). Moreover, unemployed persons often report a low level of psychological well-being (46% of short-term unemployed persons score above the General Health Questionnaire (GHQ)-critical value), have an increased risk of developing psychiatric disorders, and are clearly overrepresented among mental health care patients (Masschelein & De Witte, 1997). De Pauw (1988) has also described comparatively more common psychosomatic complaints among unemployed persons.

Social contacts often decrease in case of unemployment (Van Loon et al., 1982; Vilrokx, 1983; Elchardus & Glorieux, 1995) leading to loneliness and social isolation (Vettenburg et al., 1984; De Pauw, 1985; Verhaegen et al., 1994) or even "social death" (Alaluf, Desmarez & Domb, 1982). These devastating consequences may not be due to shame or low self-esteem, but rather to structural factors (Elchardus & Glorieux, 1995; Traisnel, 1997). Stigmatisation of unemployed persons appears to affect these persons (Van Loon et al., 1982; Pissart, Poncelet & Voisin, 1990). Vettenburg et al. (1984) describe unemployed youngsters as a 'socially vulnerable group', who experiences the confrontations with social institutions as controlling and discriminating. De Pauw (1988) adds that youth unemployment may lead to a compulsory marginalisation of youngsters. In the beginning of the 80s, it was generally believed that youth unemployment lead to aggression and delinquent behaviour (Vanheerswynghels, s.d.; Lagrou, 1982). However, this assumption has not been confirmed in Belgian research (Vettenburg et al., 1984; HIVA-stuurgroep, 1986).

Loss of income is an obvious consequence of unemployment (De Pauw, 1988; Hoger Instituut voor de Arbeid, 1988; Deliens, 1989; De Witte, 1989). A detrimental financial situation is perceived as the most dramatic aspect of unemployment, as it interferes with the (financial) subsistence in many families (Deliens, Bosman & Louckx, 1988). Financial losses not only affect savings, but also psychological well-being and the desire to have children (Van Loon et al., 1982).

The association between employment status and suicidal behaviour is well-documented (see e.g., Hawton & Rose, 1986; Platt, 1986; Moesler, Pontzen & Rummler, 1990). Based on their well-known studies, Platt & Kreitman (1985) state that unemployment acts as a vulnerability factor for attempted suicide, and that there is no sufficient evidence to assume a direct causal link or to support a self-selection hypothesis. A number of studies indicate that the association between unemployment and (attempted) suicide is confounded by variables such as age, gender, duration of unemployment, ecological factors, financial distress, marital status, and temporal factors (Platt, Hawton, Kreitman, Fagg & Foster, 1988; Moesler et al., 1990). Moreover, Platt & Kreitman (1985) demonstrate that unemployment is more strongly associated with suicidal behaviour if unemployment is less common. A case-control study in Gent has confirmed these findings and indicates that unemployment is associated with attempted suicide, although this association is confounded by age, marital status, and living situation (van Heeringen & Jannes, 1993). On the other hand, unemployment has also been found to be associated with positive consequences, as 15-30% of a group of unemployed individuals have reported a better health status due to loss of job-related stress (Masschelein & De Witte, 1997).

1.2.5 The role of mediating variables

Not only unemployment as such but also unemployment-related factors including socio-economic status, stigmatisation, work ethics, and personal strength can influence health. De Pauw (1988) has reported a number of mediating variables such as age, length of unemployment, work involvement, financial distress, gender, social class, lack of recreational activities, personal vulnerability, and social stress. De Witte (1994) also states that several factors increase or weaken the impact of unemployment, including work ethics, social network, financial strength, activities, and personality characteristics. Indeed, several confounding variables appear to affect the association between unemployment and health. The role of gender, education, and length of unemployment will be discussed in more detail in Chapter 2.

Research on the consequences of unemployment has mostly been limited to unemployed men, which is a surprising finding since females are traditionally overrepresented in unemployment statistics. Unemployed men appear to suffer more than unemployed women (De Pauw, 1988; De Witte & Wets, 1993; Traisnel, 1997) as they commonly report more loneliness, more problems with structuring their time, and a lower level of psychological well-being (De Witte, 1994). Women appear to be psychologically affected by unemployment to a lesser extent than men, which may be due to two factors, namely the familial and financial situation (De Witte & Hooge, 1995). Women appear to easily take up an alternative role in the family and to feel less financially responsible.

Lower educational levels are associated with more negative perceptions of unemployment (HIVA-stuurgroep, 1986; Deliens et al, 1988). Unemployed persons with low school qualifications are found to be more pessimistic and to complain more commonly about social isolation and loss of self-esteem. This can be due to a stronger work involvement and to a higher regard of paid work.

A strong commitment to paid work has been reported to be strongly and positively associated with a decrease in psychological well-being (De Witte, 1993). In their review, De Witte and Hooge (1997) demonstrate significant differences on psychological well-being, experience of unemployment, work involvement and job-seeking intensity between short-term and long-term unemployed persons. Short-term unemployed persons often report a lower level of psychological well-being, a more negative experience of unemployment, and are more commonly work-oriented and searching for a job. Finally, unemployment and especially long-term unemployment can interfere with re-employment (Van Loon et al., 1982).

1.2.6 'Causal' versus 'selection' hypothesis

Possible explanations for the association between 'unemployment and health' can be mainly found in causal and selective hypotheses. Several authors have contributed to this debate (De Witte, 1994; Masschelein & De Witte, 1997). Masschelein and De Witte (1997) agree that several selection processes are involved in finding or keeping a job. Employees with a poor health are more prone to dismissal and are less likely to find a job once they are unemployed (De Witte, 1994). Thus, unemployed persons with ill health remain unemployed, which can lead to a stronger association between unemployment and health. However, the selection hypothesis provides only a partial explanation since unemployment unambiguously burdens the psychological well-being of unemployed persons. The fact that a substantial proportion of persons (20%) does not report any problems due to their unemployment can only moderately affect this causal inference (De Witte, 1994). Verhaegen et al. (1994) conclude that the direction of the association between unemployment and depressive symptoms still remains unclear. Unemployment can cause depressive symptoms through, among others, financial hardship, isolation from peers, and loss of self-esteem. However, depressive symptoms might also cause unemployment by impairing the ability to work. Hopelessness might be an important mediator in this process.

Studies on health inequalities among social groups may help to understand the role of different variables in explaining the association between unemployment and health. The explanation for health inequalities can be reduced to the causal and the selection hypotheses (Polus & Louckx, 1991; Raes, Kerkhofs & Louckx, 1993). The health selection hypothesis considers health as the cause rather than the consequence of socio-economic inequalities. Health thus appears to exert this influence through social mobility (Polus & Louckx, 1991). Although the effect of selection appears to be rather limited, and although it is not clear how such a selection might occur, the role of selection has been stressed by different authors in Belgium.

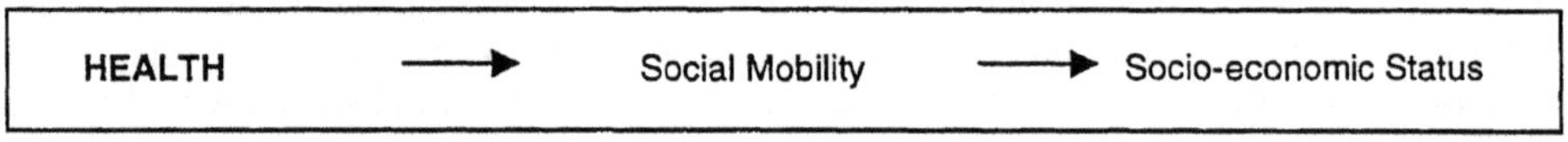

The causal hypothesis states that socio-economic status (SES) causes health inequalities and includes two different orientations. According to this hypothesis, cultural aspects such as behaviour, lifestyle attitude, and knowledge are unequally distributed among social groups, thus mediating the influence of the SES.

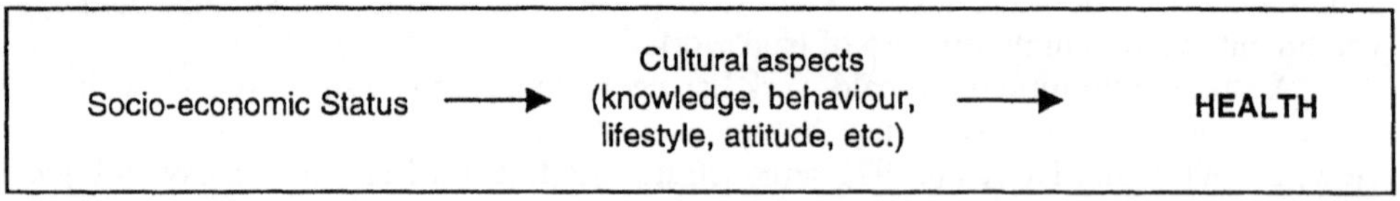

The structural hypothesis argues that structural or environmental (living and working conditions) and material (lodging) factors are unequally distributed, thus causing health inequalities. As unemployment is more common among persons with low qualifications, unemployment can be regarded as such a mediating factor.

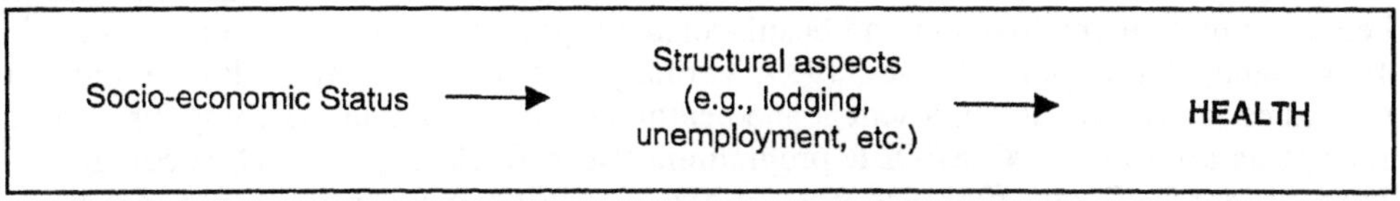

Polus and Louckx (1991) state that the selection hypothesis and the causal hypothesis both consider a dynamic and integrated problem from a narrow and static scope. Thus, it is argued that both viewpoints should be integrated. As no empirical evidence to accept a selection hypothesis is available, Dutch researchers have recently stated that selection is not to be regarded as a valid explanatory variable (Stronks, van de Mheen & Mackenbach, 1993). A causal model including different causal factors is preferred in order to explain the association between SES and health. These factors include working and living circumstances, psychosocial factors, unequal access to health care, etc. The effect of SES on health seems rather indirect and caused by determinants such as behavioural (e.g., health-related behaviour), material (e.g., lodging), structural (e.g., working conditions, unemployment) and psychosocial characteristics.

From studies on the association between unemployment and suicidal behaviour results in favour of both hypotheses have been found (van Heeringen, 1993; van Heeringen & Jannes, 1993). The self selection hypothesis is supported by the higher risk of attempted suicide among unmarried or divorced individuals. Further evidence for a selection hypothesis (health status leads to both inactivity and attempted suicide) can be derived from the particularly strong association between economic inactivity and attempted suicide among individuals inactive due to chronic illness. Causal inference is supported by the finding of a lower risk among married individuals since social support is widely believed to reduce the negative impact of unemployment (van Heeringen, 1993).

1.3 Conclusion

Belgium is confronted with relatively high unemployment rates, and youth unemployment rates are even two to three times higher than the overall rates. The overview of the debate concerning unemployment and health provides some theoretical and epidemiological evidence for an association between unemployment and health in Belgium. The theoretical debate appears to be based mainly on the work of Jahoda which, however, has been refined in two ways. First, people adapt to unemployment after some time. Second, several categories of long-term and short-term unemployed persons are to be distinguished, and only unemployed individuals belonging to specific categories appear to show detrimental effects of unemployment. A limited number of Belgian publications have addressed the possible consequences of unemployment showing a clear association between unemployment and health, but hardly any study has provided evidence in favour of a causal or selection hypothesis.

2 Analysis of research on youth unemployment and health

In this second chapter all available Belgian research on youth unemployment and health is reviewed. Prior to a discussion of the main findings from these studies, the design and methods of the available studies are described. Only three studies on the association between youth unemployment and health-related aspects were found (Vettenburg et al., 1984; Sand, Verhaegen & Meyer, 1989; Verhaegen et al., 1994). An additional number of studies focuses on unemployment and health, however, without matching the criteria for age as used in the YUSEDER programme (Born & Gavray, s.d.; Opvoeding, s.d.; Jeuris, 1984; De Pauw, 1988; De Witte, 1992b; De Witte & Wets, 1993; van Heeringen & Jannes, 1993; Hooge, 1995; Gavray, 1996; Wets & De Witte, 1997). Other studies are found not to include many health-related aspects (Alaluf et al., 1982; Van Loon et al., 1982; Deliens et al., 1988; De Witte, 1992a; Elchardus & Glorieux, 1995), whereas other studies report only indirectly on the association between unemployment and health (Moens, Haenen & Van de Voorde, 1988; Mackenbach & Looman, 1994; Gavray, 1997; Born, Gavray & Cattelino, 1998).

2.1 Description of the available data (design and methods)

Nearly all Belgian studies are cross-sectionally designed surveys. The most obvious disadvantage of a cross-sectional study is the fact that it is limited to a single data collection (except when a follow-up study is performed) thus reducing opportunities to study causal mechanisms. Unfortunately, no Belgian longitudinal study on unemployment and health has been conducted. Two studies in this report are based on aggregated data from WHO (Moens et al, 1988) and Eurostat (Mackenbach & Looman, 1994).

2.1.1 Cross-sectional studies

The first report on youth unemployment was published in 1982 by Alaluf et al., who studied unemployed youngsters and their culture in the region of Charleroi, a former mining area with high rates of unemployment (Alaluf et al., 1982). Life-style and attitudes were studied in a random sample of 89 unemployed youngsters with very low qualifications. These first results on youth unemployment indicate that self-esteem among unemployed persons is affected by unemployment and that feelings of dependence and worthlessness are commonly experienced. In the same year, Van Loon et al. (1982) studied the effects of unemployment on the family in a sample of 298 married unemployed persons (less than 35 years old) living in Antwerp who were unemployed for at least four months and entitled to employment benefits. Unemployed persons often report financial stress, social isolation, and a decreased self-esteem. At a time of rapidly increasing rates of youth unemployment, Vettenburg et al. (1984) studied the association between unemployment and juvenile offences in a sample of 207 boys and girls, 17 to 19 years of age, from the Leuven-Herent region. The group consisted of equal numbers of unemployed, working, and studying youngsters. None of them were married or living with a partner. All came from lower classes as defined by the professional status of the father. The findings show that no direct relation can be identified between unemployment and delinquent behaviour, but that school achievement rather acts as a confounding variable.

In the same period, the Socialist Health Insurance Fund interviewed a representative sample of 403 unemployed persons less than 36 years of age and enrolled in the

Socialist Health Insurance Fund (Opvoeding, s.d.). The sample consisted of unemployed men and women from Flanders, except from the province of Brabant (including Brussels). The fact that men and single persons report more problems emerges as an important finding from this research. Deliens et al. (1988) studied the effect of unemployment and social environment on social behaviour in 592 youngsters (aged 24 to 26 years) with low educational levels, living in the district of Brussels-Halle-Vilvoorde. Besides social behaviour, data on health-related topics were collected from these youngsters and their partners. It was found that unemployed youngsters have less contact with their parents and other family members. De Witte (1992a) performed a secondary analysis of data from a survey on attitudes of young adults towards the Christian Labour Movement (ACW) including their socio-political orientation. The sample consisted of 756 Flemish young adults (536 employed and 220 unemployed persons), aged 18 to 35 and enrolled in the Christian Labour Movement. Unemployed youngsters were found to show more sympathy for left wing parties. Sand et al. (1989) studied the prevalence of depressive symptoms among 900 adolescent boys and girls, categorised according to employment status (students, workers, and unemployed youngsters). Depressive symptomatology was measured in adolescents, aged 16 to 21 years from the region of Brussels, using the 20-item CES-D self-report scale (Centre for Epidemiological Studies – Depression) as developed by Radloff (1975) (in Sand et al., 1989). It was concluded that Belgian adolescents often reach the level of clinical depression and that unemployed adolescents commonly show significantly more depressive symptoms than studying or working adolescents. Some years later the same research group published a more elaborate and in-depth version of this cross-sectional study (Verhaegen et al, 1994). The sample consisted of 300 unemployed subjects who were registered at the Brussels Department of Employment and Welfare, 298 employed workers, and 300 students. This in-depth analysis confirmed that unemployment is associated with a substantial degree of depressive morbidity.

Van Heeringen and Jannes (1993) studied the association between employment status (stratified to economic inactivity, unemployment, and employment) and attempted suicide in a case-control study. Data from a random sample of the 1981 Population Census records for Gent (n= 1,608) were compared to the records for all attempted suicide referrals (residents of Gent city aged 15 years or older, n= 508), referred to the University Hospital during the period 1986-1990. Unemployment was identified as a risk factor for attempted suicide in both males (15-34 years old and 35-49 years old) and females (35-49 years old).

At the Higher Institute for Labour (Hoger Instituut voor de Arbeid; HIVA), several studies on the psychosocial profile of short- and long-term unemployed men and women were conducted. De Witte (1992b) studied the psychosocial profile of long-term unemployed persons and persons involved in an employment initiative for very long-term unemployed persons in Flanders (the 'Work Again Action' = WeerWerk). A stratified sample of 309 long-term unemployed men were interviewed concerning their experience of unemployment, psychosocial well-being, work expectations, and work involvement. A sample of 199 long-term unemployed persons enrolled in the 'Work Again Action' were interviewed using the same questionnaire. It appeared that, in general, long-term unemployed persons do not suffer from being unemployed, but a small subgroup of unemployed persons really suffers. De Witte and Wets (1993) studied psychosocial characteristics of long-term unemployed women (n= 407) aged up to 35 years who had been unemployed for more than one year and who were living in the German-speaking community of Belgium. Only a small minority of these women experienced their unemployment negatively and showed a lower psychosocial well-being. Moreover, having one or more children and having a higher family income level are variables with a significant positive influence on the experience of unemployment. In the same research institute, Hooge (1995) studied the psychosocial profile of 1,109 unemployed individuals who participated in the so-called Individual Counselling Plan ('Individueel Begeleidingsplan'), a governmental initiative to employ persons who have been unemployed for at least 10 months. The results indicated that short-term unemployed persons experience their unemployment very negatively and have a low level of psychological well-being. Wets and De Witte (1997) performed a similar study among 579 unemployed men and women of all ages living in the German-speaking community of Belgium, focussing on the experience of unemployment, psychosocial well-being, and work expectations. They also observed that most unemployed persons do not suffer from unemployment and that only a small group is strongly affected by being unemployed.

In two studies on the consequences of unemployment (Jeuris, 1984; De Pauw, 1988), patient records were used in a cross-sectional design. Jeuris (1984) performed a socio-economic analysis of three community mental health centres in Antwerp by studying 1,040 client records, categorising the sample according to professional status: employed, unemployed, living in a family of an unemployed person, and persons entitled to welfare benefits (excluding employment benefits). Unemployed patients reported more relational and financial problems and feelings of social exclusion. De Pauw (1988) studied the client records of 11,938 patients who were registered at one of 18 community mental health centres during the period 1979-1983. The sample consisted of 5,360 men and 6,578 women, categorised according to professional status in the same way as in the study described above. It appeared that the proportion of unemployed persons among patients of mental health centres is significantly larger than in the normal population.

A few studies include a follow-up period of several years based on a cross-sectional design. Elchardus and Glorieux (1995) performed three such studies. The original study was a time-budget study among 206 unemployed men living together with their partner and at least one child. The focus was on the direct consequences of unemployment. The sample included 95 employed, 56 short-term unemployed, and 55 long-term unemployed men from the district of Halle-Vilvoorde (near Brussels). Unemployed men reported more boredom and spent more time in activities with their partner and children. Ten years later, 177 men from this sample participated in a follow-up study that focussed on the lasting consequences of unemployment. A large majority was employed (n= 151) at the time of the follow-up, while 26 men were not or only part-time employed. The results showed an improved psychosocial well-being after (re-)employment. In this follow-up study Elchardus and Glorieux also studied the effects of paternal unemployment on the children by interviewing 94 children who were born before 1982. Apparently, unemployment of the father can have a negative influence on the school results of their children.

Recently, Born et al. (1998) studied the relation between adolescent and young adult psychosocial well-being in a follow-up study. The original sample included 618 youngsters from the city of Liège, aged 14 to 21 years. Among them, 139 (41 students, 52 workers, and 46 nonworkers) were re-interviewed at the age of 21 to 25 years. The results showed that depression in adulthood is not related to employment status. Gavray (1997) studied the prevalence of deviant behaviour in adolescence and adulthood according to employment status in the same sample in Liège. No significant interaction between professional status and type and rates of delinquent behaviour could be demonstrated.

2.1.2 Longitudinal studies

As far as can be determined by the authors, no longitudinal study has been performed in Belgium concerning youth unemployment and health. Born and Gavray (s.d.) and Gavray (1996) report on a secondary analysis of the data from the Panel Study of Belgian Households, a longitudinal study. However, as research material from only one study year has been used, these studies should be regarded in the strictest sense as cross-sectional. Born and Gavray (s.d.) performed a secondary analysis of the data from the Panel Study of Belgian Households focussing on divergent variables of psychosocial well-being among a sample of 6,319 Belgians between 16-65 years of age. The results from this study indicate that status and professional situation of men are largely conditioned by their psychosocial well-being. Gavray (1996) has conducted another secondary analysis on the data of the Panel Study of Belgian Households, studying the association between socio-professional status and the presence of depression, thus showing that the level of depression depends linearly on the quality of the socio-professional involvement.

2.1.3 Aggregated studies

Moens and colleagues (1988) studied the epidemiological aspects of suicide among youngsters (aged 5-24 years) in 21 selected countries. Trends in reported suicide rates were extracted from the WHO yearbooks for the periods 1970-74 and 1980-84. It appeared that youth suicide is strongly associated with indicators of anomia and social isolation, but less with socio-economic variables. Mackenbach and Looman (1994) assessed the influence of living standards on mortality ratios in 133 European regions based on the standardised regional mortality ratios (SMRs) and the Eurostat data on living standards (gross domestic product, car access, and unemployment rates). The mortality rates covered the period 1980-1984, while the living standards covered the period 1985-1988. Thus it was demonstrated that unemployment rates have the strongest association with mortality after controlling for confounding variables.

2.1.4 Types of statistical analysis

The first empirical studies (e.g., Opvoeding, s.d.; Alaluf et al., 1982; Jeuris, 1984) on youth unemployment are characterised by limited statistical interpretations, presenting only frequencies and cross tabulations. Later, the influence of the independent variables has been studied using variance (e.g., Van Loon et al., 1982; Verhaegen et al., 1994) and regression analysis (e.g., Vettenburg et al., 1984), whether or not controlling for confounding variables. Recently, more powerful statistical analyses such as factor analysis and cluster analysis are, among others, used to define profiles of short-term and long-term unemployed individuals (e.g., De Witte, 1992b; Hooge, 1995; Wets & De Witte, 1997).

A number of methodological shortcomings in the study of the association between unemployment and health must be addressed. Ten years ago Rosseel (1988) already criticised the studies on unemployment and health as lacking a coherent theoretical and methodological basis. Although the lack of a comprehensive and universally accepted theoretical basis is apparent, the theoretical framework on unemployment and health has, since then, been elaborated and refined. Thus, recent findings concerning unemployment and health are far less contradictory than 10 years ago. However, a number of topics such as social isolation still awaits further clarification.

Unemployment is a dynamic and transient process (periods of employment precede and follow episodes of unemployment) which is usually approached as a rather static concept. Moreover, research on unemployment and health has mainly used a quantitative design, while more qualitative approaches would be appropriate for the study of subjective feelings, the quality of life of unemployed persons, and other subjective characteristics. Currently available data are also almost exclusively descriptive, often making use of retrospective and cross-sectional designs. The possibility that the association between unemployment and health is spurious or caused by the choice of methods and instruments, the research concept, or another variable should be taken into account when interpreting the results. Mistakes can also be due to incorrect definitions of studied variables such as unemployment and to errors in the data collection (Polus & Louckx, 1991). The lack of control for confounding variables is a major methodological shortcoming. Indeed, unemployment rates are associated with many other characteristics linked to deprivations which are usually not accounted for in the analyses.

A final problem which has to be mentioned in this context is the relative generosity of the Belgian unemployment insurance, potentially leading to international differences in the experience of unemployment (De Witte, 1993).

2.2 Overview of present studies

2.2.1 Objective health indicators

2.2.1.1 Mortality rates

Data on the influence of unemployment on mortality are extremely scarce in Belgium. In the study of Mackenbach and Looman (1994) on the association between living standards and mortality in the European Union, unemployment emerges as the variable that is most strongly associated with mortality after controlling for confounding variables. This is particularly true for the situation in the southern part of Belgium (Wallonia). This part of the country is characterised by a relatively high mortality rate, a living standard below the EC average, and a relatively high unemployment rate.

2.2.1.2 Morbidity

A number of studies provide information on morbidity among unemployed persons in Belgium. Different instruments are used to measure morbidity (e.g., CES-D scale, GHQ-12). The study of patient records in community mental health centres reveals that unemployed persons have many more problems than other patient groups (Jeuris, 1984). According to MACLA diagnoses (a psychiatric diagnostic classification system developed in Louvain), 67% of all unemployed persons suffer from neurotic disorders, personality disorders, and other nonpsychotic disorders including addiction and depression.

Depression and *depressive symptoms* have frequently been comparatively studied. Sand et al. (1989) used the CES-D scale (Centre for Epidemiological Studies – Depression; Radloff, 1975) to assess the prevalence of depressive symptoms among adolescent boys and girls. The prevalence rates of depressive symptoms were found to be much higher among Belgian adolescents than among American adolescents, with 18.9% of the Belgian adolescents in this study reaching the level of 'clinical depression'. When the sample was studied according to employment status (student, worker, and unemployed person), significant differences in rates of depressive symptoms were found between unemployed youngsters (27%), students (15.3%), and workers (14.4%).

Some years later the same research group published a more elaborate and in-depth analysis of the 1989 research material (Verhaegen et al., 1994). It was concluded that primary unemployment is associated with a substantial degree of depressive morbidity and that belonging to the group of unemployed Belgian youth carries a substantially higher risk of depressive symptoms and especially of long-lasting symptoms than with workers or students. A more detailed analysis of the employment status of these adolescents revealed that the group of unemployed persons scores significantly higher than the students and the employed youngsters. Unemployed persons report more depressive symptoms of any duration and of long duration (5-7 days), 51.6% and 27% respectively, than students (43.3% and 15.3%) and employed youngsters (32.5% and 14.4%). The data showed a 40% excess risk of depressive symptomatology for students and almost a 70% excess risk for unemployed persons. The nature of depressive symptoms was similar in the three groups, suggesting a common occurrence of affective problems such as hopelessness, low self-esteem, and unhappiness in young adults. Born et al. (1998) used the Depression Scale of Moos to measure the level of depression in a follow-up study and concluded that employment status is not related to depression in adulthood, but rather to depression in adolescence. Subjects who are relatively more depressed during their adolescence have a more active and efficient strategy of searching for a job. Depression among adolescents seems to be more related to personal characteristics than to external characteristics. Another striking finding from this study is the fact that long-term maternal unemployment has a significant influence on depression in adolescence. Gavray (1996) used the Moos Scale to assess the level of depression among different socio-professional groups (see Table 4) and stated that the level of depression depends on the quality of the socio-professional involvement. These results indicate a more vulnerable psychosocial status among individuals who are, to a lesser extent, involved in work and underline the role of financial allowances for psychological well-being.

Table B-4: Association between socio-professional status and level of depression

Socio-professional status	Level of depression (Moos Scale)
Full-time workers	15.9
Part-time workers	17.8
Unemployed persons with allowance	18.5
Unemployed persons without allowance	21.7
Persons with no official status	22.3

Source: Gavray, 1996.

Wets and De Witte (1997) used the General Health Questionnaire (GHQ) to measure the *psychosocial well-being* among unemployed men and women in the German-speaking part of Belgium. Relatively high scores were found. In other studies of the HIVA (De Witte, 1992b; De Witte & Wets, 1993; Hooge, 1995) the GHQ-12 was used to assess psychological well-being, thus allowing a comparison of the findings (see Table 6). Hooge (1995) observed that short-term unemployed persons generally experience their unemployment as negative, potentially leading to a very low level of psychosocial well-being. The psychosocial well-being of long-term unemployed persons appeared to be less affected (De Witte, 1992b).

Table B-5: Comparison of GHQ scores in 4 different studies

Population	Average score	% above critical value*
Unemployed persons in the German-speaking community	13.2	46.6
Short-term unemployed persons in Flanders	12.7	45.9
Long-term unemployed persons in Flanders	10.6	25.6
People living from social security benefits in Flanders	12.3	33 to 39

* The critical value is computed by recoding the scores 1 and 2 from the questionnaire to 0 and 3 and 4 to 1. The sum of these new values gives a score between 0 and 12, with 2 as critical value. 46.6% has a score greater than 2.

Source: Wets & De Witte, 1997.

2.2.1.3 Suicidal behaviour (suicides and attempted suicides)

Van Heeringen and Jannes (1993) identified unemployment as a risk factor for attempted suicide in both males (OR 9.00) and females (OR 3.38) in the age group between 35 to 49 years (OR 13.26). Unemployment emerges as a risk factor for attempted suicide in males aged 15 to 34 years (OR 4.00), but not in females in the same age group. Economic inactivity was not identified as a risk factor except for people with chronic illness. Moens et al. (1988) found that youth suicide is less associated with socio-economic variables such as unemployment than with indicators of anomia and social disintegration in both males and females.

2.2.1.4 Utilisation of health services

A further analysis of client records from community mental health centres shows that young unemployed men make less use of these services than older unemployed men (45 to 49 years) (Jeuris, 1984). Unemployed women with relatively high qualifications make most use of these services. De Pauw (1988) observed a higher proportion of unemployed persons among the client population of community mental health centres than in the general population. As opposed to the findings of Jeuris (1984), De Pauw (1988) stated that young unemployed men are more often registered in these centres including unemployed persons with higher educational levels.

2.2.2 Subjective health indicators

2.2.2.1 Psychosocial strains

According to Van Loon and colleagues (1982), *financial distress* is one of the most obvious consequences of unemployment affecting savings for clothes and recreation. Moreover, deprivation of all kinds of activities becomes a daily rule among unemployed youngsters (Alaluf et al., 1982). 80% of the unemployed young adults from the Socialist Health Insurance Fund study report that they experience financial distress, especially in case they had worked before and have been jobless for a longer time (Opvoeding, s.d.). This financial distress affects savings for clothes, holidays, transport charges, and spare time which also indirectly affects social relationships. The same study reveals that young and short-term unemployed persons are most *optimistic*, but after two years of unemployment the frequency of job applications decreases and feelings of *insecurity and hopelessness* become ubiquitous. Another reported disadvantage of unemployment is *stigmatisation* (Van Loon et al., 1982).

Unemployed patients attending community mental health centres experience more *relational and financial problems* than other patient groups (Jeuris, 1984). De Pauw (1988) underlines these results by finding that unemployed married men especially suffer from financial distress. Interestingly, she observes fewer relational problems among unemployed persons than among the other groups. Unemployed youngsters with low educational levels do not appear to experience extreme financial distress (Deliens et al., 1988). However, unemployment undeniably affects the living situation of households with an unemployed partner, as demonstrated by the fact that 44% define themselves as living in insecure living circumstances, while the (financial) subsistence of 33% of the unemployed young families is endangered according to more objective measures. Unemployment also has a clear influence on the patterns of consumption and affects savings for housing, clothes, transport, and food. The secondary analysis of the Panel Study of Belgian Households (Gavray, 1996) revealed that 17% of the families of which the head of the family is unemployed live below the poverty level.

Work appears to be of major significance especially for unemployed persons (Elchardus & Glorieux, 1995). Unemployment causes *boredom* and problems with *time consumption*. Unemployed persons tend to search for job-replacing activities and focus on the household. Alaluf et al. (1982) observed that behaviour, interests, and reactions of unemployed youngsters are nearly totally focussed on their unemployment and potential reemployment. A classification of long-term unemployed persons reveals that two particular types of unemployed persons, that is, the adapted and withdrawn individuals, are not involved in work and searching for a job (De Witte, 1992b; Wets & De Witte, 1997). This appears also to be the case among young, long-term unemployed women (De Witte & Wets, 1993). Finally, Vettenburg et al (1984) described unemployed youngsters as 'socially' more vulnerable than their working and studying peers insofar as they have a much bigger chance to experience successive *negative contacts with social institutions*.

2.2.2.2 Subjective well-being

Jeuris (1984) stated that unemployed individuals commonly show more *psychosomatic complaints* and that unemployed men report more *stress* than other groups. In contrast with these findings, Vettenburg and colleagues (1984) did not find an association between unemployment and psychosomatic status among youngsters, although unemployed youngsters reported more *subjective health problems*. De Pauw (1988) observed more problems concerning *addiction* and *social integration* among unemployed persons. Moreover, unemployed women and persons living from welfare benefits commonly reported psychosomatic complaints. It was concluded that unemployment does not cause psychosocial problems, but nevertheless constitutes a serious risk, especially among unemployed men aged 25-35 years. The most direct influence of unemployment on the family was a *decrease in the desire to have children* (Van Loon et al, 1982). Moreover, unemployed women tended to delay employment at times when having children.

Born and Gavray observed a direct link between the level of professional integration and *psychosocial well-being*. This relation was only found among males and not among females. Psychosocial well-being of women was mainly influenced by the living conditions of their household. De Witte (1992b) found a relatively high level of psychosocial well-being among long-term unemployed persons. However, the 'desperate seekers' experienced their unemployment as extremely negative, probably due to *social isolation* and *financial problems*. 75% of the "desperate seekers" showed a critical score on the GHQ-12. "Withdrawn" and "adapted" unemployed persons reported a more positive experience of unemployment. Almost half of all interviewed unemployed persons agree that health limits their working abilities (48%), and 1 in 15 unemployed persons reported that this is due to psychological complaints (depression, sleeping, and concentration disorders).

Interesting results were revealed by De Witte (1992b) who compared the psychosocial profiles between long-term unemployed persons and participants of the 'Work Again Action', finding substantial differences between these two groups. The 'Work Again Action' participants experienced their unemployment more negatively, scored significantly higher on the GHQ-12, and thus have a lower level of psychosocial well-being. 55.6% of the 'Work Again Action' participants scored above the GHQ critical value, while only 24.8% of the long-term unemployed persons scored above this value. A study of the psychosocial profile of young long-term unemployed women (De Witte & Wets, 1993) showed that only few unemployed women suffer due to unemployment (11%). Only the group of "desperate seekers" had a negative experience of unemployment and a low level of psychosocial well-being, as opposed to the "withdrawn women" and "postponers". Hooge (1995) conducted a similar study among short-term unemployed persons and found lower levels of psychosocial well-being and a more negative experience of unemployment.

In general, it can be concluded that the psychosocial well-being of unemployed persons is not seriously affected by the experience of unemployment, although a subgroup of unemployed persons clearly suffers from this situation (Wets & De Witte, 1997). Moreover, differences in well-being between unemployed and employed persons tend to disappear after re-employment (Elchardus & Glorieux, 1995).

2.2.2.3 Self-esteem

Unemployment definitely causes a decrease in self-esteem (Van Loon et al., 1982), with this negative self-image clearly being associated with *financial deprivation*. Moreover, long-term unemployment is associated with increased *concerns, feelings of dependency*, and *lack of self-reliance*. Alaluf and colleagues (1982) reported that the self-esteem among unemployed youngsters decreases, thus leaving them feeling worthless, dependent, and inferior. However, the study of Vettenburg et al. (1984) revealed no differences in self-image among unemployed, working, and studying youngsters. Elchardus and Glorieux (1995) did not find evidence of social withdrawal among unemployed men due to shame or low self-esteem. On the other hand, unemployed persons appeared to be less *self-confident*, to feel more *vulnerable,* and to be prone to feelings of *losing control.*

2.2.2.4 Alienation (political orientations)

A survey of political attitudes among employed and unemployed young adults showed that unemployed persons become more *leftist*, develop more *radical ideas* (either left- or right-oriented) on socio-economic issues, and vote more often for the socialist party (De Witte, 1992). However, only a small minority of unemployed persons appear to vote in a more radical manner, especially if this political orientation matches the original attitudes. The large majority of unemployed young adults becomes apathetic and experiences feelings of resignation. This attitude can be defined as a kind of *learned helplessness* due to social isolation and loss of control over one's own life. Among very young unemployed persons, a lack of political interest was observed. A limited analysis of the voting behaviour by Elchardus and Glorieux (1995) showed that long-term unemployed persons vote for nontraditional parties out of protest.

2.2.2.5 Social deviation (delinquency)

Vettenburg and colleagues (1984) could not demonstrate a direct relation between unemployment and delinquency, although it appears that unemployed persons have more contacts with the police and the judicial system. School was found to be an important confounding factor since it usually reinforces an already unfavourable starting position in the family and increases the probability of juvenile offending. Unemployment can only have an influence after school exerted its influence. Gavray (1997) stated that the employment status of young adults shows no significant interaction with types and rates of delinquent behaviour, although students and nonworkers report four times more drug-related offences compared with nonworkers. Rather than a causal relation between employment status and delinquency, a causal relation between the lack of financial resources and delinquent behaviour was demonstrated.

2.2.2.6 Health behaviour

The study of the Socialist Health Insurance Fund (Opvoeding, s.d.) among unemployed young adults did not demonstrate a difference in the consumption of alcohol and stimulants or sedative drugs before and after unemployment. On the other hand, 29% of the unemployed persons reported *smoking* more. The same study revealed changes in *sleeping patterns* ranging from sleeping less to sleeping substantially longer. *Nutritional behaviour* was affected by unemployment in the sense of a reduced consumption of meat and of irregularly eating due to a decrease in income and to psychosomatic complaints.

2.2.3 Mediators (demographic variables)

2.2.3.1 Age

Age was identified as a potential confounding variable in the association between unemployment and *attempted suicide* in both males and females (van Heeringen & Jannes, 1993). Age was found to influence the experience of unemployment and the level of *psychosocial well-being* among short-term unemployed persons (Hooge, 1995). Older unemployed persons (i.e., aged 40 to 46 years) experienced their unemployment more positively and appeared to be affected by it to a lesser extent. Younger long-term unemployed persons tended to be more optimistic than older ones (De Witte, 1992b). Wets and De Witte (1997) reported that unemployed persons aged 25 to 34 years have comparatively fewer problems with being unemployed than unemployed persons under 25 years and unemployed persons aged 35 to 44 years. A curvilinear relationship between age and having problems with being unemployed was found, indicating that older and to a lesser extent young unemployed persons experience their unemployment less negatively.

2.2.3.2 Gender

Unemployed young men experienced their unemployment more negatively than women (Opvoeding, s.d.; De Witte, 1992b; Hooge, 1995). Moreover, unemployment was a greater risk factor for *attempted suicide* among young men than among young women (van Heeringen & Jannes, 1993). Gender emerged as a potential confounding variable in the association between unemployment and *depressive symptoms* (Verhaegen et al., 1994). Females were almost twice as likely as males to experience depressive symptomatology of brief duration, but they were only slightly more likely than males to report symptoms of long duration.

2.2.3.3 Education

Unemployed persons with higher educational levels appeared to be less affected by unemployment (De Witte, 1992b). In studying the association between unemployment and juvenile delinquency, Vettenburg and colleagues (1984) concluded that earlier unfavourable school experiences have a more negative impact than the employment status thus suggesting a substantial association between a low educational level and *delinquency.*

2.2.3.4 Social class (social milieu)

No studies have been published in Belgium on unemployment and health in which the effect of social class was controlled for as a mediating variable. This is probably due to the lack of a satisfactory classification system of social class in Belgium.

2.2.3.5 Length of unemployment

Short-term unemployed persons evaluated their unemployment more negatively than long-term unemployed persons (Hooge, 1995). A comparative study demonstrated significant differences between these two groups concerning the experience of unemployment and psychological well-being with lower *well-being* scores among the short-term unemployed (De Witte & Hooge, 1997).

2.2.4 Moderators (psychological variables)

2.2.4.1 Work and job orientation

The studies of the Higher Institute for Labour (De Witte, 1992b; De Witte & Wets, 1993, Hooge, 1995; Wets & De Witte, 1997) suggested differences in psychological well-being and job orientation between different types of unemployed persons. These profiles were based on the dimensions 'wishes and expectations concerning work' and 'job-seeking behaviour'. Types of unemployed persons ('desperate' and 'discouraged' persons) who are intensively searching for a job and who are strongly job-oriented (persons who really want to work) had a much lower level of *psychological well-being* and a more negative experience of unemployment.

2.2.4.2 Financial strain/stress

Empirical evidence to support the hypothesis that financial stress is an important mediating factor in the association between unemployment and health is found in a number of Belgian studies. The family's own income appeared to be significantly associated with the level of *psychosocial well-being* of young long-term unemployed women (De Witte & Wets, 1993). In another study, the same authors stated that the experience of unemployment and the level of psychosocial well-being depend partially on income (Wets & De Witte, 1997). In their study on the psychosocial profile of long-term unemployed persons, a linear relationship between a negative experience of unemployment and the income level was found (De Witte, 1992b). Moreover, the financial dimension appeared to be a major factor in explaining gender differences in *health status* among unemployed persons. Men usually have more financial responsibility. Unemployment threatens the financial situation, which can cause a decrease in psychological well-being and a more negative experience of unemployment. This question of financial responsibility can also explain the more negative experience among unemployed single women.

2.2.4.3 Social support

Social support may well be another very important moderating variable as young persons living alone appear to be substantially more affected by their unemployment due to feeling more *isolated* and experiencing more *stress in their relationships* (Opvoeding, s.d.). Besides age, marital status and living situation were found to confound the association between unemployment and *attempted suicide* (van Heeringen & Jannes, 1993). Unemployment was a greater risk factor among married and widowed individuals than among unmarried or divorced persons. Moreover, unemployment was a greater risk factor among unemployed individuals living alone than among those living together with others. The relationship between unemployment and *delinquency* can be confounded by the fact that unemployed youngsters often come from families which do not conform to societal norms (Vettenburg et al., 1984). Research at the Higher Institute for Labour on psychosocial profiles suggested that, besides the income level, the family type affects the experience of unemployment. Having one or more children appeared to have a significant effect on the experience of unemployment (De Witte & Wets, 1993). Caring for children appeared to reduce the stressful character of unemployment. In another study, the same authors stated that the experience of unemployment and psychosocial well-being partially depend on the family type (Wets & De Witte, 1997). 'Withdrawn' persons who demonstrated a relatively high level of psychological well-being were almost all mothers with small children (De Witte, 1992b).

A striking finding from one of the first Belgian studies on youth unemployment concerns the radical social changes observed in the environment (Alaluf et al., 1982). Unemployed youngsters compared unemployment with a grave, and they experienced unemployment as a social death ("décès social"). However, the family relations remained unchanged. Vettenburg et al. (1984) observed that unemployed youngsters report more *problems at home* and with the family and that they have fewer friends. Moreover, unemployed individuals (especially single persons) reported more *stress in their direct relationships* and felt more *isolated* (Opvoeding, s.d.). Jeuris (1984) found that unemployed individuals and individuals on welfare benefits often feel socially isolated. Deliens et al. (1988) added that unemployed youngsters with low educational levels have less *contact with their parents* than their working peers. However, Elchardus and Glorieux (1995) stated that unemployment does not cause social isolation. On the contrary, unemployment leads to an increase in the time spent with family and children. The study of the children of the subjects from the original sample revealed that paternal unemployment has a negative influence on the school achievements of the children and that these children more commonly report racist and individualistic attitudes.

3 Summary of results

Belgium has been confronted with the substantial problem of unemployment since the 70s, reaching peak figures in the early 80s and 90s. Although at present the level of unemployment has stabilised, approximately one in seven persons is currently unemployed. Specifically youngsters, females, long-term unemployed persons, and persons with low qualifications are common among the unemployed. There are striking regional differences with unemployment rates in Wallonia and Brussels being much higher than those in the Flanders. Youth unemployment rates are two to three times higher than the overall unemployment rates. Among them, females, the very young with often minimal qualifications, and youngsters from Wallonia and Brussels appear to be most affected by youth unemployment.

The consequences of a lack of work have not been extensively debated in Belgium, but at least some researchers have provided interesting theoretical viewpoints for this discussion. The Belgian debate originated from the 'Marienthal' study of Jahoda, and her work still partially defines the actual debate. De Witte is the Belgian author who has contributed most to the debate on (youth) unemployment and health by reviewing the international literature on this topic and by putting forward an adaptation theory which includes a decrease of psychological well-being shortly after unemployment and a later stabilisation at a certain level. Only re-employment can break this circle. Later, De Witte and other researchers at the Higher Institute for Labour (HIVA) have studied the psychosocial profile of short- and long-term unemployed persons and have observed that especially 'desperate' and 'discouraged' persons suffer from their unemployment, while 'withdrawn' and 'adapted' persons are less affected by it.

As the association between youth unemployment and health – especially regarding availability of empirical data – is poorly documented in Belgium, those studies also had to be discussed in this overview which do not match precisely the YUSEDER age criteria. The first theoretical publications concerning youth unemployment and health warned of the devastating consequences of youth unemployment, but since then these points of view have been refined. Although many (young) unemployed persons appear not to be affected by unemployment, this experience causes psychological, financial, physical, and social problems for them. Several authors use selection and causation hypotheses to explain the association between unemployment and health. Although 'selective' factors may be involved, unemployment has a direct detrimental effect on psychological well-being.

No empirical evidence of an association between unemployment and mortality rates has been found, although a European comparative study shows that the high mortality rates in Southern Belgium are associated with high unemployment rates. Concerning morbidity, a large proportion of the studies has focussed on the psychological well-being of unemployed persons using the GHQ-12, demonstrating relatively high scores especially among short-term unemployed persons and certain groups of unemployed persons. Significant differences in depressive symptomatology between unemployed, employed, and studying youngsters have been observed.

Unemployed persons are at a six to seven times higher risk of attempting suicide than employed persons. Particularly, young unemployed men appear to be at risk. Moreover, unemployed persons are overrepresented within the client population of community mental health centres. Many unemployed youngsters experience financial distress, but only some groups of unemployed persons seem to be no longer job-oriented ('withdrawn persons'). Well-being is affected by unemployment, which can lead to psychosomatic complaints and a decrease in psychological well-being and self-esteem, thus inducing feelings of dependency and powerlessness. The political orientations of unemployed youngsters appear to be only slightly influenced by unemployment, while their social life may be subject to substantial changes. Youth unemployment is not associated with juvenile offending, and only a limited influence on health behaviour has been demonstrated. The association between youth unemployment and health appears to be confounded by mediators such as age, gender, education, and length of unemployment, and by moderators including work and job orientation, financial strain, and social support. Particularly, social support and financial strain appear to affect the experience of youth unemployment.

Overall, unemployment emerges as a risk factor and stressor, thus affecting divergent health-related aspects. This review of the Belgian debate shows that unemployment confronts individuals with a new reality which challenges their adaptational capacities.

Youth unemployment and health: Belgian studies – an overview

Studies on youth unemployment and health

Author	Sample	Instruments/ Methods	Population	Dependent Variables	Results
Vettenburg, N., Walgrave, L., & Van Kerckvoorde, J. (1984)	= 207 Flemish youngsters from lower social classes (random sample) students (n = 70) workers (n = 66) unemployed youngsters (n = 71)	Cross-sectional study In writing self-report questionnaire	– 17 to 19 years – region of Leuven and Herent (urban and rural)	Self-reported delinquent behaviour Self-esteem Psychosomatic health Social vulnerability	– no direct relation between unemployment and delinquency; school achievement was identified as a confounding variable – unemployed youngsters seemed more socially vulnerable – no differences in self-esteem, psychosomatic health and delinquent behaviour
Sand, E., Verhaegen, L., & Meyer, J. (1989)	N = 900 Belgian adolescents (random sample) students (n = 300) workers (n = 300) unemployed youngsters (n = 300)	cross-sectional study CES-D scale in writing questionnaire and brief interview	– 16 to 21 years – urban population (Brussels area)	prevalence of depressive symptoms	– Belgian adolescents often reached the level of clinical depression – unemployed adolescents presented significantly higher rates of depressive symptoms than studying and working adolescents
Verhaegen, L., Deykin, E., & Sand, E. (1994)	N = 898 Belgian adolescents (random sample) students (n = 300) workers (n = 298) unemployed youngsters (n = 300)	cross-sectional study CES-D scale in writing questionnaire and brief interview	– 16 to 21 years – urban population (Brussels area)	prevalence of depressive symptoms	– primary unemployment was associated with a substantial degree of depressive morbidity – depressive symptoms were of longer duration among unemployed youngsters

Studies on unemployment and health without matching the age criteria (up to 36 years)

Author	Sample	Instruments/ Methods	Population	Dependent Variables	Results
Opvoeding en Vrijetijdsbeste-ding der Jongeren-MJA (s.d.)	N = 403 unemployed young adults (representative sample), enrolled in the Socialist Health Insurance Fund (Bond Moyson)	cross-sectional study structured in writing questionnaire	– 15 to 36 years – Flanders (except Brabant) (urban and rural)	health-related behaviour psychological well-being social relations	– men and single living persons reported more problems – unemployed persons experienced much stress in their social relations – no changes in alcohol and drug use after unemployment
De Witte, H., & Wets, J. (1993)	N = 407 long-term unemployed women from the German-speaking community in Belgium (representative sample)	cross-sectional study psychosocial profile of long-term unemployed women General Health Ques-tionnaire (GHQ-12) 3 different scales (experience of unemployment, wishes, and expectations concerning work and intensity of job-seeking) in writing questionnaire	– 18 to 35 years – urban and rural parts of Belgium	experience of unemployment psychosocial well-being work-involvement intensity of seeking a job	– only a small minority of long-term unemployed women experienced their unemployment negatively and showed a lower psychosocial well-being – most women were only moderately involved in the labour market and showed no intensive job-seeking behaviour – having one or more children and having a higher income-level were two variables with a significant positive influence on the experience of unemployment

Other studies which include only some health related aspects

Author	Sample	Instruments/ Methods	Population	Dependent Variables	Results
Alaluf, M., Desmarez, P., & Domb, I. (1982)	N = 89 unemployed youngsters with very low qualifications (random sample)	cross-sectional study face-to-face interview with structured questionnaire	– 16 to 25 years old – region of Charleroi (urban)	life style attitudes	– unemployed persons' self-esteem was affected by unemployment and they often experienced feelings of dependency and worthlessness – unemployment strongly disturbed the social relations of these youngsters – attitudes and behaviours of unemployed persons were almost exclusively work-oriented
Van Loon, F., Pauwels, K., & Van Humskerke, H. (1982)	N = 298 married unemployed persons, entitled to unemployment benefits random sample)	cross-sectional study face-to-face interview with structured questionnaire	– less than 35 years – jobless for at least 4 months – urban population (Antwerp)	experience of unemployment social and family relations desire to have children	– unemployed persons often reported financial stress, social isolation and a decreased self-esteem – long-term unemployment caused increased concern, feelings of dependency and a lack of self-reliance – unemployment affected the desire to have children
Deliens, L., Bosman, E., & Louckx, F. (1988)	N = 592 independently living male youngsters with low qualifications (stratified sample) unemployed youngsters employed youngsters	cross-sectional study face-to-face interview with structured questionnaire	– 24 to 26 years – district urban Brussels-Halle-Vilvoorde	socioeconomic behaviour (subsistence, patterns of consumption, social relations, etc.)	– unemployed youngsters had less contacts with their parents and other family-members – unemployment had a clear influence on the subsistence of families and on their patterns of consumption
De Witte, H. (1992a)	N = 756 young adults (random sample) workers (n = 536) unemployed persons (n = 220)	cross-sectional design secondary analysis of a survey concerning the political attitude of youngsters structured in writing questionnaire	– 18 to 35 years – all urban and rural Flemish regions, – enrolled in Christian labour movement (ACW)	political attitudes attitudes concerning the Christian labour movement (ACW)	– unemployed youngsters showed more sympathy for left-wing parties – most unemployed persons became apathetic due to social isolation and only a small minority presented radical political opinions – among very young unemployed persons a relatively high level of political indifference was found

Author	Sample	Instruments/ Methods	Population	Dependent Variables	Results
Elchardus, M., & Glorieux, I. (1995)	N = 206 men living together with their partner and at least one child (original sample) employed (n = 95) short-term unemployed (n = 56) long-term unemployed (n = 55) N = 177 men follow-up sample), of which full-time employed (n = 151) part-time employed or unemployed men (n = 26) N = 94 children of these men, born before 1984	cross-sectional study, including the original study, a follow-up study and study of the children time-budget study (24h) structured in writing questionnaires	– 24 to 37 years – urban district (Halle-Vilvoorde)	time-consumption psychological well-being	– unemployed men reported more boredom and spent more time in activities with their partner and children – unemployment didn't cause shame or social isolation, but feelings of insecurity and vulnerability – follow-up results showed an improved psycho-social well-being after (re-) employment – unemployment of the father could have a negative influence on the school results of their children

Studies on unemployment and health without matching the age criteria (all ages)

Author	Sample	Instruments/ Methodes	Population	Dependent Variables	Results
Born, M., & Gavray, C. (s.d.)	N = 6,319 persons from 4,439 Belgian households (representative sample) categories according to socio-professional status	longitudinal design secondary analysis on the Panel Study of Belgian Households face-to-face interview with structured questionnaire Moos Depression Scale	– 16 to 65 years – all different Belgian regions (urban and rural)	psychosocial well-being	– status and professional situation of men largely conditioned by their psychosocial well-being – link between professional integration and psychosocial well-being remained insignificant for women
Jeuris, W. (1984)	N = 1,040 patients administered in one of 3 mental health care centres (Centra Geestelijke Gezondheidszorg) –working group –unemployed group –family-group –remaining group	cross-sectional study study of patient files	– all ages – urban population (Antwerp)	registered problems at the intake in a mental health care centre	– Unemployed patients reported more relational and financial problems and feelings of social exclusion – 67.4% of the unemployed persons could be diagnosed as having a neurotic, personality or other non-psychotic disorder (addiction, depression, etc.), according to the MACLA-diagnosis – especially unemployed women with a relatively high education seemed to make use of these mental heath care centres
De Pauw, M. (1988)	N = 11,938 patients, administered in a mental health care centre (Centrum Geeste-lijke Gezondheidszorg) working group unemployed group family-group remaining group	cross-sectional study study of patient files	– all ages – 5.360 men 6.578 women – urban and rural	registered problems at the intake in a mental health care centre	– significantly higher proportion of unemployed persons among patients of mental health care centres – unemployment was identified as a risk factor for psychosocial problems: unemployed persons report more problems concerning social integration, addiction and material situation, but less concerning relations – unemployed men suffered more than unemployed women

Author	Sample	Instruments/ Methodes	Population	Dependent Variables	Results
De Witte, H. (1992b)	N = 309 long-term unemployed persons (stratified sample) N = 199 long-term unemployed persons (stratified sample)' enrolled in an employment action for long-term unemployed persons (WeerWerk) [control group]	cross-sectional study psychosocial profile of long-term unemp. GHQ-12) 3 different scales (experience of unemployment, wishes, and expectations concerning work and intensity of job-seeking) face-to-face interview	– region of Flanders (urban and rural)	experience of unemployment psychosocial well-being work-involvement intensity of seeking a job	– generally, long-term unemployed persons didn't suffer from unemployment, but a small hard core of unemployed persons really suffered – experience of unemployment was related to family type, income and gender – 48% stated their health status limited their ability to work; in 1 in 5 persons this was due to psychological complaints – "Desperate seekers" experienced their unemployment as extremely negative and 75% of them scored higher than the critical value on the GHQ-12 – the WeerWerk-clients scored significantly higher on the GHQ-12 and had a more negative experience of unemployment, compared with other long-term unemployed persons
Van Heeringen, C., & Jannes, C. (1993)	N = 1,981 (random sample) of the Population Census record for Gent (n= 1.608), linked with records for all attempted suicide referrals, residents of Gent city (n= 508) and admitted to the University Hospital from 1986-1990 economically inactive unemployed persons employed persons	cross-sectional study case-control studystudy of attempted suicide referrals	– 15 years or older – admitted to the University Hospital due to attempted suicide	attempted suicide	– unemployment identified as a risk factor for attempted suicide in both males (15-34 years old and 35-49 years old) and females (35-49 years old) – age and living situation were identified as potential confounding variables

Author	Sample	Instruments/ Methodes	Population	Dependent Variables	Results
Hooge, J. (1995)	N = 1,109 short-term (10 months) unemployed persons, participating in a government's employment action (Individueel Begeleidingsplan) (representative sample) N = 583 persons from the original sample (follow-up sample)	cross-sectional study including follow-up after 6 months study of the psychosocial profile of short-term unemployed persons General Health Questionnaire-12 3 different scales (experience of unemployment, wishes, and expectations concerning work and intensity of job-seeking) in writing questionnaire	– less than 46 years – jobless for 10 months and entitled to unemployment benefits – Flanders (urban and rural)	experience of unemployment psychological well-being work-involvement intensity of job seeking	– short-term unemployed persons experienced their unemployment very negatively and had a very low level of psychological well-being – age, gender and family situation partially determined the experience of unemployment and the psychological well-being – recovery of the psychological well-being after (re-) employment
Gavray, C. (1996)	N = 6,319 persons from 4,439 Belgian households (representative sample) categories according to socio-professional status	longitudinal design secondary analysis on the Panel Study of Belgian Households structured questionnaire Moos Depression Scale face-to-face interview	– 16 to 65 years – all different urban and rural Belgian regions	level of depression	– level of depression depended linearly on the quality of the socio-professional insertion – lower level of psychosocial well-being was observed among persons less involved in work

Author	Sample	Instruments/ Methodes	Population	Dependent Variables	Results
Wets, J., & De Witte, H. (1997)	N = 579 unemployed persons from the German-speaking community of Belgium	cross-sectional study study of the psychosocial profile of unemployed persons General Health Questionnaire (GHQ-12) 3 different scales (experience of unemployment, wishes, and expectations concerning work and intensity of job-seeking) in writing questionnaire	– German-speaking community of Belgium – urban and rural	experience of unemployment psychological well-being work-involvement intensity of seeking a job	– most unemployed persons did not suffer from unemployment. Only a small core group was strongly affected by their unemployment – decrease of income strongly influenced the psychological well-being among unemployed persons – experience of unemployment and psychological well-being among unemployed persons was affected by family type and income – persons from 25 to 34 years old and persons under 25 seemed to suffer less from unemployment

Studies only indirectly related to unemployment and health

Author	Sample	Instruments/ Methods	Population	Dependent Variables	Results
Moens, G., Haenen, W., & Van de Voorde, H. (1988)	sample based on mortality rates for suicide in the WHO-yearbooks (for the periods 1970-1974 and 1980-1984)	aggregated study reported mortality rates for suicide (WHO-yearbook)	– 5 to 24 years – 21 European countries – urban and rural	mortality rates for suicide	– youth suicide was strongly associated with indicators of anomia and social isolation in both sexes, but less with socioeconomic variables
Mackenbach, J. & Looman, C. (1994)	– sample based on the data of all cause mortality for 133 European regions	aggregated study standardised regional mortality ratios (SMRs) Eurostat data on living standards (gross domestic product, car access and unemployment rates)	– Standardised mortality rates for 133 regions in the EC (1980-84) – Eurostat data on regional living standards (1985-88)	mortality ratios	– unemployment rates had the strongest association with mortality, after controlling for confounding variables – high mortality rates were found in the Southern regions of Belgium. Most of these regions have living standards below the EC-average and relatively high unemployment rates
Gavray, C. (1997)	1 N = 618 youngsters (original sample) 2 N = 139 youngsters (follow-up sample) of which: – students (n = 41) – workers (n = 52) – non-workers (n = 46)	cross-sectional study, including the original study and a 4-year follow-up study International Self-Reported Delinquency in writing questionnaire	– 14 to 21 years (1. sample) – 21 to 25 years (2. sample) – city of Liège	delinquent behaviour	– no significant interaction between the professional status and type and rates of delinquent behaviour – students and non-workers reported 4 times more drug-related offences – causal relation was found between the lack of financial resources and deviant behaviour
Born, M., Gavray, C., & Cattelino, E. (1998)	1 N = 618 youngsters (original sample) 2 N = 139 youngsters (follow-up sample) of which – students (n = 41) – workers (n = 52) – non-workers (n = 46)	cross-sectional study, including the original study and a 4-year follow-up study Moos Depression Scale in writing interview	– 14 to 21 years old (1. sample) – 21 to 25 years old (2. sample) – city of Liège	depression	– depression in adulthood was not related to employment status – depression among adolescents was more related to individual rather than to external characteristics – long-term unemployment of the mother had a significant influence on depression in adolescents

Youth Unemployment and Health in Germany

Thomas Kieselbach & Gert Beelmann[1]

1 In collaboration with *Birgitt Erdwien*.

1 Introduction to youth unemployment and health

1.1 National development of youth unemployment

1.1.1 Unemployment in general

Throughout the 1990s the condition of the German labour market has suffered continuous deterioration. The labour force participation rate declined; the unemployment rate rose, and an increasing number of long-term unemployed has plagued the Federal Republic's economic situation for years. The real extent of unemployment in Germany as a whole is well over the given figure of 4.4 million for 1977. The so-called hidden labour force (jobseekers who are willing and able to work but who are not registered with the employment office) is around 1.6 million (not including job scheme participants). On top of this there are over 2 million people involved in labour-oriented sociopolitical schemes. If these figures are taken into account, Germany has a current shortfall of some 7 million jobs (Kieselbach, 1998).

The differing evolutional paths in the East and West are clearly reflected by the numbers of the country's workers and its unemployed (cf. Table 1). In West Germany the number of people employed rose slightly between 1989 and 1997 (the labour force participation rate remained constant). In the same period the number of unemployed rose from 2 million to a record 3 million. The situation that evolved in East Germany was far worse. Between 1989 and 1997, the workforce decreased by almost 4 million (1989: 9.8 million – 1997: 6.1 million). At the same time the number of unemployed rose continuously (1990: 0.2 million – 1997: 1.4 million).

Table GER-1: Employed and unemployed persons in West vs. East Germany in millions

	West Germany		East Germany	
	employed	unemployed	employed	unemployed
1989	27.6	2.0	9.8	–
1990	28.4	1.9	8.9	0.2
1991	29.2	1.7	7.3	0.9
1992	29.5	1.8	6.4	1.2
1993	29.0	2.3	6.2	1.2
1994	28.7	2.6	6.3	1.1
1995	28.5	2.6	6.4	1.1
1996	28.2	2.8	6.3	1.2
1997	27.9	3.0	6.1	1.4

Source: Bundesanstalt für Arbeit/Federal Labour Office, 1998.

The length of the period of unemployment is indicative of whether structural problems in the labour market are becoming entrenched. When someone is unemployed for a year or longer we speak of long-term unemployment. The figure for long-term unemployment in the Federal Republic rose sharply between 1996 (1.2 million) and 1997 (1.5 million). In the meantime, in West Germany, the proportion of long-term unemployed has reached 34%, a record high for the postwar period. In East Germany, 28% of all unemployed are long-term unemployed, a smaller proportion than in the West (because of the greater emphasis of publicly subsidised job-creation schemes).

1.1.2 Youth unemployment

Germany's youth unemployment also increased dramatically in the 90s, albeit to a differing degree in East and West Germany. The problem of German youth unemployment has, in recent times, taken on an increasingly high profile political dimension. It is seen as "the unemployment of young people that results from their attempt to move from the world of being educated into the job market system" (Wolfinger, 1997, p. 150). It is becoming increasingly difficult for young people in Germany to successfully master the transition between scholastic education, job-oriented training, and the workforce. In East Germany the switch from job training in state-run concerns to that of a market economy has led to major problems in the availability of apprenticeships. The second step, from training into the workforce, is greatly impeded by a lack of jobs to satisfy the pressure of growing demands (cf. Wolfinger, 1997). The proportion of youth unemployed in the Federal Republic is comparable to the proportion of unemployed for all ages. In 1997 the overall unemployment rate was 12.7% ("West" Germany 11.0% vs. "East" Germany 19.5%). By comparison, the rate for 20-24 year olds was 12.4% in the West and a much higher 22.3% in the East. The rate for the under 20 years age group was somewhat lower, yet still with a large West-East difference: 10.5% and 16%, respectively (ANBA, 1997).

Table 2 shows the progression of the rate of unemployment in the Federal Republic since the 1970s. Apart from the oil crisis in the mid-70s and the economic downturn in the early 80s, the unemployment of under 25 year olds has increased at a steady rate, although rather more alarmingly among the 20-24 year olds than among the under 20 year olds. The situation is particularly grim in the East, where the 1997 rate was some 10% higher than in the West. These figures make two things very clear: There is a large discrepancy between West Germany and the new German states on the one hand and an increasingly critical situation of the labour market per se on the other.

Figure GER-1: Young unemployed people below the age of 25, West vs. East Germany (1974-1976: values from September of the respective year; 1977-1994 yearly average values)

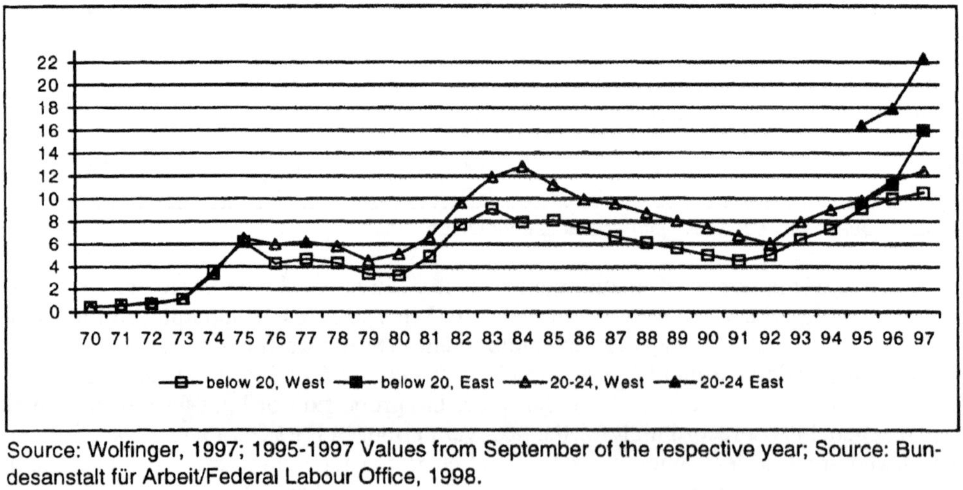

Source: Wolfinger, 1997; 1995-1997 Values from September of the respective year; Source: Bundesanstalt für Arbeit/Federal Labour Office, 1998.

Long-term youth unemployment, however, plays a lesser role than long-term unemployment where all ages are considered. At the end of September 1997, the long-term unemployment rate for under 25 year olds was 9% in the West as well as in the East.

1.2 Unemployment and health – some theoretical considerations

As a result of the continual increase in unemployment in most western industrialised nations since the 1980s there has been an ever increasing study of the social and individual repercussions of unemployment. In Germany, numerous seminar publications document a branch of study within the realm of psychology that comes under the heading "differential unemployment research" (Wacker 1983; see also Holzhüter, Hickel & Kieselbach, 1997; Kieselbach & Wacker, 1991; Schindler, Wacker & Wetzels, 1990). The central argument in favour of a differentiated method of focussing on the repercussions of involuntary unemployment is the differing perception, reaction, and assimilation (according to the individual concerned) of the various phases of unemployment. Here, criteria such as age, gender, and level of training give rise to totally different levels of stress and pressure. Krieger and Schläfke (1987) point out a negative aspect of a differentiated judgement of the social consequences of unemployment, namely the question of to what extent unemployment is self-inflicted and the resulting guilt feelings. The fact remains that public discussion of overcoming the negative experiences of unemployment (which can lead to self-fulfilment in some cases) gives rise to a climate of scepticism among the unemployed who are faced with the real (financial, psychosocial) world of what unemployment entails.

Youth unemployment and unemployment in general can no longer be seen as a temporary phenomenon. The situation has to be considered entrenched (cf. Kieselbach, 1985). The proportion of youth unemployed in the Federal Republic is about the same as that for all ages. While the proportion of unemployed for the entire civilian labour force in November 1997 was 11.3%, the proportion for under 25 year olds was 11.6%. Regarding the West-East division, the proportion of unemployed under 25 year olds was 10.5% (West) and 15.7% (East) (ANBA, 1997). These contrasting tendencies are tied in with the differing economic climates and structures in East and West Germany. In 1997 the growth tendencies due to increased exports benefited West rather than East Germany. On top of this, the crisis in the building sector hit the East harder than the West. The unemployment rate for the entire German civilian labour force (average for 1996) was 12.7%, with the figure for East Germany (19.5%) almost double that of the West (11.0%).

There are different levels of debate on the effects of youth unemployment in Germany. On the socio-psychological level, Kieselbach (1985) developed three scenarios of how society deals with youth unemployment:

1. Trivialisation: The real extent of youth unemployment is belittled by means of biased statistical representation,
2. Naturalisation: Unemployment is considered an inevitable natural phenomenon subject to regular cycles (e.g., "the spring upturn", "flood of trainees"),
3. Individualisation: Youth has only itself to blame for the onset and duration of youth unemployment.

On the social level, Hahn and Schön (1996) point out two further aspects crucial to the health-related consequences that unemployment has on young people:

1. Where poverty is concerned, young unemployed people are increasingly hit hard (e.g., they receive less unemployment benefits than the older unemployed)

2. Unemployment at a young age can be seen as setting the tone for later working life and can increase the risk of social marginalisation.

It is assumed that young people are less vulnerable in the context of psychiatric morbidity. Where long-term unemployment is ongoing, there is danger of an increasing gap between youth who are unemployed and those who have jobs. Those who are cut off from the labour market see themselves, in the long run, as stigmatised. Their personal development is therefore impaired. More often than not the experience of unemployment is accompanied by an accumulation of other daily hassles (Kieselbach, 1988). By way of contrast, those who do manage to enter the workforce experience positive effects resulting from the latent functions inherent in work. Acquired skills can be put to good use. The young people are financially and socially independent and their days are structured. These psychosocial aspects appear to enhance personal development.

As regards East Germany it has been pointed out that, on top of the far greater vulnerability to unemployment, there are youth problems specifically tied in with East Germany's process of transformation (cf. Hahn & Schön, 1996). For some of the youth, growing into adulthood coincided with this period of social upheaval. The new possibilities that life offered, following East Germany's integration into the Federal Republic, were destroyed for many by their being cut off from the workforce. Demands were placed on the young people that they "quickly reorient themselves and individualise their plans and decisions for the future" (Hormuth, 1997, p. 565).

In the context of theoretical (re)orientation, since the 1970s, there has been a broad forum of debate in Germany concerning unemployment and health. This still inconclusive debate remains wide open regarding the causes, effects, and indeed, the extent of the phenomena. Health is seen as a dynamic entity and indicates "the condition of a person when that person's objective and subjective state of being, his physical, mental and social development are in harmony with his personal potential, goals, and environmental living conditions" (Hurrelmann, 1988, p. 16).

Wacker (1985) sees merit in the argument that unemployment can be the first step in a continuum of numerous mental and social symptoms of disintegration; but he also sees merit in the argument of discontinuity, that is, unemployment does not inevitably lead to isolation. Wacker (1985) also expresses doubts about the relevancy of results of dated research studies (Jahoda, Lazarsfeld & Zeisel 1975) for the present-day situation. He considers the methodological incompatibilities alone reason enough to invalidate comparisons between older and newer studies. Apart from this, it appears difficult to draw a complete or accurate picture of the health-related stress brought about by youth unemployment, given the paucity of empirical, up-to-date studies.

A review of German literature on the subject reveals that in many cases unemployment is a critical experience in the life of the individual concerned, and one "which contributes to a marked deterioration in the person's mental and physical well-being" (Kieselbach, 1985, p. 48; Elkeles & Seifert, 1992; Kieselbach & Wacker, 1985). As for the question of an interrelationship between unemployment and health, there are basically two theoretical lines of approach:

1. The hypothesis of causality, according to which unemployment leads to psychological deterioration; i.e., the onset, continuance, or indeed, the anticipation of a period of unwanted unemployment is the direct cause, in the short or in the long term, of psychiatric and psychosocial disturbances to an individual's well-being.

2. The hypothesis of selection, according to which unfavourable living conditions and less robust health bring about unemployment or, as the case may be, reduce the unemployed person's chances of re-entering the workforce.

Research that concentrates solely on lines of impact neglects not only the social and psychological effects of youth unemployment, but also the lifestyle patterns, behavioural patterns, and coping strategies of the people affected. The real course that unemployment takes always depends on whether and to what extent alternative options can be perceived and acted upon (cf. Hahn & Schön, 1996).

2 Analysis of research studies on youth unemployment and health

There are very few empirical analyses examining the interrelationship between youth unemployment and health in Germany. In contrast to the studies carried out in other countries, those available in Germany are heterogeneous in their methodology and, for the most part, descriptive. Furthermore, there is very little current data available. Most of the studies date back to the 1970s and are directed primarily towards the general effects and consequences of a labour market which has been continually strained since that time. They fail to deal explicitly with the health-related effects of unemployed youth.

2.1 Description of the available data (design and method)

Over the last 20 years, a total of 17 studies dealing with youth unemployment and health could be found. In addition, there is also a classical representative survey from the 1950s (Schelsky, 1952). Of the studies found, 8 were supposed to be qualitative and 10 quantitative. For this period there was only one longitudinal study and four of the studies carried out were representative.

Table 1 in the Appendix gives a detailed overview of the German studies and describes random samples, instruments used for measurement, methods, population groups, the dependent variables taken into account, as well as the main results.

2.1.1 Cross-sectional studies

2.1.1.1 Quantitative studies

In Germany the most important and comprehensive study of youth unemployment was carried out in the mid-1970s and early 1980s by the IAB (Institute for Labour Market and Career Research). The first phase was conducted in Autumn 1975 with 1,000 unemployed youths participating. The period for the second phase of the IAB study was November 1981 to November 1982, with a total of 2,500 unemployed youth participating. Both investigations were representative surveys conducted by mail, and they dealt exclusively with under 25 year olds registered as unemployed. In the second study, the participants had only been registered as unemployed for a few weeks.

The aim of the first IAB study was to ascertain the participants' social and career background, the changes experienced by the young people following their unemployment, and most importantly, the financial and psychosocial strains suffered during the period of unemployment. This study was carried out at a time when the rate of unemployment of under 25 year olds was at its highest since World War II. In 1975 the rate of youth unemployment was 6.4% compared to 4.7% for all age groups. The mid-1970s saw, for the first time since World War II, the onset of massive economic problems largely caused by the "oil crisis" and the global recession. This led to considerable imbalances in the labour market with youth being particularly disadvantaged. In 1974, 28% of all the people registered as unemployed were under 25 years of age.

The second IAB study was carried out at the time of the next economic crisis in Germany. Among other factors, a large increase in the number of people seeking work in the early 1980s led to disparities in the labour market. Baby boomers stormed the available training programmes and job positions causing bottlenecks in the labour market (Wolfinger, 1997). The fact that both IAB studies were concurrent with periods of economic crisis darkened the spectrum of gloom as perceived by the young unemployed. Both studies found that the primary strain suffered was financial. Other consequences were family tensions and conflicts as well as a general feeling of malaise. These studies still form an important basis for the consideration of the relationship between youth unemployment and its associated psychosocial burdens (Schober 1978, 1987).

Apart from these representative studies are yet two more, albeit from different historical contexts. The first can be seen as pioneer work on the effects of youth unemployment in Germany. In 1950 Schelsky and his colleagues, with the support of the DGB (Federation of German Trade Unions), carried out an extensive study of the financial situation and psychosocial stress of unemployed youth. 1,978 young jobless people were questioned along with a comparative or control group of 308 young people who were employed (Schelsky, 1952). Results showed that 60% of the young unemployed paid board and lodging within their family. Consequently, lack of money was a major stress factor. Another was the increased difficulty in developing and maintaining social relationships. The DGB study is still considered a classic in the field of unemployment research in Germany but its validity is obviously limited to the immediate postwar period of reconstruction.

The most up-to-date empirical data comes from an East German survey carried out in three series of surveys between 1993 and 1995. The second series, conducted in Summer 1994, concerns a group of 84 officially registered unemployed youths. They were questioned about their financial situation, psychological strains, and countermeasures. By way of comparison, young people in employment were also surveyed (Hahn, 1996). Results showed that the major concern of 50% of the unemployed was fear of not finding a job. Also, their financial situation was far worse than that of their employed counterparts. However, the specificities of the East German labour market must be taken into account. In the East there is far more youth unemployment. The increased psychosocial stress must be viewed against the background of the transformations undergone by East Germany's youth and labour market as a result of its integration into the Federal Republic.

A series of noteworthy, quantitative empirical investigations emerged in the late 1970s during a period of economic downturn. Indeed, most of the data available for Germany is from the 1970s. Until that time the topic of youth unemployment as a psychosocial problem was largely unexplored. In order to remedy this, several methodologically ambitious investigations were conducted using between 252 and 855 young respondents. In two of the investigations control groups were used.

In the Spring of 1976 Heinemann conducted a large-scale study in southwest Germany with 293 unemployed and 277 employed youths. Most of those questioned were male because there were only few young females registered as unemployed. The main aim of the study was to ascertain the influence of unemployment on young people's personality. Important traits such as feelings of self-worth, aggression, and moodiness were taken into account. It appeared that negative changes in personality occurred as a result of long-term, but not short-term, unemployment. The researchers also interviewed experts from various institutions and organisations. Finally, they sought the employers' views on youth unemployment.

In Autumn 1976, Wilhelm-Reiss (1980) investigated 15-24 year olds in order to ascertain the psychological changes resulting from the failure to enter the workforce. She interviewed 252 youths, dividing them into five subcategories: (1) trainees/apprentices, (2) young workers, (3) unemployed, (4) participants in special training courses, and (5) vocational school students. The survey was conducted in weakly structured regions of southern Germany. The survey brought to light increased somatic and psychosomatic disorders of and lower self-esteem among the unemployed.

Baumann, Becker, Gerstenmainer, Schickle and Tippelt, (1979) examined the political attitudes of unemployed youth and how these young people could (re)act to their situation, as well as the social and psychological problems resulting from unemployment. The groups compared were apprentices and young unskilled workers, 436 respondents in all. The political leanings of the unemployed were basically limited to spontaneous actions. With regard to self-esteem, only minimal differences were found between the two groups.

In 1978 Eichenhofer and colleagues examined the causes and consequences of youth unemployment in a southern German state (Saarland). This extremely complex study investigated, among other things, psychosocial repercussions and political attitudes. A strong correlation was found between unemployment and social destabilisation. The unemployed also displayed increased tendencies towards depressive and aggressive behaviour (Arbeitskammer des Saarlandes, 1980).

The above studies are seminal (even though dated and limited to particular regions of southern Germany), but at this point two more quantitative studies should be mentioned: Grieswelle (1977) investigated 1,033 youth (15-19 years old) who were classified as either (a) vocational school students who had never had a job or an apprenticeship, (b) those who had a job at the time of the survey, or (c) vocational school students who had had a steady job and then become unemployed. The study focussed mainly on work and career orientation. What emerged was the parental influence on the respondents' systems of values. Mruck and Mey (1992) investigated the material and social living conditions of young people in two districts of Berlin. Of the 454 participants, 49 were unemployed. 95% of all respondents considered a paid job very important. Financial restrictions were considered the worst repercussion of unemployment.

2.1.1.2 Qualitative studies

In unemployment research there has been an increasing demand for a qualitative, rather than a purely quantitative approach. It is easy to discern the shortcomings of quantitative methods which make generalisations about results while totally neglecting respondents' life histories (cf. Vonderach, Siebers & Barr, 1992). Likewise, the German qualitative studies that do exist also fail to pay enough attention to respondents' backgrounds.

Due to its extensive random sampling, Burger and Seidenspinner's 1975 study (published 1977) is considered the most comprehensive qualitative study in Germany. 314 youths of 9th grade school age were interviewed, both in group discussion and in one-on-one interviews. The study was conducted in two distinct regions: one urban industrial, the other a small southern German town. The sample group studied included youth in assistance programmes, trainees, young workers, and secondary school-leavers, as well as 75 unemployed adolescents. The study's main focus was on how the young experienced unemployment and its repercussions on their career perspectives and outlook for the future. The study brought to light the unemployed respondents' fear of career failure, attitude of resignation, and their loss of self-confidence.

In the mid-1980s Siebers and Vonderach (1991) extensively interviewed 64 long-term unemployed youth. The study examined how young people in rural areas of northern Germany reacted to and coped with recurring or long-term unemployment. In order to examine continuity and progression (in the sense of a longitudinal study), 20 of the participants were re-interviewed one and a half years later. This biographical perspective indicated a certain stigmatisation and feelings of social isolation.

In addition to these qualitative studies are a series of papers that are less extensive and culturally specific and will be only briefly summarised here. Opaschowski (1976) questioned some 130 unemployed adolescents from an industrial working class environment as to future prospects, career orientation, and social relationships, thus underlining the buffer effect of family support. In a study commissioned by the Federal Ministry for Youth, Family, and Health, 50 unemployed youth were questioned about their day-to-day psychosocial stress, work preferences, and political attitudes. This study indicated that the effects were increased if the adolescents concerned had already been previously subjected to massive psychosocial stress before (Sinus, 1983). Alheit and Glass (1986) investigated the unemployment of 15 youths in a biographical context, concentrating on their subjective experiences. The authors created a typology of patterns for explaining the youths' means of coming to terms with their situation. Krieger and Schläfke (1987) examined the situation of 13 unemployed youth living in an urban area and receiving welfare assistance. Their aim, using a structured interview technique, was to measure the subjective impact of unemployment. The main finding was a reduction in social contact due to inadequate financial means. In March 1987, Christe (1989) questioned 78 participants in a reintegration programme about the tangible consequences of unemployment on day-to-day life. What the 18 to 26 year olds feared most was being sidelined or becoming pariahs.

All in all, there is much diversity in the data of these quantitative and qualitative studies, both in the size and composition of their sampling. Apart from the studies of the IAB (Schober, 1978; 1987) and Hahn (1996), the above-mentioned investigations are not based on standardised measurement criteria and therefore do not permit viable generalised conclusions. The findings are almost exclusively based on cross-sectional studies and thus fail to investigate the consequences of unemployment.

2.1.2 Longitudinal studies

The paucity of long-term measurements in the context of youth unemployment and health represents a huge deficit in any psychological research into the problem. Only one qualitative longitudinal study exists that was carried out by Diezinger, Marquardt, Bilden and Dahlke (1983) by conducting panel interviews with 52 unemployed young women. In the first instance, between September 1978 and April 1979, they were asked about their psychosocial stress, social relationships, and work preferences. Three subgroups with differing work experience were compared: (a) school-leavers or those who had no work experience, (b) those who had worked or who had begun but not completed apprenticeships, and (c) those who had completed occupational training. In the second phase 18 months later, 29 women aged 15-19 years were interviewed and analyses revealed that feelings of boredom and futility, as well as increased teenager-parent conflict were results of the unemployment. The importance of peer group relationships increased at the expense of parental relationships.

2.1.3 Aggregated studies

Secondary data can be obtained from a variety of sources. Among the most comprehensive investigations from which relevant data can be gleaned are those of the Socio-economic Panel (SOEP), the Mikrozensus (Sample Census), the Arbeitsmarkt-Monitor für Ostdeutschland (Labour Market Monitor for East Germany), the Wohlfahrtssurvey (Welfare Survey), and the statistics available from the Federal Institute for Employment (BA).

The SOEP is an annual cross-sectional survey of households in Germany. A part of this survey consists of a questionnaire dealing with socioeconomic factors and subjective evaluations based on family income. The Mikrozensus, a government survey, furnishes data concerning the social and economic structure of the population. The statistics from the Mikrozensus, an annual cross-sectional sampling, are used as an important source in analysing Germany's employment/unemployment situation. The Arbeitsmarkt-Monitor is a representative survey of 10,000 "East" German inhabitants aged between 16 and 64 years. Between 1990 and 1994 it was carried out five times with the aim to monitor and report on the progressive changes in the East German labour market from the point of view of workers and those seeking work. Finally, the Wohlfahrtssurvey was conceived to measure the objective living standards of Germans and their subjective judgement of their quality of life. The survey conducted in 1993 questioned 3,062 respondents in the East and West.

2.1.4 Methods of statistical analysis

The above studies use predominantly descriptive methods of analysis. The largest group – nine – are purely descriptive. Six studies are qualitative-interpretative in character and three use a combination of descriptive and multivariate methods of analysis.

2.2 Overview of present studies

2.2.1 Objective health indicators

2.2.1.1 Mortality rates

In order to conclusively settle questions as to the effects of unemployment on mortality rates data is required from longitudinal studies, regular panel studies, or statistics on causes of death. International data analyses on a wide scale indicate a correlation between increases in unemployment and mortality rates, albeit with varying time lags (Brenner, 1987; Moser, Goldblatt, Fox & Jones, 1990). In a number of macro-sociological studies Brenner attempted to test the correlation. Brenner and Mooney (1983) demonstrated the relationship between increased cardiac and chronic disease as cause of death and unemployment in industrialised countries such as France, Germany, and Sweden. Morell et al. (1993) examined collected international data for a relationship between unemployment and suicide. The analyses were based on a comparison of OECD countries from 1966 to 1987. For France, Australia, the USA, and Canada, a high correlation, with variances between 58% and 77%, was found in the case of 16-24 year old males. Countries with low unemployment rates (Japan, Sweden, and Germany) showed only weak correlations (explained variance less than 1%).

2.2.1.2 *Morbidity*

Because of insufficient existing data, connections between the prevalence of ill health and unemployment in Germany can only be guessed at. There is, nonetheless, no doubt that ongoing long-term unemployment has a deleterious effect on psychological and physical health, especially where financial hardship and psychosocial stress is involved (cf. Kieselbach, 1998). This has been tested empirically predominantly for adults. On the whole, it is difficult to decipher cause and effect conclusions about health from German studies of unemployment (cf. Elkeles & Seifert, 1992). For youth in particular, however, there is some subjective data to be found (cf. Chapter 2.2.2.2.).

2.2.1.3 *Suicidal behaviour*

Until now, the relationship between unemployment and suicide in Germany has only been examined by means of aggregated data. For the period 1950-1985, no correlative trend has been discerned (Häfner, 1988). Over this period the suicide rate for both sexes remained stable. If we look at age, the highest increase in suicide rate occurred in males aged 20 to 29 years. The highest level of unemployment occurred in the age group 20 to 25 years, and here no correlation with the rate of suicide was detected (cf. Häfner, 1988). In statistics on suicide attempts unemployed people are overrepresented. However, it may be that the correlating factor is chronic mental illness (schizophrenia, alcoholism, and drug abuse) which carries a risk of both increased unemployment *and* attempted suicide (Häfner, 1988).

2.2.1.4 *Utilisation of health services*

The unemployed generally tend to avoid seeking professional services to help combat their psychosocial problems. The feeling of low self-esteem concomitant with unemployment would possibly be reduced even further when seeking such help (Kieselbach, 1998). This is confirmed by the First National Health Survey of the German Cardio-Circulatory Prevention Study. Kurella (1992) points out a dichotomy here, that is, two subgroups of unemployed: one that noticeably avoids going to the doctor and the other group that goes to the doctor far more frequently than employed people. It is not clear if this finding is age-dependent nor to what extent it can be applied to unemployed youth. There is as yet no empirical data that either confirms or refutes a finding of increased medical services for unemployed youth in Germany.

2.2.2 *Subjective health indicators*

2.2.2.1 *Psychosocial strains*

Development of identity is determined largely by what a person experiences in his or her private life, career training, and working life. Abilities and competence developed depend largely on the chances a person has to learn new skills and put to use skills previously learned. Unemployment prevents people from showing what they can and what they cannot achieve. The destructive consequences of unemployment are to be seen less in the unemployment itself than in the non-use of skills and qualifications, and in particular, in the wasted potential of young people (Kieselbach, 1988). The psychosocial stress resulting from loss or denial of work, disappointment, and a blighted future is manifested at various levels. The main stress factors are uncertainty about finding a new job, inability to use acquired skills, lack of structure to one's day, increased social tensions, and not least, financial hardship. (See Chapter 2.2.4. for a more detailed account of financial hardship and welfare support.)

German studies indicate a multitude of varying psychosocial stress tied in with unemployment. The most comprehensive studies on this topic are those of the IAB. In the mid-1970s and early 1980s (both periods of economic downturn), 1,000 and 2,500 unemployed youth, respectively, were questioned concerning their financial and psychosocial hardships and the ways in which they tried to cope with them. No direct analysis of the relationship between youth unemployment and health was undertaken because it did not appear to represent a quantifiable problem (Schober, 1978; 1987). In response to the question as to what they found most unpleasant during the period of unemployment, 26% of the respondents in the second study stated feelings of uselessness and lack of structure to their day. 20% also reported trouble within the family (Schober, 1987). From seven possible choices of what was considered a major stress, 74% indicated the uncertainty of finding another job; two thirds indicated uselessness and lack of fulfilment; 50% indicated lack of social contacts; and 25% being cut off from friends and acquaintances. Trouble in the family (44%) and parental reproach (30%) were also experienced as stressful. A factor analysis reveals two main stress factors: "lack of fulfilment and isolation" and "strained family relationships". In the case of the first of these two, the correlation with separate items was between 0.39 ("worried about new job") and 0.60 ("being at home gets on my nerves"). The second factor displayed coefficients of 0.54 ("family tensions") and 0.66 ("parents reproach me").

The first IAB study revealed stresses pertaining to general feelings of insecurity (80%), that is, in time-breakdown, career, and day-to-day life. Added to this was the stress factor of family tension (50%). Comparisons between the two IAB studies – with an interval of 6 years between them – revealed a high degree of concurrence. The unemployment rate of under 25 year olds was slightly higher at the time of the first study. Other studies differ somewhat in their estimates of the extent of repercussions.

There is general agreement, however, that unemployment has undesirable repercussions both for the individuals concerned and for society at large. Half the respondents in a Labour Market Monitor for East Germany study had doubts about finding another job (Hahn, 1996). The current problems of the East German labour market could reasonably be compared with those of the West German labour market in the 1970s and 1980s. A study about fears for the future (which 40% of unemployed youth expressed) conducted during the 1970s economic downturn showed that the fears increased the longer the period of unemployment and the lower the unemployed person's level of education (Arbeitskammer des Saarlandes, 1980). Fear of career failure and society's contempt, according to Grieswelle (1977), is slightly more widespread among unemployed youth than among their employed counterparts in the control group.

The most serious repercussion of unemployment in almost all studies, and independent of economic cycles, appears to be financial constraint. Studies using totally different methodologies arrive at very similar findings for this point. According to Hahn (1996), the young sorely miss their accustomed income; in Sinus' study (1983), having to forego holiday travel is what the respondents find worst; in Mruck and Mey's (1992) it is "having to watch every penny we spend". Financial constraint in turn leads to changes in consumer habits and leisure activities. It becomes difficult to maintain the living standards of one's peers (Opaschowski, 1976; Christe, 1989).

Along with the economic drawbacks, the stigmatising nature of unemployment is sorely felt. For the unemployed young women in Diezinger's study (1983), their reduced self-esteem, real or anticipated, is a strain above all on other members of their family. Becoming independent of the parental home is difficult and brings about conflicts in close relationships (Christe, 1989). Twenty percent of Mruck and Mey's respondents have a fear of not belonging, 50% complain about boredom, 15% about having less frequent contact to others and one third say that, without the support of their friends they would "bomb out".

Hahn (1996) finally points out that the young unemployed are unable to put their skills to use, and this is particularly hard felt. It is a crucial aspect of youth unemployment. At the same time, those who have entered the labour market have increased their chances of utilising and developing their skills, thus doubling the speed of leaving the unemployed to drift away and, in the long run, become completely sidelined. Another psychosocial problem is the loss of days that are scheduled. Many of the young unemployed do not know what to do with their free time. It is not uncommon for the lack of a daily regimen to destroy the person's potential for meaningful activity and participation in sports and hobbies (Klink & Kieselbach, 1990; Diezinger et al., 1983, Heinemann, 1978).

Unemployed youth in Germany are subject to numerous psychosocial stresses, the crucial one being financial constraint through loss of earnings. Despite government welfare, the financial stress factor is common to all studies of youth unemployment. This leads to family conflicts and a reduction in the number of friends and acquaintances. Career insecurity and concomitant fear of the future is an added stress factor, along with the concern that one will be permanently cut off from the shrinking labour market. Other factors that are perceived as a great burden are society's placing blame on the unemployed individual, the feeling of uselessness, and the inability to bring one's skills and capabilities into play.

2.2.2.2 Subjective well-being

It is essential to investigate not only objective health parameters, but the subjective ones too, that is, how the unemployed person feels or experiences his own health. It may be that, because of the generally better state of health of young people, their unemployment-related stress only take its toll in later years. This would lead to a considerable underestimation of unemployment-related psychosocial stress (Kieselbach, 1988). It would also explain why there is far less systematic, primary data on how the young unemployed feel than on the subjective health of the older jobless in Germany. Here and there in the data are indications of changes in subjective health resulting from unemployment.

Data from the 1970s clearly demonstrates that physical and psychological complaints are more frequent and health is generally poorer in young people who are unemployed. Wilhelm-Reiss (1980) found a high prevalence of psychosomatic complaints in her investigation. Based on subjective findings, unemployed youth suffer more, somatically and psychosomatically, than those who have work. They are altogether psychologically worse off (displaying, e.g., a higher state of nervousness); especially those from broken homes. In another study, 13% of the respondents reported a subjective deterioration in their state of health, the rate being highest for the long-term unemployed and for females. Females (14%) mentioned psychosomatic ill-effects more frequently than males (11%). Moreover, 51% of respondents declared themselves ill at ease and dissatisfied; here, too, rates were higher among the long-term unemployed, the less educated, and females (Arbeitskammer des Saarlandes, 1980). The Welfare Report Nordrhein-Westfalen (1998) demonstrates, on the basis of data from the Socio-economic Panel (SOEP), that employed people across all age groups are subjectively healthier than the short- and long-term unemployed. In response to the question "How would you describe your present state of health?", 60% of the employed answered "good" or "very good", whereas 53% of short-term and only 27% of long-term unemployed answered positively. Within the framework of the "First National Health Survey", a representative cross-sectional study comparing employed and unemployed West Germans aged 25 to 69 years, Bormann (1992) found the frequency of health complaints to be 16% among the employed and a significantly higher 24.8% among the unemployed.

Results concerning the subjective health gleaned from these representative studies cannot simply be carried over to conclusions about youth. However, on their basis it is reasonable to assume that, in the long run, more frequent physical and psychological complaints among unemployed youth will be detrimental to their subjective health.

2.2.2.3 Self-esteem

The self-esteem of young people appears to be more vulnerable to unemployment than that of older people. There are, however, inconsistencies in the findings on damage to the self-esteem of unemployed youth that are more dependent on the mode rather than the period of inquiry.

According to Hahn (1996), half of all unemployed youth feel redundant as a result of their unemployment. This corresponds with results from the 1970s (cf. Schober, 1987). They miss the feeling of being needed. They are moodier, less sure of themselves, and less sociable and outgoing (Wilhelm-Reiss, 1980). Diezinger et al.'s (1983) respondents also felt useless and different from the norm. Another study showed that 17% had feelings of inferiority and these rates were higher for females, the long-term unemployed, and for those youth who had not completed secondary school (Arbeitskammer des Saarlandes, 1980). Grieswelle (1977) found lower self-confidence in unemployed than in working youth. According to Heinemann (1978), the unemployed have lower self-esteem than the employed, but these results only become significant in the case of longer-term unemployment.

Baumann et al. (1979), on the other hand, found hardly any differences among the subgroups unemployed youth, apprentices, and unskilled employed youth. All three groups had the same score for self-esteem using the Rosenberg scale, although for some specific items the score was appreciably higher for apprentices than for the unemployed. The item "I feel I can't really be proud of myself" was rejected by 82% of the apprentices but by only 60% of the unemployed and 56% of the unskilled employed. There were also significant differences found for the item "I like myself" (apprentices 50%; unemployed 23%; unskilled 18%). Sinus (1983) found that self-esteem could be damaged by the job-hunting entailed in unemployment. A third of the respondents didn't see the point in looking for a job and their fatalistic approach probably damaged their self-confidence even further (Arbeitskammer des Saarlandes, 1980).

We may conclude from the studies that increasingly drawn out periods of unemployment are devastating to self-esteem. The young unemployed often feel redundant and lacking in self-confidence; they feel that they are not needed, and therefore inferior.

2.2.2.4 Alienation (political orientation)

Whereas research into alienation normally deals with the processes of social disintegration, and research into the psychology of unemployment assumes work to be at the crux of social integration (with the corollary that lack of work organised by society entails being cut off from it) (Kieselbach, 1998), this chapter is more concerned with the political aspect of socialisation. The extent to which unemployment of young people dangerously influences their political leanings has been often discussed (cf. Baumann et al.,

1979). In the health-related studies of youth unemployment in Germany there is only scant information about this possible relationship.

Baumann et al. (1979) were able to demonstrate that unemployed youth showed a higher disposition toward spontaneous political action, for example, through their lack of adherence to institutionalised behaviour and principles of legality. Independent of unemployment, the variables 'social background' and 'education' had the greatest influence on the development of political orientation. Baumann et al. could only vaguely confirm the assumption that unemployment leads to radical political attitudes. However, the Saarland study (1980) demonstrated a relationship between the threat of unemployment and the growth of prejudices as on the value of democracy. A third of the respondents held the democratic political system responsible for unemployment.

In a study of right-wing extremism, Heitmeyer, Buhse, Liebe-Freund, Möller, Müller, Ritz, Siller and Vossen (1993) show that the young respondents, according to their degree of social or career disintegration, fall into patterns whereby their political credo becomes social, demanding the redress of society's unjust treatment. Sinus (1983) showed that political dissatisfaction was highest (34%) among those unemployed for over six months. In general, unemployed youth don't display stronger tendencies towards political extremism than the employed. The study also points out that unemployment is not the detonator of a sudden and critical change of values.

Political alienation would appear to be more dependent on schooling and social background. There is no hard evidence of the radicalisation of youth through unemployment. It would appear, however, that in comparison with the employed, unemployed youth show a higher tendency toward political dissatisfaction, doubts about the value of democracy, and spontaneous political action.

2.2.2.5 Social deviation (delinquency)

Deviant behaviour is predominantly understood as delinquent behaviour. It is a widely held and much discussed belief that unemployment is the principal cause for the rise in criminality. This is an assumption that, so far, has not been empirically confirmed (cf. Albrecht, 1988). It is truer to say that "openly aggressive behaviour represents one of the strategies (and certainly not the main one) with which the individual seeks to counter the stresses of being unemployed" (Wacker, 1979, p. 165).

In investigations of youth unemployment, unemployment is viewed as a risk factor that can be propitious to forms of criminal behaviour (Sinus, 1983). Other risk factors are crucial to the rise in delinquent behaviour (e.g., negative family environment and general social circumstances). It could be shown that 31% of unemployed youth expressed their aggressive potential verbally and 7% physically (Arbeitskammer des Saarlandes, 1980). Unemployment is seen as a marginal aspect of the cause of delinquent behaviour. Heinemann (1978) views unemployment and criminal behaviour as signs of young people's failure to adjust, the counterpart to which would be stabilising social conditions such as positive family structures, neighbourhood self-help, and so on (Opaschowski, 1976).

There is no proven correlation between unemployment and deviant behaviour among adolescents in Germany. Unemployment is one factor among many which facilitate the onset of such behaviour. A positive social environment would play an important counteractive or preventive role.

2.2.2.6 Health behaviour

Behaviour relating to health is made up of a multitude of habits which directly and indirectly influence an individual's health. Classic examples are alcohol consumption, smoking, use of legal and illegal drugs, physical activity or lack thereof, and food and beverage consumption. In Germany there are only vague assumptions that unemployment is propitious to risky health-related behaviour.

From the results of the Sinus Study (1983), it is assumed that the risk factors when added together favour a progressive slide towards addictive habits. Factors such as low self-esteem, lack of structure to one's day, financial difficulties, dependency upon parents, spending too much time in pubs and bars, etc., combined with the exclusion from the labour market, play an important role. In this context unemployment also has its influence, but the actual cause of drug addiction lies elsewhere. The study published by the Arbeitskammer des Saarlandes (1980) examined the increased risk of drug abuse as a result of unemployment. In general, 53% of unemployed youth agreed that there was indeed a link. However, when asked about their own personal drug consumption, only 11% considered unemployment a causal risk factor. Several studies expressed doubts about a link between unemployment and a general increase in alcohol/drug consumption – or a decrease in the use of sporting and other youth facilities (Opaschowski, 1976; Grieswelle, 1977). The Siebers and Vonderach study (1991) reports on one particular type of unemployed person (mainly married or divorced mothers aged 25 years or older, job-trained) whose failed or failing partner relationship, in conjunction with financial difficulty and unemployment, result in deviant behaviour such as alcohol/drug addiction and criminality.

There is no proof that youth unemployment in Germany leads to behaviour that is deleterious to health. Periods of unemployment, however, constitute one of the many risk factors favourable to the development of addictive behaviour.

2.2.3 Mediators (demographic variables)

2.2.3.1 Age

Age is a decisively important variable since "the young unemployed" comprise a very heterogeneous group, ranging from 15-year-old school-leavers to married mothers and fathers with considerable occupational experience. Therefore, health-related stresses, their intensity and frequency, must be assessed accordingly. Whereas the most frequent problem facing the under 20-year-old age group is to enter an apprenticeship or training programme, that of the 20 to 25 year olds is, first and foremost, getting and holding down a job. The 26 to 29 year olds can, in turn, be divided into two subgroups: newly qualified academics on the one hand and long-term unemployeds on the other.

The relationship between the intensity of psychosocial stress and age is usually shown by way of a curved graph. The highest stress values coincide with median age; the median stress values with the youngest unemployed; and the lowest stress values with the oldest unemployed. The youngest, despite their median stress value, tend to display a high prevalence of psychiatric morbidity (Kieselbach, 1985).

2.2.3.2 Gender

As a rule, unemployed females appear to display a more positive attitude towards work and have a higher level of education, but also have greater difficulty obtaining a job or training position and suffer less stress during periods of unemployment than their male counterparts. It is not personal shortcomings that deny them more jobs but the strongly male oriented labour market (Klink & Kieselbach, 1990). The tendency to link unemployed females to the traditional roles of housewife and mother was confirmed by Burger and Seidenspinner (1977). They also found that females had stronger feelings of isolation and spent a lot of time at home, especially those with a limited circle of friends or none at all. This led to more reliance on family ties. They often lack self-confidence and have strong bonds to their boyfriends. Marriage and early pregnancy are not uncommon. The social maturation process of the females is often impaired by a fixation on their family of origin.

2.2.3.3 Education

The level of education – schooling and professional training – is an important variable with respect to the way in which unemployment can influence health. The possibilities for those who have fared badly at school to go on and obtain occupational qualifications are severely limited (Burger & Seidenspinner, 1977). In comparison with employed youth, the unemployed have lower qualifications (Mruck & Mey, 1992). Lower formal qualifications also increase a person's risk of becoming unemployed and staying unemployed longer (Arbeitskammer des Saarlandes, 1980). Krieger and Schläfke (1987) demonstrate that unemployed youth with higher levels of schooling and education encounter fewer problems dealing with social administration (e.g., welfare and employment authorities) and cope better with financial difficulties.

2.2.3.4 Social class (social milieu)

Like education, social milieu, too, is an important variable with respect to the way in which unemployment can influence health. Several studies have established a relationship between social background and the risk of unemployment (Arbeitskammer des Saarlandes, 1980). Wilhelm-Riess (1980) points out the psychosomatic problems of young people who come from broken homes and of those from families already blighted by unemployment. The Sinus study (1983) refers to the aggravated consequences of unemployment in adolescents lacking education and training *and* from socially disadvantaged families. Mruck and Mey (1992) point out that the higher marriage rate among the unemployed compensates job insecurity.

2.2.3.5 Length of unemployment

Duration is a variable that is crucial to the degree and intensity of stress brought about by unemployment. German researchers of unemployment all agree that the longer the duration of unemployment, the worse it is for the health of the person concerned. The depression and resignation of young people increase along with the duration of their unemployment (Burger & Seidenspinner, 1977). Job applications decrease or cease altogether, as the job-seeker no longer sees any chance of a breakthrough (Siebers & Vonderach, 1991). Financial difficulties also increase (Sinus, 1983). In almost all cases, symptoms of ill health increase with the duration of unemployment (Arbeitskammer des Saarlandes, 1980). Wilhelm-Reiss (1980) found a moderate correlation between incompleteness of the family unit and duration of unemployment (0.20); she also detected increased nervousness among long-term unemployed youth.

2.2.4 Moderators (psychological variables)

2.2.4.1 Work and career orientation

According to the Shell study (Jugendwerk der Deutschen Shell, 1997), almost every second young person considers unemployment as *the* major current problem. In East Germany, the lack of opportunities for professional qualification due to lack of trainee positions is considered the second most important problem. It is worth noting that especially the older range (22 to 24 years) consider unemployment as the main problem. These results show how important young people consider work which bears out what is generally assumed. This finding is also confirmed by more recent studies of unemployed youth in the Federal Republic. Hahn (1996) found that young East Germans were extremely job and career oriented. The respondent's job (career) was placed third on a scale of the most important things in his/her personal life, following 'a feeling of belonging to society' and 'income'.

The Socioeconomic Panel (SOEP) shows that the importance of the role that work plays in a person's overall satisfaction and subjective well-being is generally higher in East than in West Germany; it is also slightly less important for younger than for older unemployed people. Young West Germans are nevertheless highly work orientated. Mruck and Mey (1992) report that work is of great importance to 95% of unemployed youth; 75% want another job as soon as possible, and 50% are interested in the prospects of promotion. Long-term unemployed youth also considered a job and career a very important aspect of life (Siebers & Vonderach, 1991). Surveys from the 1970s showed similar findings. According to the Sinus study (1983), almost all the respondents desired a steady job and were trying to find work. Another investigation reported that 80% were willing to train for an occupation and intended to seek an apprenticeship on completing their schooling (Arbeitskammer des Saarlandes, 1980).

In general, the young people's perspective of work is that they see it as an economic instrument. Their orientation is basically materialistic. Their crucial need is to get a job as a means of earning money (Opaschowski, 1976; Heinemann, 1978). It can therefore be assumed that the economic strain and financial deprivation resulting from unemployment are seen as its most serious consequence. Burger and Seidenspinner (1977) differentiate between unemployed adolescents who continued to seek a training position and those who had given up trying. The former usually had clear career intentions and planned beyond their training. The latter primarily wanted to earn money, the sooner the better; their intentions were very vague, except that work was seen as a means to an end.

Grieswelle (1977) postulates a strong parental influence over young people's scale of values in matters of work and occupation. The parents in question were often poorly qualified, dissatisfied with their work, and regarded it merely as a means of earning money. These attitudes were passed on to their children, who in turn preferred a job with higher immediate pay to a position offering training and qualification. According to Diezinger et al. (1983), females were more attuned to the multifaceted, occupational nature of work (e.g., planning one's own future). All female respondents wanted to work.

To sum up, unemployed youth in both East and West Germany have a strong job and career orientation. Gainful employment is considered a high priority in one's personal life, primarily as a means of satisfying material needs.

2.2.4.2 Financial strains/stress

Financial strain appears to have a crucial linking influence in the relationship between unemployment and health. According to the IAB studies (Schober, 1978, 1987) and Labour Market statistics, it can be assumed that about 80% of young people registered as seeking employment actually receive some sort of social welfare (unemployment benefits).

Going by what the respondents themselves say, then only a mere 60% receive social welfare. For many, this source of income is inadequate to meet their needs, and they have to resort to further financial help from their family. In the case of the single, adolescent jobless this means getting money from their parents, whereas those who are married and somewhat older receive support from their partners or are forced to dig into their savings. The respondents reported that social welfare hardly counted for them as a source of support.

The financial consequences of unemployment was reported to be experienced as a particular hardship (one third reported money difficulties right at the start of their unemployment). The sorry financial situation resulted in numerous restrictions in important facets of everyday life, for example, in leisure activities and buying power (Siebers & Vonderach, 1991; Krieger & Schläfke, 1987). More recent studies have confirmed the 1970s findings as to the difficult financial situation of unemployed youth. Their financial means are considerably lower than those of employed youth (Hahn, 1996; Mruck & Mey, 1992; Grieswelle, 1977). Numerous studies indicate that this leads to family conflict. To be dependent on parents is experienced as a great discomfiture (Sinus, 1983; Opaschowski, 1976). For unemployed females who have previously earned their own money the situation is far worse than for those who have just left school (Diezinger et al., 1983).

The financial situation of youth during periods of unemployment is most painful. Economic dependency upon parents is felt as a great burden. Many leisure activities and forms of fun have to be sacrificed.

2.2.4.3 Social support

The extent of social support is an important moderator and variable when it comes to coping with critical life events. During periods of unemployment, social networks (family, circle of friends, spouse) assume a multitude of functions in the individual concerned's coming to grips with this stressful life situation. Studies from the 1970s show that unemployed youth have fewer social contacts with friends and acquaintances than do the employed (Grieswelle, 1977; Heinemann, 1978). Increased conflict within the family and less real interest in other members of the family are further by-products of unemployment. According to Burger and Seidenspinner (1977) most unemployed adolescents can expect scant help from their parents. Preexisting conflict is aggravated by unemployment, and the worse the conflict was before, the worse it will get (Arbeitskammer des Saarlandes, 1980).

In contrast to the above, other studies indicate that close emotional ties to one's partner – or to friends and acquaintances – offer considerable support (Sinus, 1983). The family, in particular, fulfils an important supportive function within the social network during periods of unemployment. Indeed, it can be seen as a protective social retreat. As a rule the family doesn't hold their adolescent son or daughter personally responsible for his or her unemployment. The greater the perceived isolation from outside, the more binding and supportive the solidarity from within the family. However, this finding reflects the social structure of the industrial worker milieu to which the respondents belonged (Opaschowski, 1976).

Schelsky (1952) points out the influence of the level of expectation, that is, the more that was expected of the young person then the greater he perceives his social isolation in times of unemployment.

Unemployed young females often find themselves in a situation of family conflict. Parents and siblings tend to hold them in low regard, resulting in strengthening relationships with their peers (Diezinger et al., 1983). The unemployed woman's contact is often reduced to her partner's circle of friends, to the detriment of social contact in her own right (Krieger & Schläfke, 1987).

To sum up, youth unemployment is detrimental to fundamental social contact. Little can be expected in the way of moral support from the family, thus the reliance on contact with friends and acquaintances tend to strengthen, especially in the case of unemployed males.

3 Summary of results

This report examines the research that has been carried out in Germany on the relationship between youth unemployment and health. In comparison to research concerning people of more mature age, little attention has been paid to the subject. Even in times of mass unemployment, the connection between unwanted joblessness and its deleterious effects on the health of young people has only been treated marginally. This lack of attention has meant a scarcity of systematic investigations, and the heterogeneity of the existing data makes it difficult to draw generalised conclusions.

Causal relationships between youth unemployment and health-related effects cannot be established because scarcely any longitudinal data exists. The investigations which have been conducted vary greatly in concept, content, and methodology, but nonetheless point to the general finding that phases of unwanted unemployment go hand in hand with numerous psychological, physical, financial, and social disadvantages which, in the long run, can lead to increased rates of psychosocial destabilisation.

These undesirable effects, as the above analysis demonstrates, can be detected at several levels and may be summarised as follows:

1. Among the various *psychosocial stresses*, fear of career disintegration is the main one. Others are boredom, the absence of a structured day, and parental conflict due to the burden of increased financial dependence.
2. The *subjective state of health* of unemployed (in comparison with employed) youth is shown to suffer increased somatic and psychosomatic impairments.
3. Unemployment in young people appears to lower their *self-esteem* and self-confidence and bring about feelings of resignation and aimlessness.
4. Young respondents in almost all the studies complain about the gravity of *financial hardships* brought on by unemployment, especially as regards their leisure activities and buying power. Social interaction is reduced and increased financial dependence on parents creates conflict. The material situation of unemployed youth is notably worse than that of working youth, but not worse than that of unemployed elders.
5. During periods of unemployment, peers – not parents – fulfil the crucial function of *social encouragement and support,* notwithstanding a general reduction in the social circle of friends and acquaintances. Some studies report a reduction in the circle of friends, stronger family dependence, and a resultant increase in conflict.
6. The *work-oriented attitude* of unemployed German youth is shown by the studies to be very high. This orientation is predominantly economic and materialistic. Their crucial need is to have a job in order to earn money.

Going by these results it is apparent that further investigations are urgently needed to precisely clarify the relationship between youth unemployment and health. The investigations must take the individual personal background and history into account in order to monitor the psychosocial changes brought about by unemployment in young people as compared to working people of the same age.

Youth unemployment and health: German studies – an overview

Author	Sample	Instruments/ Methods	Population	Dependent Variables	Results
Schelsky (1952)	N = 1,978; comparison group employed adolescents: N = 308	cross-sectional design; representative sample; intensive survey and biographical investigation	15-25 years of age; unemployed: male (n = 1,177), female (n = 801); employed:male (n = 185), female (n = 123); representative	– social support – financial situation – psychosocial stress (time structure)	– greater instability of relationships among unemployed adolescents – extent of isolation dependent on personal demands – 60% of the unemployed adolescents are more or less responsible for supporting the family – boredom and financial restrictions as greatest stress
Opaschowski (1976)	N = about 130	cross-sectional design; in-depth-interviews, participatory observations	middle-sized city	– social support – financial situation – psychosocial stress (financial consequences) – deviant behaviour	– family is regarded as socially stabilising place of retreat – financial dependency from the parents – reduction in leisure time activities and social relationships – buffering effects of support systems (family, neighbourhood) on deviant behaviour – behaviour typology: – confident (10%) – pragmatic (50%) – resigned (30%) – apathetic (10%)
Burger & Seidenspinner (1977)	N = 314 (unemployed, ado-lescents in assistance programs, trainees, juvenile workers, post secondary modern school finishers)	cross-sectional design; interviews, group discussions and individual interviews	approximately 15 years of age. (9th graders); male (n = 203), female (n = 111); from urban areas (n = 181), from rural areas (n = 133)	– career orientation – social support	more or less general statements regarding: – fear of career risks – disorientation – resignation – employed peers have high status – loss of self-confidence – role as a housewife considered real perspective

Author	Sample	Instruments/ Methods	Population	Dependent Variables	Results
Grieswelle (1977)	N = 1,033; including vocational school students who had not found a job after completion of education (n = 233), juvenile workers (n = 571); vocational school students who had a job before becoming unemployed (n = 229)	cross-sectional design; standardised survey	15-19 years of age; male (52.7%), female (47.3%); urban and rural regions of Southern Germany	– work orientation – psychosocial stress (career failure; stigmatisation) – social support – health behaviour – financial situation	– value orientations shaped by the parents – less amount of leisure time activities among adolescents who successfully completed school – fear of career failure and social contempt is greatest among the unemployed and the adolescents who successfully completed school – concern for the financial situation is greatest among the unemployed – amount of social contact is greatest among juvenile workers
Heinemann (1978)	N = 293 comparison group (employed adolescents): N = 277	cross-sectional design; standardised survey; group discussions	15-20 years of age; urban (56%), rural (44%)	– financial stress – social contacts – personality traits (e.g., aggressiveness)	– financial losses are considered most serious consequence – reduction in social contacts and increasing isolation – aggressiveness decreases in short-term unemployment and increases in long-term unemployment
Schober (1978, first IAB Study)	N = about 1,000	cross-sectional design; representative postal survey	under 25 years of age; representative	– financial stress – psychosocial stress (uncertainty about the future)	– extreme stress due to the financial situation – general uncertainties about career, life, and time perspectives – family stress – stress because of qualifications and social status of the parents

Author	Sample	Instruments/ Methods	Population	Dependent Variables	Results
Baumann, Becker, Gerstenmaier, Schickle, & Tippelt (1979)	N = 289; comparison group: N = 147, including trainees (n = 83) and employed adolescents lacking vocational training (n = 64)	cross-sectional design; standardised survey Rosenberg Scale for self-esteem	14-20 years of age; male (64%), female (36%); rural areas (29%), small cities (23%), large cities (48%)	– self-esteem – political orientation	– a generally high value for self-esteem in all three groups – only minimal differences between the comparison groups (e.g., unemployed and the unlearned employed adolescents have lower self-esteem than trainees) – orientation toward spontaneous political actions
Arbeitskammer des Saarlandes (1980)	N = 855 (788 registered and 67 not 'registered unemployed); within the group of 788 unemployed, a subgroup of n = 143 ("seeking a training position")	cross-sectional design; standardised survey	15-19 years of age; male (44.5%), female (55.5%); fewer than 5,000 inhabitants (22%), 5,000-50,000 inhabitants (58.4%), more than 50,000 inhabitants (5.9%)	– alcohol consumption and drug use – aggressiveness – self-esteem – political orientation – subjective state of health – psychosocial stress (uncertainty about the future) – social support	– impairments in social surroundings (dependency on the family, limited circle of friends, limited possibilities for organisation of own leisure time) – fear of the future – feelings of helplessness and a lack of prospects strengthen apathetic and fatalistic reactions – depressive and aggressive behaviour – symptoms of psychosomatic illnesses – use of alcohol, drugs, or delinquency as an escape in reaction to the socialisation related classification of, or respectively, the actual situation of unemployment
Wilhelm-Reiss (1980)	N = 252; including trainees and apprentices (n = 58) juvenile workers (n = 42) unemployed (n = 52) course participants (n = 68) students (n = 32)	cross-sectional design; standardised survey, Freiburg Personality Inventory (FPI) for the measurement of the psychological consequences of unemployment	15-24 years of age; males (n = 105), females (n = 147); regions with less well-developed infrastructures in Southern Germany	– nervousness, depression (subjective health) – composure, inhibition (self-esteem)	– subjectively, increased somatic and psychosomatic disorders and an unfavourable psychological state of mind – psychosomatic problems particularly in incomplete families – ill humoured and insecure – less sociability and outgoingness

Author	Sample	Instruments/ Methods	Population	Dependent Variables	Results
Diezinger, Marquardt, Bilden, & Dahlke (1983)	T1: N = 52; including unemployed who have never worked but have completed school successfully (n = 10) unemployed with working experience from a training program or in their chosen occupation (n = 39) unemployed with a completed training (n = 3) T2: N = 29	longitudinal design; qualitative open interviews	15-19 year old girls from the region Munich	– psychosocial stress (discrimination experiences, time structure) – financial stress – self-esteem – social support – work orientation	– feelings of boredom and futility – financial reductions in the area of leisure time – conflicts with the parents – others have a low opinion of one's self – peers increase in importance as support group – work has a variety of meanings for girls (e.g., planning for the future)
Sinus Study (1983)	Interview study: N = 50; including unemployed without professional experience (n = 28); unemployed with professional experience (n = 22); additionally representative survey: N = 2,012; including n = 391 (experience with unemployment) and n = 123 (unemployed for more than six months)	cross-sectional design; interview study; representative survey	15-30 years of age; males (n = 26), females (n = 24)	– psychosocial stress (financial consequences) – social support – work orientation – political attitudes	– financial consequences constitute the greatest stress – maintenance of work orientation and search for work – circle of friends plays largest role in regard to social support (difficulty in assessing the relationship with parents because of prior conflicts) – political dissatisfaction with increasing length of unemdployment

Author	Sample	Instruments/ Methods	Population	Dependent Variables	Results
Alheit & Glaß (1986)	N = 15	cross-sectional design; narrative interview (qualitative biographical approach)	15-24 years of age; male (n = 7), female (n = 8)	– biographical course	– Patterns of coping with unemployment: – biographical break – difficult socialisation conditions – perspectives due to employment exchange measures – a criminal "subcareer" – political union commitment
Krieger & Schläfke (1987)	N = 13	cross-sectional design; structured interviews	19-31 years of age large city area	– financial situation – social contact	– limitations due to financial situation – reduction in social contact because of financial limitations
Schober (1987, second IAB Study)	N = about 2,500	cross-sectional design; representative postal survey	under 25 years of age; representative	– financial stress – psychosocial stress (job search)	– financial situation is particularly stressful – limitations of psychological well-being as the main stress (feelings of uselessness and unfulfillment) – family tension and conflicts
Christe (1989)	N = 78	cross-sectional design; narrative interview	18-26 years of age; rural areas	– psychosocial stress (identity development, exclusion)	– separation from the family/leaving home is hindered – fear of stigmatisation
Siebers & Vonderach (1991)	N = 64 (after 1,5 years a second interview with 20 chosen respondents)	semi-longitudinal design; narrative interview	18-30 years of age; rural areas	– biographical course	– negative experiences because of unemployment (withholding the status of adulthood) – financial restrictions in the leisure and consumption – biographical disintegration tendencies (stigmatisation, marginalisation, feelings of social isolation) – the accumulation of unemployment, poverty, and stressful relationships promotes drug use and delinquency

Author	Sample	Instruments/ Methods	Population	Dependent Variables	Results
Mruck & Mey (1992)	N = 49; entire sample: N = 454	cross-sectional design; standardised survey	15-30 years of age for N = 454 approximately equal numbers of male/females; two districts in Berlin	– psychosocial stress (financial consequences, job search) – social support – work orientation	– 95% consider work very important – worst consequence is the financial restrictions – diversity of psychosocial stress – one third would be in a "slump" without social support
Hahn (1996)	N = 83; comparison group: N = 45, including reemployed (n = 21), employed who have never experienced unemployment (n = 24)	cross-sectional design; standardised survey; within the framework of a representative investigation	18-25 years of age; representative (urban and rural areas of East Germany)	– financial situation – psychosocial stress (fear of failure in the job search)	– material situation of young unemployed clearly worse than employed peers, although not worse than older unemployed – every second unemployed is concerned about finding a new job

Youth Unemployment and Health in Greece

Katerina Sokou & Valentine Papantoniou[1]

1 in collaboration with *Demetra Bayetakou* and *Katerina Christofi*

1 Introduction to youth unemployment and health

1.1 National development of youth unemployment

It is necessary to incorporate an overview of the Greek economy and labour market situation in this report. This will allow for an understanding of the rudimentary character of both political and scientific initiatives on the issue of unemployment in general and youth unemployment specifically. This information is also important in order to understand how the social and public institutions can influence the state of health of young people (age group 16-29) in Greece.

After the Second World War, and especially, the Greek civil war – which lasted until 1949 –, the Greek economy experienced more than two decades of almost continuous growth. Until that time, Greece operated along preindustrial and feudalistic patterns of social and economic organisation (Mouzelis, 1978). Investments were high, new infrastructure was built, and industrialisation was at a higher rate compared to any other period in the history of Greece. High economic rates reached their peak in the beginning of the 70s, when the phenomenon of virtually zero unemployment appeared. Nonetheless, the effects of this relatively late entry into the process of economic development are still evident in the country's economic (and social) organisation, which has occupied a peripheral position as compared to the other postindustrial Northern European countries (Sokou, 1987).

In 1973 the growth process was suddenly halted. The monetary crisis of 1973 and the first oil crisis caused the slowing down of development rates worldwide. In Greece, in particular, two more reasons caused a further slowdown: the fall of the seven year dictatorship (1967-1974), and the Turkish invasion in Northern Cyprus. The political instability was followed by the necessity of establishing a stronger democracy based on social stability. The idea that the public sector should play a prominent role in the economy was then widespread in all European countries. In Greece, it led to an enormous expansion of the public sector which started in the mid-70s and continued until recently. This expansion of the public sector (40% of the economically active population in the mid-80s were civil servants) had dramatic and successive effects on the Greek economy. Public consumption was 40% higher in 1980 than in 1974, whereas public investment remained at the same level. Labour unions – particularly those of public companies – were reinforced, especially under the 80s socialist rule, and began to demand salary increases higher than the level of productivity. Labour costs increased and companies did not have enough liberty to adapt to market demands. In addition, bankrupt companies were not allowed to shut down and instead were passed to state ownership (the so-called "problematic" ones). Private investment which was 16% in 1974, fell to 11.5% of the Gross National Product (GNP) in 1987.

Without productive investments, and with a deficient secondary sector under bankruptcy, the Greek economy was doomed to fail. In 1989, expenses for financing the public debt exceeded state revenues. Unemployment was still not addressed by increasing production and encouraging investment, but through hiring people in the public sector (the hiring of public servants increased by 3.1% annually for 12 years from 1977 to 1989). However, the ongoing shrinkage of the primary sector (agriculture) during the 90s, due to common agriculture and competition policies of the European Union (EU), kept many people without jobs (KEPE, 1990). Heavily subsidised public industries and other businesses were forced to shut down or to sharply downsize on employees and production. Many companies that had not adapted to the new market demands went bankrupt. This also led to high levels of unemployment and the downgrading of city regions. Unemployment soared from 1.5% in 1975 to 7.8% in 1985 and to 10% in 1995 (see Table 1 below).

Table GR-1: Unemployment rates in Greece, 1975-1995

1975	1977	1979	1981	1983	1985	1987	1989	1991	1993	1995
1.5	1.7	1.9	3.9	8.0	7.8	7.4	7.5	7.7	9.7	10.0

Source: ESYE, Labour force surveys.

In the past 4 years Greece's unemployment rate has almost reached the corresponding figure of the European Union. Apart from women, who comprise two thirds of the approximate figure for unemployment, young people are the most severely affected. The unemployment rate of young people in Greece aged 15-24 years is almost 10% higher than the European average of 12.1%. Moreover, the long-term unemployment rate is also higher than the European rate, being 57% as compared to 48% (Eurostat, 1998). Thus, the labour market data in its entirety calls for the promotion of a multilevel employment strategy, emphasising the improvement of the ability of young people and especially women to enter or re-enter the labour market.

The 90s are characterised by the change of the economic policy and the effort to impose economic reforms so that Greece can meet the Maastricht criteria in order to be accepted in Europe's Economic and Monetary Union (EMU). However, in the present decade, past economic policies pose almost insurmountable barriers to economic reforms. Productive investments are still discouraged but the growth rate, for the past two years, has exceeded that of the E.U. New jobs are created and the rate of employment is changing.

The issue of unemployment was not seriously tackled in Greece until very recently. Still, the problem is not presented in the official statistics in its full extent. Policies were short-termed, geared towards suppression and not prevention of the problem. Furthermore, the problems created by unemployment differ among the different regions of the country and among population groups. In large cities, the unemployed can survive by working in the underground economy. However in rural areas and in cities far from the capital Athens, the unemployed have only limited options. They are jobless but have the support and sympathy of the family and the surrounding community. Bearing in mind that until 1985 unemployment was not given enough publicity but was rather faced by the individual as a personal problem, one can easily understand the rudimentary character of both political and scientific initiatives on the issues of unemployment and youth unemployment respectively. Concerning the latter, that is, youth unemployment, one can also understand why primary social institutions such as the family play such a dominant role as a central redistribution and primary support unit. Despite all the above, though, Greece is going through a transitional period; new employment policies are initiated, scientific research is in progress, and the traditional function of the family is being questioned.

1.2 Unemployment and health – some theoretical considerations

It is estimated that economic loss and downward mobility typically associated with economic instability (insecurity at work, unemployment, or underemployment) can seriously affect social functioning, health, and well-being, particularly for lower status people. There is a vicious circle of poverty, unemployment (and other forms of lack of meaningful work), other social and economic symptoms of inequality, discrimination, social vulnerability, and chronic illness. The socio-economically excluded are less likely to attain health, while the chronically ill are less likely to fulfill their socioeconomic roles and may thereby become impoverished (Svensson, Westcott & Zöllner, 1985). Hence, there is a causal versus selective hypothesis which explains the unambiguous dualism between ill health and unemployment. Unemployment may be the result of lower health prerequisites. People with health problems have limited access to the labour market, deprived of mechanisms that would promote their adaptation (selection hypothesis). On the other hand, unemployment, underemployment, and insecurity at work affect the condition of people in general (causal hypothesis) by preventing them from developing as autonomous individuals with high self-esteem, having a decent social and economic participation in society (see Figure 1).

Figure GR-1: The process from unemployment to ill health

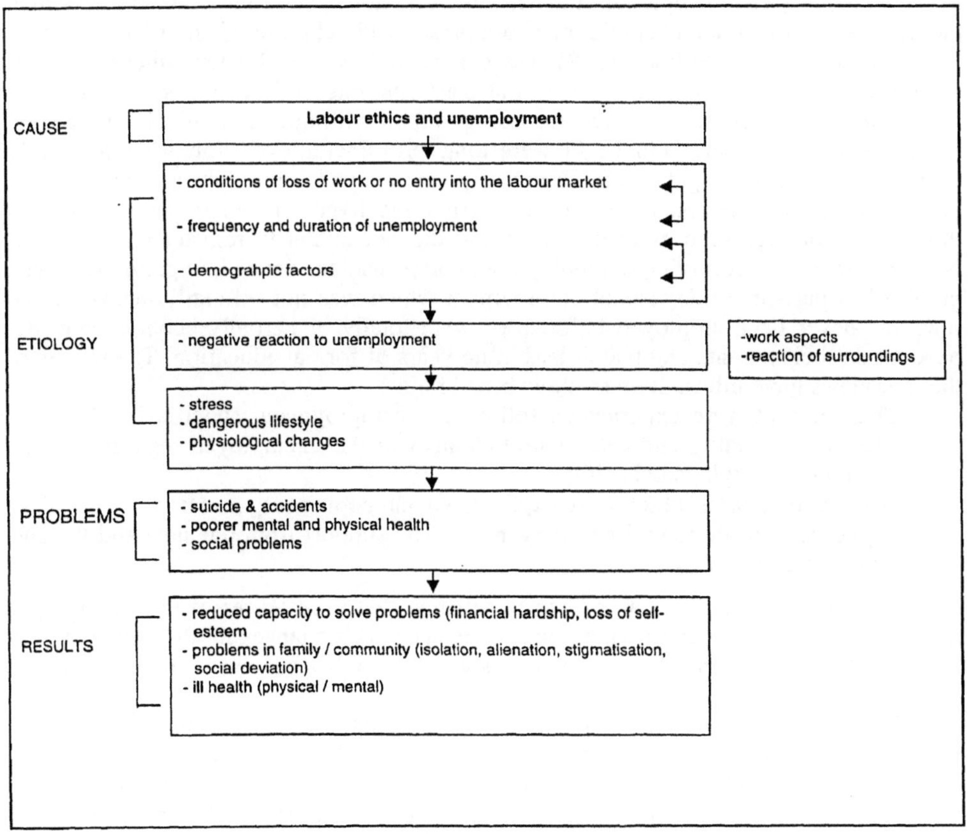

2 Analysis of research on youth unemployment and health

In Greece, research on the relation between youth unemployment and health is scarce. The main reason is that unemployment has not been considered as problem that needs to be seriously tackled. Consequently, political initiatives and scientific research remained rudimentary – with the exception of the past few years. The studies that are going to be presented in this report are studies that have been conducted during these past 10 years. A number of them are still in progress, while others need further analysis, taking health and occupational status as main variables. However, despite being merely descriptive, what becomes rather evident in these studies is some kind of relationship between unemployment and health deterioration, especially mental health.

2.1 Description of the available data (design and methods)

After reviewing several scientific projects, no references were found devoted especially to unemployed young people and their health conditions. The following studies which include issues of health and employment are presented in chronological order.

The study from Sokou (1989) was carried out in the Greater Athens Area. A sample of 24 people was interviewed in at least one lengthy in-depth, semi-structured interview. The sample was selected according to their willingness to talk about their experiences. Of the 24 individuals, 11 were long-term unemployed young people 20-27 years old. The remaining 13 were chronically unemployed from older age groups. The younger subgroup members were all unmarried and lived with their parents. All but three were not registered as unemployed and did not intend to register in the future. None of them were receiving unemployment compensation. Seven had previously been involved in part-time or seasonal employment which was not officially declared, and four had never been employed before. All were totally or partially economically dependent on their parents and had at least nine years of formal education. The results of the interviews gave information on three broad fields:

1. Changes that were experienced following unemployment, specifically those related to personality and behavioural changes of the unemployed regarding social relations, life style, and health;
2. Data on the phases which were experienced and coping responses;
3. Suggestions made regarding interventions and support from the state and the surrounding community.

Regarding the first field and according to self-reported experiences of the unemployed in the study, chronic unemployment was associated with changes in attitudes and feelings about one's self and the surrounding society, social behaviour, and health-related parameters.

Table 2 shows 16 aspects which came up in the interviews, all expressing negative feelings either towards one's self or society as a whole. Nine of them were expressed by both the younger and the older unemployed: feelings of uselessness, frustration, lower status, disorganisation of time structure, lack of social support, work exploitation, loss of self-esteem, self-confidence, and trust in social institutions. Two were expressed only by the younger unemployed: sense of low prestige and feelings of dependency, and five were expressed only by the older unemployed: expressions of suspiciousness and helplessness, feelings of a lack of justice and lack of respect, loss of faith. In the overall number of negative expressions, the younger and older unemployed were nearly equal (11 and 12, respectively).

Table GR-2: Self-reported feelings about being unemployed (n = 24)

Change	Younger unemployed	Older unemployed
Sense of uselessness	+	+
Feelings of frustration	+	+
Sense of lower status	+	+
Sense of disorganisation of time structure	+	+
Feelings of a lack of social support	+	+
Sense of work exploitation	+	+
Loss of self-esteem	+	+
Loss of self-confidence	+	+
Loss of trust in social institutions	+	+
Sense of low prestige	+	–
Feelings of dependency	+	–
Expression of suspiciousness	–	+
Expression of helplessness	–	+
Sense of lack of justice	–	+
Feelings of lack of respect	–	+
Loss of faith	–	+

Health-related behaviours were also reported to have changed (Table 3). Both younger and older unemployed mentioned their irregularities in sleeping and mealtimes, neglect of regular showers (as defined by each group), neglect of personal grooming such as face washing, shaving, or hair washing. Both groups remarked on their prolongation of time spent in bed and their higher consumption of coffee and alcohol. The younger group added that they neglected even brushing their teeth (while for the older group, this health-related behaviour was not an issue because for many of them, regular bathing is not defined as being necessary for health). It is important to note that the younger unemployed expressed a higher exposure to narcotics while only the older unemployed talked about somatic and psychosomatic problems such as abdominal pains, changes in blood pressure, sleep disturbances, tiredness, and nervous breakdowns.

Table GR-3: Changes in health and health-related habits (n = 24)

Change	Younger unemployed	Older unemployed
Irregularity of sleeping time	+	+
Irregularities of mealtimes	+	+
Neglect of regular showering	+	+
Neglect of daily face washing and/or shaving	+	+
Neglect of hair washing	+	+
Prolongation of time spent in bed	+	+
Higher consumption of coffee and alcohol	+	+
Neglect of daily brushing of teeth	+	–
Higher exposure to narcotics	+	–
Abdominal pains	–	+
Change in blood pressure	–	+
Sleep disturbances	–	+
Tiredness	–	+
Nervous breakdowns	–	+

All in all, it can be said that unemployment affects the well-being of both the younger and older age groups. However, young people tend to report lower self-esteem, health satisfaction, and depression while their older counterparts have a tendency to face more serious health-related problems.

The study of the National School of Public Health by Agrafiotis, Tselepis, Pantzou, Avgeridis, Papastamou, and Siontora (1994) was carried out in Athens and Patras (the 4th largest city in Greece) under the title "Sexuality & Social Representations: Contribution to AIDS Prevention" (see Tselepis & Agrafiotis, 1997). A total of 90 people all between 18 and 30 years of age took part in this study, equally divided into three subgroups: the first group was composed of long-term young unemployed persons (between one to three years of unemployment), between the age of 24-30 years who had completed the nine-year obligatory education; the second group were blood donors; and the third consisted of young people who voluntarily asked for an HIV test. The sample was randomly selected and interviewed. The aim was to investigate their perception on AIDS in relation to their sociodemographic characteristics (age, gender, education, occupational state), health behaviour, use of licit and illicit drugs, and life styles. The results showed that the group of young unemployed sometimes identified unemployment with a situation similar to AIDS. Fear of alienation and social isolation, depression, use of licit and illicit drugs, no utilisation of health services, and an overall risky health behaviour composed the main differences among this group as compared to the other two subgroups of the study.

Since 1996 the Greek Monitoring Centre for Drugs and Drug Addiction publishes an annual report on the condition of drug use in Greece. Part of the survey from 1997 records the sociodemographic characteristics of people seeking help in therapeutic centres. For that purpose, a total sample of 3,092 people has been examined during the years 1994-1997 using a 10 minute face-to-face interview and a structured questionnaire designed by the Pompidou Group of Epidemiology and the European Centre for Drugs & Drug Addiction (EMCDDA). The results show that among those young people (the majority between 20-29 of age) enrolled in therapeutic programmes, more than half are unemployed and only one quarter is fully employed.

The study conducted by Kouveli, Armenakis, and Sakellaropoulos (1997) was a cooperative project between the National Centre for Social Research (EKKE) and the Ministry of Environment (Department for the Rehabilitation of Earthquake Victims). The aim was to record the housing problems of earthquake victims in Aigion (a city of approximately 25,000 inhabitants, located 150 km from Athens). The 602 households used as a sample consisted of all the homeless population, that is, those whose houses were either destroyed or severely damaged and therefore were unsuitable to live in. The structured questionnaire was addressed to the head of each household in order to record the sociodemographic and economic states of the family and its previous housing conditions. The survey showed that all earthquake victims belonged to lower socioeconomic groups with poor housing conditions prior to the earthquake. Although homeless, they perceived unemployment – especially of their younger family members – as the main reason for their deprived situation.

The aim of the study conducted by Kouveli, Tsakiris, and Sakellaropoulos (1998) from the National Centre for Social Research is to analyse the consumption standards of an Agrarian population by taking, as a case study, the entire population of a village (Mavromati). The sample consists of the total number of households (approximately 300 inhabitants). The semi-structured questionnaires uses demographic/economic state and household condition as the main variables for the examination of the family financial distribution. Although quantitative analysis is still in progress, the first results show poor consumption standards, no utilisation of health services, and a large percentage of unemployed young people.

The programme from Ioannidi and Mestheneos (1999, 2000) under the title SOSTRIS (Social Strategies in Risk Societies) is a TSER project that is aiming at analysing the social strategies in risk societies. Seven countries are participating in the programme (U.K. – coordinators, France, Italy, Germany, Spain, Sweden, and Greece) and the sample taken in each country is from different groups, all vulnerable to social exclusion. In Greece, six categories are examined, taking six people from each of the following groups: unemployed graduates, unemployed unqualified young people, single parents, early retirees, migrants, and ex-industrial workers. The qualitative research is based on the biographical-interpretative method and is now at the last stage where researchers work on flagship projects responsible for the groups under study in each country. Regarding the first two groups of unemployed graduates and unqualified youth, the first outcomes indicate the importance of education and social milieu as major mediators in the social exclusion process. The second group of unqualified young people experience the risk of social exclusion more due to the lack of specific skills and training and the lack of support (financial and sometimes emotional) from their poor families. They feel much more isolated, marginalised, and have lower self-esteem. In contrast, the group of unemployed graduates experience the buffering effects of family support, lack of pressure in relation to having to earn money, and an attitude that a degree is an achievement in itself.

2.2 Overview of present studies

2.2.1 Objective health indicators

2.2.1.1 Mortality rates

No specific data on mortality rates is available in Greece. The classification by profession from the National Statistics Office does not take into consideration the unemployed as a separate group. Instead, there is a broad category of "people with undeclared occupation". In the 15-30 year age group this broad category has higher mortality rates caused by transport accidents, suicides, and self-inflicted injuries. However, due to the heterogeneity of this category, the above mentioned assumption provides only some information which may serve as a guide for further analysis.

2.2.1.2 Morbidity

In Greece, there exists an association between low socio-economic conditions and bad health conditions among adults. The lower socio-economic groups have a 1.5 times higher possibility of having a chronic disease and they experience depression twice as often as the higher socio-economic groups (see Sissouras, Deligianni, Kalomenidis, Karokis & Mitropoulous, 1995). In addition, after reviewing the records of the outpatient department at a public general hospital situated in the centre of Athens, it could be shown that during periods of economic recession and massive dismissal there was an increasing flow of patients suffering from heart and hypertensive diseases (e.g., during the 1992 massive dismissal of personnel from the public transport organisation which was under privatisation). However, also with regard to this variable, no specific data on young unemployed persons is available.

2.2.1.3 *Suicidal behaviour (suicides and parasuicides)*

No direct correlation between unemployment and suicide among the young population could be found in any of the studies. There is only an ambiguous assumption (described under mortality) which needs further investigation. However, in the article by Tselepis and Agrafiotis (1997) based on the 1994 study, unemployed young people may display a tendency to health-related risk behaviour that sometimes leads to accidents and – indirectly – to suicide. Further, there are studies on other issues which conclude that hidden, unconscious suicide attempts are higher than the national average in cities in general and specifically in cities and regions with a high unemployment rate.

2.2.1.4 *Utilisation of health services*

The same study mentioned above (Tselepis & Agrafiotis, 1997) showed that unemployed young people do not care about their general health condition and seldom visit doctors. They display an overall indifference about their state of health, and they do not utilise the health services as compared to the employed population. However, this assumption may change by taking into account the socio-economic variables (education, social class, and economic state). The studies conducted by Linos (1998) and Athanassouli, Kounari, Homata, and Panagopoulos (1990) showed that the unemployed and the lower socioeconomic groups use fewer health care services for preventive reasons. The sociodemographic analysis within the report by the European Monitoring Centre for Drugs and Drug Addiction (1997) showed, among other things, that more than 50% of those enrolled in therapeutic programmes are unemployed (only one quarter is fully employed). This finding supports the argument above that lower socio-economic groups including the unemployed use health care services mostly for therapeutic (as compared to preventive) purposes.

2.2.2 *Subjective health indicators*

2.2.2.1 *Psychosocical strains*

According to Sokou (1989), young unemployed people report a sense of lower status, *feelings of frustration*, *dependency*, and a lack of possibilities to demonstrate their capabilities. They feel that the situation of unemployment prevents them from the opportunity to use their abilities and to have a well-ordered day. This disorganisation of *time structure* along with feelings of *financial dependency* reinforce the sense of *uselessness* and are regarded as key stress factors. However, there are other factors which affect the level of tension generated by unemployment. These factors are going to be discussed in the following chapters (regional differences, education, social milieu, length of unemployment).

2.2.2.2 *Subjective well-being*

The results regarding health satisfaction in the studies show that unemployed young people have a greater possibility of psychological disturbance and symptoms of *depression* as compared to the employed. Tselepis and Agrafiotis (1997) argue that length of unemployment and age are predominant factors in the degree of psychological disturbance. They recall a typical case of a long-term (3 ½ years) unemployed young man who lived in Athens and was suffering from depressive symptoms. He was tense, socially isolated, could not enjoy life, and had a feeling of impotence. In addition, due to the health-related issue of the study (AIDS prevention), many of the interviewees (all Athens residents between 25 and 30 years old and chronic unemployed for at least one or more years) had the tendency to associate the consequences of unemployment with the consequence of AIDS: "no joy of life", "unable to live decently", "stigmatised by society", "injustice", "death". The Patras report, on the contrary, shows an overall satisfactory health state among the young population regardless of occupational state. The latter reinforces the argument that mechanisms of community support and the sense of belonging (family, relatives, and peer relations) is stronger in smaller communities.

2.2.2.3 Self-esteem

In the studies by Sokou (1989) and Tselepis & Afrafiotis (1997) it was found that self-esteem is substantially harmed among the young unemployed. However, the level also depends upon other factors such as education. In the study by Ioannidi and Mestheneos (1999), for example, the group of unemployed graduates enjoy a relatively high degree of self-esteem since the university degree is socially valued and considered as an achievement in itself.

2.2.2.4 Alienation (political orientation)

Due to lack of sufficient data, assumptions can only be made about the relation between political alienation and youth unemployment. There is a feeling that unemployed young people are less politically active compared to employed ones, although political apathy is a generalised phenomenon. In the study of Tselepis and Agrafiotis (1997), unemployed young men express also feelings of injustice and marginalisation. Sokou (1989) argues in her report that younger unemployed seek justification by constructing their own closed society – a type of ghetto that incorporates elements of social and political alienation.

2.2.2.5 Social deviation (delinquency)

In Greece, there exists no direct relationship between youth unemployment and delinquency. Unemployment must be viewed as one of the aspects that encourage deviant behaviour. However, there are unpublished studies estimating that delinquency is higher than the expected average in cities and regions of high unemployment.

2.2.2.6 Health behaviour

Health behaviour is related to cultural and social factors as well as to issues of accessibility and availability of services. In Greece, there are studies showing that unemployed young people neglect health-related daily activities. Sokou (1989) reports that unemployed people do not wash and/or shave themselves and do not brush their teeth each day. They tend not to eat and sleep regularly and to use alcohol, tobacco, and drugs more frequently. The reason for the worse health behaviour cannot always be related to a lack of interest. Several young unemployed persons do not have any health insurance to cover the cost of social services. Furthermore, the cost of transportation to health care services is also a reason since many unemployed persons live in the outskirts of the cities which are often deprived of any health facilities. Finally, Tselepis and Agrafiotis (1997) report a higher licit and illicit drug use among the unemployed subgroup as compared to the other groups. They also report that the unemployed use condoms less often and take more risks in their sexual behaviour (regarding AIDS).

2.2.3 Mediators (demographic variables)

2.2.3.1 Age

The studies available on young unemployed people do not make a clear distinction on age subgroups. However, what has been observed in the Tselepis and Agrafiotis study

(1997) is a tendency to find people with more significant *psychological disturbances* (stress, isolation, depression) among the older age group 25-29 years.

2.2.3.2 Gender

Gender is an important mediator that differentiates the results significantly. The impression from the studies mentioned above is that unemployed women present an overall better health state than men. The Annual Report on Drugs showed that the ratio of men to women enrolled in therapeutic communities is 6:1. Women have not been socialised to be the breadwinners. Society accepts marriage and childbearing as an equally important role, enabling them to feel useful and socially integrated (Sokou, 1988). Usually, the health condition of older age groups is more substantially affected by unemployment, especially when their spouse is unemployed or when they are financially responsible for the family (single parenthood).

2.2.3.3 Education

Education is one of the most influential variables in relation to the extent of health consequences caused by unemployment. In the study by Ioannidis and Mestheneos (2000), significant differences are observed with regard to *psychological well-being* according to level of education (in relation to social class) among the young unemployed. The subgroup of unqualified youth is the one at most risk of social exclusion. The lack of specific skills and training, especially when combined with coming from a poor family who cannot offer any material support, has consequences for the subjective well-being, *self-esteem,* and *social isolation* of the affected person. Contrary, the subgroup of unemployed graduates is experiencing a lack of pressure in relation to having to earn money because the family is willing to bear the cost of unemployment for several years. Furthermore, these young people enjoy a high level of self-esteem and emotional support from their families and social surroundings since a degree is understood as an achievement in itself in Greece. In addition, educated young people report fewer risk behaviour attitudes. In the report of the Greek Monitoring Centre for Drugs and Drug Addiction it is clearly shown that education is an important mediator in the *drug addiction* process. Although the percentages of university students and graduates have increased during the last four years (4.4% and 5.5% respectively during 1997), still the vast majority (2/3) of those enrolled in therapeutic programmes have not completed secondary education.

2.2.3.4 Social class (social milieu)

Similar to the degree of education, importance is attached to social class as a significant mediator between young unemployed persons and health. Family income and living standards are predominant factors that influence the state of health among young people. In both studies conducted by the National Centre for Social Research (EKKE), what became evident is that unemployment affects more the *well-being* of young people from lower socio-economic status groups. In the study by Kouveli et al. (1997) on earthquake victims of Aigion (a city of approximately 25,000 inhabitants near Patras) it was found that the households that were the most severely damaged were those belonging to the lowest socio-economic status. Those households had a significantly higher number of young unemployed who lived under deprived living and housing conditions, thus facing the consequences of a vicious circle. Similar results are found in another study by Kouveli et al. (1998) on the consumption standards of Mavromati village (an agrarian village of approximately 300 inhabitants): The lower income families are also the ones most affected by unemployment. In addition, their younger members have no access to training or other alternatives in order to extend their capabilities leading to multiple psychological strains (financial hardship, insecurity about finding a job, psychosocial stress).

2.2.3.5 Length of unemployment

There is no specific study that subcategorises the group of long-term unemployed. However, in the Tselepi and Agrafiotis study (1997), age and duration of unemployment were detected as being important variables. Among the persons between 24 and 30 years of age with one to three and a half years of unemployment those persons facing the longest periods of unemployment were suffering the most from psychosomatic disturbances.

2.2.4 Moderators (psychological variables)

2.2.4.1 Work and job orientation

There is no direct study which examines how the degree of work and job orientation affects the health condition of young unemployed persons. Yet the study on chronic unemployed young people (Sokou, 1989) showed that they are coping better with present and probably future unemployment by minimising life goals and work prospects and by moving into a social environment which was not demanding. Lower level of work commitment was linked with higher levels of *psychological well-being*.

2.2.4.2 Financial strain/stress

Financial strain is a main factor that has a negative effect mostly on the *psychological well-being* of the young unemployed. They remain dependent on financial support from their families, and this feeling of dependency creates loss of *self-esteem* and a sense of *uselessness* (Sokou, 1989). Yet activities related to the submerged economy serve as a buffer in this process enabling them to work in various part-time and seasonal activities – providing them with some kind of financial and emotional relief.

2.2.4.3 Social support

In Greece, social support is considered to be a fundamental element in order to avoid or alleviate health disorders related to unemployment. The family is the primary unit of social support and in many cases it replaces the limited state provisions. Young unemployed persons continue to live with their parents and to depend financially on them. Continued residence in the parental home is accepted and expected in Greece (Sokou, 1989). However, economic dependence on parents is accepted as long as the child behaves in the way the parents expect (Mousourou, 1985; Sokou, 1987). The psychological pressure that the family may exercise on its younger members is eliminated through the support of the circle of friends who play a significant function by justifying one another and by creating a social place of retreat. The more social support, the less deterioration in the well-being of the young unemployed.

3 Summary of results

The issue of unemployment has not been systematically and openly examined, neither within the scientific nor the political world in Greece. During the 80s several industrial units were closed down. Interestingly, although unemployed workers organised several demonstrations, unemployment was still not a public issue. Media presented only the demonstrations and the demands of the unemployed without promoting an in-depth debate on unemployment. Since 1990 unemployment, especially among the youth, started to be more openly discussed as a problem by politicians and scientists. The causes and consequences of youth unemployment is one of the issues which need further analysis since research on young people is still scarce. There are several studies that analyse facets of unemployment and others that analyse health-related issues. Yet there is *no single* study directly interrelating these two issues.

For the purpose of this report, contacts with scientists and research centres were made for the collection of relevant information. These contacts have created an awareness among the academic world and have provided a stimulus for the reorientation of existing and future studies. Several scientists whose work has been included in this report became interested in making secondary analyses of their existing data in order to investigate the relation between health condition and working status. The information given by the Greek YUSEDER team of researchers may be used as baseline data because it is expected that surveys will soon present results analysing the trends of the unemployed's health conditions.

In conclusion, considering the findings from the survey of the Greek researchers there is no doubt about the existence of a relationship between unemployment and the deterioration of health. This relationship is rather more obvious in mental (compared to physical) health problems. It is thought that there is greater proportion of depression, psychological disturbances, stress, loss of self-esteem and social disorientation among unemployed young people. It is also thought that unemployment leads to a loss of social bonds. Changes in lifestyles and reduced interest in public affairs are situations that might lead to social and political alienation (isolation and self-marginalisation).

Yet the relationship between unemployment – especially youth unemployment- and physical health still remains ambiguous and needs further research. What also requires additional investigation is the level of importance that is attributed to certain mediating variables such as education, social class, gender, and age. Nonetheless, the health-related consequences of unemployment is a dynamic issue that requires attention and further analysis, as it portrays and it interacts with society's norms, values, and preventive mechanisms.

Youth unemployment and health: Greek studies – an overview

Author	Sample	Instruments/ Methods	Population	Dependent variables	Results
Sokou (1989)	N = 24 unemployed persons 11 long-term unemployed young people 13 chronically unemployed from older age groups	cross-sectional study semi-structured interviews	20-27 years old	– education – gender – age – living condition – length of unemployment	– changes that were experienced after dismissal, specifically regarding personality and behaviour, social relations, life style, and health – data on phases experienced and coping responses – suggestions regarding interventions and support from the state and surrounding community
Agrafiotis, Tselepis, Pantzou, Avgeridis, Papastamou & Siontora (1994)	N = approx. 90; random sample 1/3 unemployed 1/3 blood donors 1/3 people who voluntarily take HIV test	cross-sectional study semi-structured interview	18-30 years	– age, gender, education, occupational state – health behaviour – use of licit/illicit drugs – life styles	– for the first group compared to the other two subgroups of the study: – identification of unemployment experienced as a situation similar to AIDS – fear of alienation and social isolation, depression, use of licit and illicit drugs, no utilisation of health services, and an overall risk behaviour.
Kokkevi, Stefanis et al. (1997)	N = 846 (1994) N = 1,130 (1995) N = 546 (1996) N = 570 (1997)	cross-sectional study face-to-face interview structured questionnaire	majority 20-29 years old drug addicts enrolled in therapeutic programmes	– education – occupational state – enrollment in therapeutic programmes	– relation between unemployment and drug addiction with 50% of population in drug centres being unemployed
Kouveli, Armenakis & Skellaropoulos (1997)	N = 602 (households)	cross-sectional study structured questionnaire	homeless population of Aigion	– demographic and economic status – house condition	– large number of young unemployed among homeless families
Kouveli, Tsakiris & Skellaropoulos (1998)	N = approx. 300 (total number of households of Mavromati village)	cross-sectional study semi-structured questionnaire	entire village	– demographic and economic state – household condition	– quantitative analysis still in progress. – first results show poor consumption standards and no utilisation of health services in combination with large percentage of unemployed young people.

Author	Sample	Instruments/ Methods	Population	Dependent variables	Results
Ioannidi, Mestheneos (1997-99)	N = 36 distinguished in six vulnerable groups: unemployed graduates unemployed unqualified youth single parents early retirees migrants ex-industrial workers	qualitative research based on the Biographical-Interpretative method		– socio-demographic state (education, age, gender, occupational state) – living standards	– first outcomes regarding unemployed graduates and unqualified young people: – indication of importance of education and social milieu as major mediators in the social exclusion process.

Other studies which include health-related aspects

Author	Sample	Instruments	Population	Dependent Variables	Results
Agrafiotis et al. (1998)	N = 2,000 people at national level	quantitative research based on questionnaire designed for the purposes of this survey on European level	– 18-45 years	– education – occupation – family status	– survey is in progress at this time
Linos (1998)	N = 1,000 young women	questionnaire	– rural population	– occupation – current health status – health problems last year – major psychological burden last five years	– first outcomes showed that unemployed and lower socio-economic groups use less health care services for preventive reasons
Linos (1998)	N = 200	questionnaire	– 20-30 years – hospitalised or seen at hospital for various reasons	– current and past health problems – all those mentioned above	– same as above

Youth Unemployment and Health in Italy

Michele La Rosa & Vando Borghi[1]

1 The Italian report is a result of a collaboration of the whole Italian research team. However, Chapter 1 can be attributed to *Michele La Rosa* while the other chapters can be attributed to *Vando Borghi*.

1 Introduction to youth unemployment and health

The present report[2] will give an overview of the issue of unemployment and specifically youth unemployment in Italy, followed by an analysis of the available research on the correlation between youth unemployment and health. It is necessary to bear in mind that until now the latter aspect has not received much attention both on a theoretical and empirical level. Therefore, the analysis will also incorporate additional useful data linked only indirectly with the subject of this report in order to understand how the condition of exclusion from work can affect the state of health of young persons in Italy.

1.1 National development of youth unemployment

1.1.1 Unemployment in general

To understand the Italian specificity regarding unemployment one has to look, first of all, at the strong regional differences, or to be more explicit, the dualism between the socio-economic situation of the North versus the South. "Perhaps the most salient feature of the Italian economy and of its employment pattern is the enormous, and increasing, regional disparity. In this country – with the notable exception of Liguria – the employment rate declines continuously as one moves from northern to southern regions; and the gap between the South and the Centre-North of the country is very wide indeed" (European Commission, 1997, p. 17). According to the data of the National Institute of Statistics (Istat), the territorial concentration of the unemployment problem in the southern area is very evident and does not show any signs of decrease over time (Table 1).

Table I-1: Unemployment rate by geographic division

	1995	1996	1997
North*	6.8	6.6	6.6
Centre*	10.3	10.3	10.2
South*	21.0	21.7	22.2
Italy**	11.9	12.0	12.1

Source: *Istat, Rilevazioni Forze di Lavoro; **Eurostat, Unemployment n°3.

In 1997, according to Eurostat data the number of people searching for a job in Italy has reached 2,757,300. From 1996 to 1997 this number increased by 26,100 persons – a number slightly lower than in 1996 (43,900) and much lower than in 1994 (225,300) and 1995 (116,400). However the incidence of the territorial dimension of unemployment in the same year has again proven to be extremely relevant: the southern regions were the only ones to register an increase in the unemployment rate (from 21% to 21.7% in 1996 to 22.2% in 1997), whereas, on the contrary, in the Centre the rate first stayed the same and then decreased (10.3% in 1995/1996, 10.2% in 1997), and, in the North, first a reduction took place which then remained unchanged (from 6.8% to 6.6% in 1996/1997).

To allow for a comprehensive understanding of the development of unemployment in Italy, the following table summarises the unemployment rates between 1975 and 1998.

2 The authors are all members of the C.I.Do.S.Pe.L. (International Centre for Documentation and Sociological Studies on Labour Issues) of the Sociology Department of the University of Bologna.

Table I-2: Unemployment rate in Italy, 1975-1998

	Total	Males	Females
1975*	4.8	3.2	8.6
1985*	8.4	5.8	13.5
1990*	9.1	6.4	13.8
1991*	8.8	6.2	13.2
1992**	9.0	6.5	13.2
1993**	10.3	7.8	14.8
1994**	11.4	8.9	15.7
1995**	11.9	9.2	16.4
1996**	12.0	9.4	16.4
1997**	12.1	9.3	16.6
01.1998***	12.0	9.2	16.5

Source: *European Commission, 1997; **Eurostat, *Unemployment*, 3, 1998; ***Eurostat, *News release*, 32, 1998.

As it can be ascertained from the data in Table 2, a second characteristic identifying the Italian model of unemployment lies in the importance and the incidence of the gender variable in the social composition of unemployment. As compared to men, women have a much higher likelihood to find themselves unemployed: in 1997 and January 1998 the percentage of unemployed females was 7.3 points higher than the corresponding males' percentage.

A third aspect that distinguishes the Italian situation in the unemployment issue is the correlation between unemployment and educational level. Contrary to most other European countries – where a lower educational level is systematically associated with a stronger risk for unemployment, and persons with a higher level seem to be more advantaged – Italy (similar to Spain and Greece) constitutes an exception to this rule: Also here the unemployment rates within the group with the highest school level are rather high (17.3%). Moreover, Italy presents an additional specificity with regard to the correlation between unemployment and educational level, inasmuch as Italy is the only country where the unemployment rate among persons with the highest educational degree (17.3%) is greater than among those with the lowest degree (15.4%). In this regard the Italian situation has been defined as a phenomenon of "intellectual unemployment"[3]. This means that Italy is facing a contradiction between an increasing upper level education and a still weak and backward economical development, leading to an economic context which offers only few highly qualified jobs (Reyneri, 1997, p. 42). However, it is also true that this interpretation (the "intellectual unemployment label") can overshadow the most serious aspect of the correlation between unemployment and educational level: exclusion and educational dispersion.

3 More generally, according to a recent study of the Giacomo Brodolini Foundation for the European Commission (1997, p.17), "the probability of being in the labour force and of being employed increases with educational level. The probability of a university graduate's being employed is 1.7 greater than that of a person with the lowest level of schooling for men and 4 times greater for women. Most striking is the probability of unemployment for labour force participants, which also increases with education – however, with the exception of university graduates whose unemployment probability is about half the overall average. Lower and upper secondary school graduates have the greatest probability of being unemployed."

A fourth constituting element of the specific Italian context is the presence of a high rate of long-term unemployment: Against the European average which is about 45%, in Italy of the persons searching for a job (64.1% of men, 67.1% of women), 65.6% have been looking for more than 12 months. Finally, the aspect, that is of main interest within this research study is also steadily increasing in the whole of Italy: Among the unemployed a much larger presence of young persons exists who are looking for their first job. This element constitutes one of the most characterising elements of Italy. In sum, with regard to the aspects discussed so far it can be assumed that the identity of the Italian unemployed person can be described as follows: It is more likely that a person affected by unemployment comes from the South. More often it is a "she" and she has been looking for a job for more than 12 months.

Considering the overall Italian situation it becomes clear that this country has to be classified as an anomaly of the model of unemployment structure defined as "Mediterranean" (Mingione & Pugliese, 1995). As compared to the "continental" situation, the "mediterranean" model is characterised by high unemployment rates in the agricultural field, persistent low levels of industrial employment (and of industrial employment in particular), low levels of female participation in the labour market and, especially for young women, high unemployment (Giannelli, Orientale Caputo & Pugliese, 1996, p.50). This situation is only true for the southern part of Italy. Therefore, the anomaly of the Italian case itself consists most of all in unifying the "continental" (in the North) and the "Mediterranean" model (in the South) in one single country. If one tries to reread some of the aspects outlined above through the territorial incidence variable, the consistency of such a territorial dualism becomes extremely evident: "Male participation rates are everywhere higher than female rates. However the gap is lower in the North (47% males and 43% females) than in the South (35% males and 24% females). Female [unemployment] rates are 66% in the South and 21% in the North. Since 1993 the rate in the southern regions has been steadily increased while in the Centre and the North there has been a slight decline. Among males, unemployment rates are four times higher in the South than in the North" (Baldacci, Gazzelloni & Inglese, 1997, p. 131). Therefore, in Italy, typologies and situations of people looking for a job cannot be understood at the national level, but have to be always referred to the two different contexts of the Centre-North and the South (Mingione, 1991, p. 54-5).

1.1.2 Youth unemployment

As it has already been at least partially outlined, the question of youth unemployment is one of the aspects characterising the specificity of the Italian labour market. The Eurostat data clearly points out an overrepresentation of the Italian youth (and even more of young women) in the social composition of unemployment when compared with the average percentages of young Europeans of the same age.

Table I-3: Unemployment rates by age groups; seeking first job rates, 1996

	EUR 15			Italy		
	Males	Females	Total	Males	Females	Total
15-19 years	21.5	24.5	22.8	31.8	42.6	36.4
20-24 years	20.6	22.4	21.4	29.5	38.1	33.3
25-29 years	12.4	15.1	13.6	15.5	21.7	18.1
15-29 years	16.5	19	17.6	22.3	30.3	25.7
Seeking first job	17.8*	23.4**	20.5***	50.6*	56.6**	23.7***

Source: Eurostat, *Labour Force Survey*, 1996; Legend: *out of 100 unemployed males; **out of 100 unemployed females; ***out of 100 unemployed persons.

Together with the territorial dualism, the prominence of young persons being unemployed in Italy is probably the most characterising aspect of the Italian labour market. The significant differences which characterise it in comparison with other European countries are rendered in the following figure:

Figure I-1: Unemployment rate by age: stylised graphs

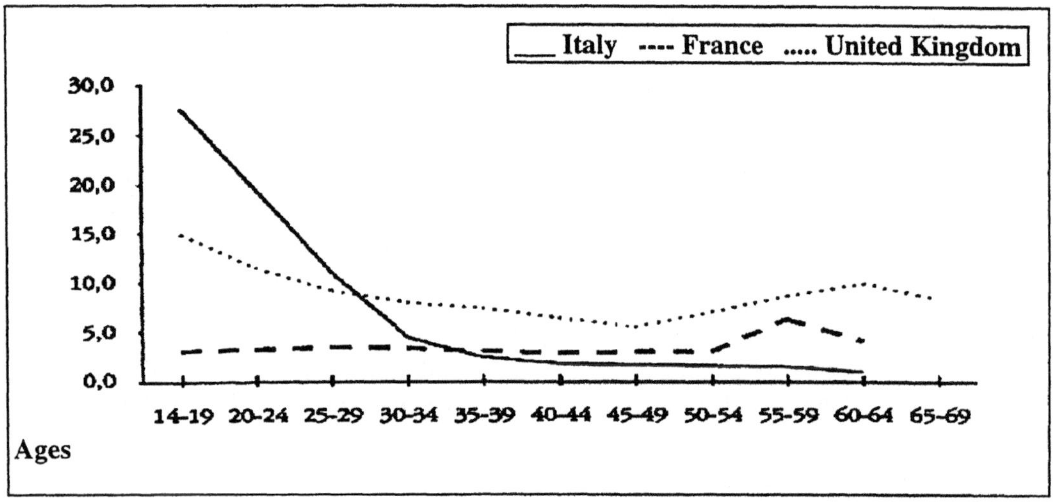

Source: Reyneri, 1996.

In 1997[4] the unemployed between 15 and 29 years of age amounted to 1,679,000, respectively 60.8% of all unemployed persons in Italy. Among these, 51.7% (869,000) were young women. When breaking down the youth unemployment rate in age brackets, 15.6% were between 15-19 years of age, 46% between 20-24 years of age, and finally 38.3% between 25-29 years of age. What is even more striking are the numbers for the length of time that young people are seeking a job. In 1997, among all unemployed persons between 15-29 years of age, 67% had been looking for a job for more than 12 months (in absolute terms these were 1,126,000). When considering that almost

4 The data source is Eurostat, provided by the co-ordinator and re-elaborated by us.

41% of the whole group of unemployed persons were in this situation, the presence of a social context in great distress becomes obvious. This means that not only each single young person has difficulties in finding a job but that this is also true for its entire social network – a network which should be able to not only give financial support for its young members, but which should also be a social area where part of the difficulties in the course of daily life can be communicated. When considering the conditions in the South where families with a single employed person have to assume support usually for more than one unemployed young person, this situation becomes even more extreme.
It is in this regard that the connection between the Italian employment and unemployment model outlined in the previous chapter comes into focus. On the one hand there is the "more employed and more employable" labourer: male, adult, head of the family to whom all forms of protection and support of the Italian welfare system in case of economical difficulties are assigned; on the other hand there is the young person looking for a job, struggling to enter the world of labour in order to build a path of autonomy for him-/herself who needs the support of the head of the family waiting to come out of precariousness. This condition of exclusion of young people from labour is at risk of adding to other sources of subjective tension (exit from the family, parents' expectations towards a path of autonomy, personal expectations of putting oneself and one's capabilities to test in the labour market, planning of an own family, etc.) which might become sources of frustration if not real and strong uneasiness. The longer that the period for young people is in which they are spending without finding a regular job, then the higher the risk is for them to be affected by processes of alienation with very serious outcomes for their personality as well as their social participation (Bezze, 1998, p. 97-98)[5].

In order to evaluate the risk dimensions of the younger generation which unemployment could provoke, imply, and intensify at a psychophysical level, the following section will deal with the knowledge accumulated in this field up to now. It has to be stressed, however, that the Italian context is characterised by a certain lack of empirical research regarding the correlation between unemployment and health.

1.2 Unemployment and health – some theoretical considerations

In the beginning, the phenomenon of unemployment was investigated in Italy by the psychological and psychosocial sphere mainly on a descriptive level. This approach tended to point out the various reactions of the persons to a situation of job loss with regard to, for example, their daily behaviour and their utilisation of time. During the second half of the 80s and the beginning of the 90s, the debate and the research on the psychological implications of job loss on the health and well-being of people started to have a stronger theoretical depth also through the reception of the international literature (Crepet, 1989, 1990; Bruzzone, 1991; Briante, 1991). This second stage of analysis led to (Sarchielli, 1995):

1. an increase in attention to the "various occupations" or the various modalities with which different actors interpret, re-elaborate, and manage the situation (socially, culturally and economically);

---

5 It is significant that the Italian Caritas Report – Zancari Foundation 1998 – provides a specific section on the issue "*The long wait for a job: when youth unemployment provokes social alienation*" – an issue which had not been debated in the previous report.

2. More interest in personal and social factors which are involved in the determination of the answer to the absence of occupation;
3. an increased effort to find the connection between the analysis of the unemployment phenomenon and other spheres on both a theoretical and empirical level;
4. an update of the present "morphology" of unemployment;
5. a broader contextualisation of unemployment studies that took into account the plurality of types of separation from work in Italy (preretirement, redundancy fund, mobility, promotion of resigning, etc.);
6. the use of unemployment study as the primary point of observation for changes in the relationship between persons and work.

If, in the studies on the social impact of unemployment, the necessity to take into account the different social, cultural, and economical conditions of persons for their ability to cope with job exclusion is pointed out (Accornero & Carmignani, 1986), it is fundamental to do the same when dealing with the implications for health such an event involves. This is also true for the more restricted sphere of youth unemployment. Considering the empirical results of the related studies, there does in fact exist an inner differentiation of youth unemployment, and the impact it has on the psychophysical well-being of the persons depends upon the *social resources* they can reach and the *potential capabilities* they can activate (Depolo & Sarchielli, 1987). In analysing a social group such as young people, the logical frame which "attributes to the condition of job absence an unquestionable causal power, with similar consequences for all those affected by it" – independent of gender, age, family situation, territorial context, etc. also has to be abandoned (Sarchielli et al., 1991, p.46). Therefore, it would be necessary to always take into account the different situations of the respective persons who underwent a condition of job exclusion with particular attention given to the main factors of differentiation: family background, educational level, and gender (ibid., p.28). In addition, when understanding health in a broader way than mere psychologically, unemployment must be comprehended not as much as a primary cause of changes in the health condition, but as a factor that "intervenes in the correlation between the individual and his own health condition" affecting it economically (impoverishment), increasing people's vulnerability to illness factors and mortality, influencing the psychological condition as well as social life leading to isolation, breaking of affective relationships, etc. (Crepet, 1990, p.57).

Therefore, despite the fact that empirical research has evidently shown a clear association between the condition of job absence and worse conditions of health in Italy – both on a subjective and a more objective level (diagnosed by a doctor) including a consequent greater frequency of medical examinations and a greater use of medicines (Figà-Talamanca & Pagano, 1987) – the causal correlation between illness and mortality increase and unemployment is not completely clear. "Illness might be both the cause and the effect of unemployment" (ibid., p. 50). Especially in the case of the correlation between health and youth unemployment, such a precaution must be maintained or maybe even accentuated. Based upon a review of national and international literature, Crepet underlined that

> "even if there is not a complete agreement among the different authors, the condition of being unemployed for a young person does not necessarily imply a high 'risk' of depressive symptoms. Several researchers agree, in fact, on pointing out that it is not so much the unemployment which provokes an unfavourable effect on the mental health of the young person producing therefore a depressive symptomatology, as it is the occupation itself which tends to mitigate it." (Crepet, 1990, p. 139).

2 Analysis of research on youth unemployment and health

2.1 Description of available data (design and methods)

The study from Crepet, Vetrone, Piazzi, Costa, and Lombardi (1992) was carried out in the province of Foggia (in the region Puglia, in the Southern part of the country) a sample of 379 (104 women and 175 men) young people between 18-26 years of age (of which 50% were between 24-26 years). The average scores of the General Health Questionnaire (GHQ) were higher (2.17 with 1.97 among males and 2.33 among females) than those scores from similar surveys carried out in other countries. This led the authors to affirm the presence of a widespread and persistent psychological uneasiness in this population sample, as it could be expected among young people of a disadvantaged region (p. 50). The survey shows a greater significance of the variable gender than age or occupational condition: The female sample systematically scored higher on the scale of Beck's depression test, the somatic symptoms, anxiety, hostility of the Fava's and Kelener's Symptom Questionnaire, and for the scales of loss of hope and self-esteem (p. 52). The unemployment condition, instead, did not seem to be in correlation with higher scores for what concerns the discomfort indicators, also because the uneasiness correlated with such a condition tends to express itself "in forms less traditionally symptomatic" and, therefore, less measurable by the scales used for the survey. However the data concerning the Hopelessness Scale, in which an extremely high score of the young unemployed persons was recorded in general, denotes a clear condition of discomfort in the perception of their future. A result of this latter situation can be seen in the tendency of "social apathy and decrease of efforts to change one's own future in a better way" (p. 51). The risk such a loss of hope implies in terms of a self fulfilling prophecy is rather obvious in the sense that it can cause a "passive adaptation" leading towards a chronic condition of marginality (p. 51).

The survey carried out by Vetrone, Crepet, Costa, Piazzi, Di Tommaso, Ferrara, Petrangeli, and Frighi (1992) in the province of Sienna (in the region of Tuscany in the centre of Italy) is similar to the one described above. The interview was given to a sample of 400 individuals (147 males, 253 females) between 18 and 26 years of age. The results confirm those obtained within the previous research: The high average GHQ score of the female sample, the nondiscriminating factor of the occupational condition in comparison with the indicators of psychological uneasiness, and the higher score of unemployed persons on the Hopelessness Scale.

Grassi, Falzoni, and Fasoli (1992) started their survey from the beneficiaries' Archive of the Health Unit of Cento (small town in the province of Ferrara in the region of Emilia Romagna). This study differentiates three different groups (all males, between 20 – 29 years of age): 30 young metalworkers exposed to mental health risk in relation to the quality of their work environment, 57 not exposed to the same risk, and 40 young persons seeking their first job or having been unemployed for at least six months. The researchers – detecting a higher score for what concerns the indicators of mental uneasiness only for the first group – concluded that regarding the mental balance and the risks for mental health, as compared with the perspective of dangerous and distressing work, the unemployment condition seems to be not particularly negative (p. 150).

The fourth survey which could be found in Italy was carried out by Sarchielli, Depolo, Fraccaroli and Colasanto (1991). The sample consisted of 96 young people from

Vicenza and 320 from Turin (region Piedmont, in the northern part of the country). Two groups were distinguished: firstly, young people between 17-19 years of age with a degree of compulsory education, and secondly, young persons with secondary level degree between 22-24 years of age. Gender, activity level in the effort toward seeking a job (number of direct activities), length of unemployment (8-32 months), occupational condition (seeking first job, unemployed, precarious labourers looking for a stable job, and employed less than 25 hours a week or with a temporary contract of less than three months duration), and level of school degree were taken into consideration. The survey confirms that the condition of job absence is a "situation of potential psychosocial stress" and this especially "if the subject thinks he is not 'equipped' to solve the situation favourably" (pp. 187-188). This means that the level of psychological stress the young people experienced in this condition was not determined by the event itself, but rather by "the correlation perceived between difficulty and complexity of the task on the one hand, and the personal and social resources available for the affected youth on the other hand". Therefore, according to the results of this research it seems reasonable to affirm that the highest psychological costs are paid when "a) the persons perceive they have only scarce resources; and b) the demand of the environment is particularly cogent". Two processes can be outlined: firstly, the persons who perceive that they have scarce possibilities to turn to regarding "psychosocial resources" (friends, family, reference persons to whom they can turn) and who have "a weaker self-esteem" (also in comparison with other social groups) are those who are more exposed in terms of psychological well-being; secondly, this dynamic intensifies in those contexts in which the environmental demand appears to be particularly overwhelming to the subject.

The survey by Depolo, Fraccaroli, and Sarchielli (1992) is part of the research described above, and focusses on the possible changes in the psychological well-being among a sample of 115 persons who took part in the first research study and who were now in a different occupational position. The following variables were utilised: a measure of psychosocial resources; scales of self-positioning; and comparison between the dimensions 'economical assets', 'social relationships', 'psychological well-being', 'self-esteem'; 'GHQ 12'. The results show: a) a significant better psychological well-being of the stable employees; b) no changes in the state of well-being among the persons with irregular or occasional jobs; and c) a stabilisation of the conditions of uneasiness among the persons without a job.

The essay by Fraccaroli (1989) is an anticipation of the results found by Sarchielli et al. (1991). The author dwells upon the analysis of the concept of work involvement meaning both a verification of the methodology used and the usefulness of the concept itself in order to examine the person's behaviour. For the survey, Warr's six item scale has been used together with some questions on the 'nonfinancial employment commitment' about the image of the ideal work and the effect of unemployment. The results show the importance of the level of school degree as a mediator for the effects of work involvement: While among those with the lowest educational level work involvement correlates significantly with "working expectations of intrinsic nature", among those with a secondary school degree, it means "to nurture expectations of social success" apart from those strictly connected with the occupation itself. With regard to unemployment the results could show that a person "who possesses a higher work involvement tends to define the relevance of the unemployment effects as stronger and more pervasive – above all as regards self-esteem and the possibility to plan projects for the future" (p. 661). Instead, work involvement does not show any relation with the threat of unemployment on aspects of daily life.

As it can be seen from the six studies mentioned above, the research attention focussed primarily on the well-being of the young people and on the effects unemployment may have in correlation with it. The results allow the conclusions to be drawn that the probable condition of uneasiness and mental suffering is more related to variables of both generation (being young as "a passage phase" which involves anxieties, fears, expectations, frustrations, etc.) and gender (an element "which makes us think of a suffering strictly correlated with the issues of women's condition" [Vetrone & others, 1992, p. 80]) apart from the occupational condition in which it is experienced[6] than to the condition of unemployment in itself.

2.2 Overview of present studies

2.2.1 Objective health indicators

2.2.1.1 Mortality rates

In the studies examined above, no data could be found with regard to mortality rates. However, on a general level, in the last 10 years – according to the data of the Central Institute of Statistics (Baldacci, Gazzelloni & Inglese, 1997, p. 138) – the mortality rate for persons between 20 and 35 years of age has increased (see Table 4). This increase has been more evident in the North of the country as a consequence of AIDS and drug abuse. The same source outlines that, for 1994, the main cause of death "for the young population are *traffic incidents* which account for more than 30% of all male deaths and 21% of female deaths". During the 90s, *AIDS*, instead of suicide, has become the second highest cause of death for males and females. Also, the mortality due to *drug abuse* has increased in the last decade.

Table I-4: Death rate standardised by sex and age

	1987	1990	1993
15-19	2.3	2.4	2.1
20-24	3.2	3.4	3
25-29	3	4.1	4

Source: Eurostat.

However, from this data it is not possible to understand the link between unemployment and the risk for mortality among young persons. In a longitudinal study carried out in Turin on a population of 1,023,957 persons in 1971, and 1,056,102 in 1981, an excess of mortality among unemployed persons of both sexes was pointed out. The investigation "documents an excess of mortality among the young unemployed seeking their first job (...) and a consistent excess among men who, having lost their job, were seeking a new one in 1981" (Costa & Segnan, 1988, p. 51). However, the authors also stressed that, unlike similar surveys carried out in other countries, in Turin "the association between unemployment and mortality among young people seeking their first job is less convincing"

6 These results are also confirmed by research on the psychosocial well-being status of young apprentices (Crepet, Baldasseroni, Zoppi, & Carnevale, 1994).

because "the excess of deaths observed is for the greatest part due to *violent deaths*", whereas more consistent results exist for "the association between mortality and unemployment for men seeking a new job" (ibid.). In addition, the risk "is higher among persons in a condition of stable unemployment" (p. 52). Costa and Segnan conclude their data analysis by affirming that in Turin, during the beginning of the 80s, job loss was associated with a "doubled risk of death" and that an excess of 50% death risk for both sexes among young people seeking their first job was already evident[7] (p. 54).

2.2.1.2 *Morbidity*

The empirical research examined does not provide any data on this issue with regard to young persons. However, without distinguishing age categories (Figà-Talamanca & Pagano, 1987), more general statistical data could show a clear association between the condition of job absence and worse conditions of health. Also the data from the National Health Survey conducted in 1983 testifies that unemployed persons report a poorer health status. However, no causal explanations could be given: "Illness might be both the cause and the effect of unemployment" (ibid., p. 50).

2.2.1.3 *Suicidal behaviour (suicides and parasuicides)*

Likewise, no data on this issue could be found in the empirical research studies examined. However, even if the general data in Italy "is different from the other European countries for the fewer suicides" (Crepet, Caracciolo, Cappi, Tugnoli, Cielo & Simonato 1995, p. 60), the suicide rates of young people are rather worrying, collocating "this cause of death as the first among adolescents"[8].

Table I-5a: Age specific suicide rates in Italy

	1977	1978	1979	1980	1981	1982	1983	1984	1985	1986
15-19	1.91	2.27	2.28	2.41	2.12	2.19	1.97	1.76	1.85	2.07
20-24	5.13	4.65	4.76	5.64	4.92	4.99	4.92	4.95	4.79	4.47
25-29	4.22	5.43	6.46	6.00	5.97	6.30	6.31	5.75	5.75	6.80

Source: Bille-Brahe et al., 1992, p. 60.

Table I-5b: Age-gender specific suicide rates in Italy

	1985-89		1990	
	M	F	M	F
15-19	3.0	0.9	3.3	1.6
20-24	7.1	2.0	8.2	2.4
25-29	9.5	2.6	10.2	2.5

Source: Istat data, in D'Avanzo, 1995, p. 17.

Therefore, the correlation between unemployment and suicide is a highly disputed question. Although several studies "have demonstrated that it is much more frequent to

7 It is useful to underline that, according to the authors of the survey, "the particularly high risk observable among unemployed persons from the middle-class born in the north – whose entry in unemployment is relatively recent in the Turin area – seems to be consistent with the hypothesis that unemployment has worse consequences for the social groups which have been less used to it historically" (Costa, & Segnan, 1988, p.54).

8 Even if, sticking to the official data, "the rate of suicide of both sexes between 15 and 24 years old (about 5/100,000) is among the lowest in Europe" (D'Avanzo, 1995, p.18).

find a status of unemployment or working instability among those who committed suicide or tried to commit suicide", it does not appear to be quite clear *how* unemployment increases the risk for suicide (Crepet, 1990, p. 148). Another study, replicating and extending previous similar research on suicide and unemployment, showed – confirming previous results – that, if we analyse the trends at a regional level, any association between unemployment and suicide disappears, and the authors conclude that unequivocal results cannot be produced even by large-scale prospective longitudinal studies (Platt, Micciolo & Tansella, 1992).

Table I-6: Suicide rates per 100,000 persons

	1988	1996
employed	5.3	5.7
unemployed	9.8	14.2

Source: Data Eurostat e Istat; our reelaboration.

2.2.1.4 Utilisation of health services

No data on this subject could be found in the empirical research examined. However, the paper by Figà-Talamanca and Pagano (1987) reports a poorer health status among unemployed people in general: this is true both for "objective" diseases (diagnosed by a doctor) and for the subjective perception of one's own health. An extrapolation of this data to young persons, however, is questionable.

2.2.2 Subjective health indicators

2.2.2.1 Psychosocial strains

Although not all instruments used within the different studies are able to grasp the issue of psychosocial strain, some of the empirical research shows a condition of psychosocial strain among young unemployed people. Crepet et al. (1992), for example, found out that the unemployment condition does not seem to be correlated with higher scores of feelings of general *discomfort.* One of the reasons mentioned by the authors for this is that the *uneasiness* correlated with such a condition tends to express itself "in forms less traditionally symptomatic", and that it is, therefore, less measurable by the scales used for the survey. However data from the *Hopelessness* Scale show extremely high scores among the young unemployed in comparison with their peers. A clear condition of discomfort in the perception of their future among unemployed youth could be denoted, resulting in the tendency to social apathy and decrease of efforts to improve one's own future. The risk such a loss of hope involves is the self-fulfilling prophecy of such feelings "with a final consequence of a passive adaptation without any inner conflicts (i.e., with an apparent psychophysical balance) towards a chronic condition of marginality" (Crepet et al., 1992, p. 51). The study of Vetrone et al. (1992) among 400 young people could also show that more hopelessness was found among the unemployed, even if occupational status seemed not to be a factor determining uneasiness.

The study by Sarchielli et al. (1991) with 416 unemployed adolescents showed that the absence of employment is "a situation of potential psychosocial stress" especially in the case that the subject thinks that he or she has not enough personal resources available to cope with the requirements of such a live event. Thus the level of individual strain is determined by an interaction of the difficulty and the complexity of the stressor unemployment with the coping resources of the individual affected. The highest psychological costs are paid when the persons have only scarce resources and the environmental demand is particularly strong (p.188).

2.2.2.2 *Subjective well-being*

The research on subjective well-being shows different results. Following the results from a review of national and international literature (Crepet, 1990, p. 139) it can be concluded that – even if the different authors do not completely agree – the condition of unemployment is not necessarily linked to a high 'risk' of *depressive* symptoms for the affected young person. It is not so much the unemployment that causes mental diseases and depressive symptomatology among young people as it is the occupation which tends to mitigate it. This latter consideration is also confirmed by the longitudinal study conducted by Depolo et al. (1992) where a significantly better psychological well-being of young people previously unemployed and now stably empolyed could be reported. At the same time the survey shows: a) an absence of any modification for what concerns the state of well-being in the persons who have found irregular or occasional jobs; b) a stabilisation of the conditions of uneasiness in the persons still without a job.

The study by Sarchielli et al. (1991) states that persons more exposed in terms of psychological *well-being* are those who perceive having scarce possibilities for themselves to turn to "psychosocial support resources" (social network of friends, family, and reference persons) and who have "a lower self-esteem (also in comparison with other social groups)". These results are opposed in the study by Grassi et al. (1992) who compared the psychological conditions of a group of young metalworkers with that of a group of young unemployed persons. Higher scores for the indicators of psychological uneasiness were detected only for the first group of persons. The researchers concluded that "the unemployment condition seems to be lived in terms not particularly negative for what concerns the mental balance and the risks for mental health – especially when compared with dangerous and distressing work." (p. 150).

2.2.2.3 *Self-esteem*

Despite a general agreement found in the literature about a negative influence of the condition of unemployment on the self-esteem of the affected person, the available surveys in Italy (Crepet et al., 1992; Depolo, et al., 1992; Vetrone et al., 1992) did not report any significant correlation between occupational status and level of self-esteem of young people.

2.2.2.4 *Alienation*

In Italy, no data was found with regard to political alienation.

2.2.2.5 *Social deviation (delinquency)*

In the Italian studies on youth unemployment and health no respective data could be found.

2.2.2.6 *Health behaviour*

No data was found in the studies on youth unemployment and health, but reference can be made to the more general data from Istat. With regard to *smoking* habits, the Istat data (1996) revealed that the percentage of smokers among young people is decreasing. Among the very young between 14-18 years of age, the percentage (8.2%) is only half when compared with that of 17.1% registered in 1991. Under 25 years of age, 24.7% of males and 12% of females are smoking. The percentage of smokers is lower in the

North and Centre of the country, and higher in the South – particularly on the Islands. Such a trend, however, is turned upside down when looking at the disaggregated data of women, who have the highest percentage of smokers in the Centre-North. With regard to occupational condition, the highest percentages of smokers are among the employed and the people seeking a job (see Table 7).

Also the empirical research on youth condition, lifestyles, and health seems to confirm the wide awareness of the risks connected with smoking habits with the result that, in Italy, since the beginning of the 80s, the smoking habit has progressively decreased (Buzzi, 1994, p. 87[9]). However, the risk distribution is still irregular without being correlated to the family's social class and cultural level in a linear way. Of importance seems to be especially the level of education with those who have only a primary school degree (about 47% of the male population) showing 59% of deaths imputable to social inequality in relation to smoking (Ponti & Faggiano, 1994, p. 194). The link between unemployment and smoking habits, however, has not been clarified.

Table I-7: Active smokers between ages 14 – 34 years (ratio for 100 persons of the same age, condition)

	Males		Females		Males and Females	
	1993	1994	1993	1994	1993	1994
Employed	41.1	40.5	23.9	24.5	34.4	34.2
Seeking job	40.8	40.0	20.7	20.1	31.8	30.6
Other condition	15.9	16.5	14.0	13.9	14.7	14.9

Source*:* Istat, 1996.

Regarding *alcohol use* and *drug consumption*, Buzzi (1994, p. 97) underlined the modest consistency of the drinking habits of young people. Drinking habits are correlated with an increase in age and male sex. Other variables affecting the phenomenon seem to belong to the working class and low cultural level. The Iard research (Buzzi, 1994, p. 101) could show that a risk for abuse exists also in the world of youth: Only 40.3% have never gotten drunk, and 30.8% have been in that condition several times. However, the profile of those who seem to fall in this last condition of greater risk – mostly males living in the northern-central regions, belonging to upper-middle class, with a good cultural background in their family of origin – does not refer to situations of marginality but chiefly to young people with indubitable elitist characteristics. A similar profile can be found for young persons who are more at risk for taking drugs: These are in particular males in metropolitan areas coming from upper classes. All in all, a clear and direct link between unemployment and alcohol consumption/drug abuse among young unemployed persons cannot be revealed from the data outlined above.

9 This is the most extensive study on the correlation between youth condition and health. The research, carried out on a sample of 1,250 persons between 16 and 30 years of age in the whole of Italy, has been realised through a structured questionnaire with 69 questions (five on basic data) concerning the conceptions of health, illness, sanitary and pharmaceutics information, health condition, prevention, sanitary attitudes and behaviours; and also expectations for the future.

2.2.3 *Mediators (demographic variables)*

2.2.3.1 *Age*

The two surveys, from Crepet et al. (1992) and Grassi et al.(1992), show that differences of age do not seem to be significantly associated with the psychosocial status of young persons. In their analysis of more general statistical data, Figà-Talamanca and Pagano (1987) found out that pathological excess is more evident in the subgroup aged 40-60 years. Sarchielli et al. (1991) reported that this variable is significant only if associated with other issues (see Section 2.2.4.1).

2.2.3.2 *Gender*

In general, some of the studies show differences between psychological well-being of males and females. In their survey conducted among young persons in the city of Foggia (Southern Italy), Crepet et al. (1992) found that the average scores of the General Health Questionnaire were higher than those in similar surveys carried out in other countries. This might be due to the more difficult situation for young persons in a Southern Italian city. In particular, the survey stressed a greater significance of the gender variable in comparison with age and also occupational condition. The female sample scored systematically higher for *depression*, *somatic symptoms*, *anxiety*, *hostility*, *loss of hope*, and *self-esteem* (Beck's test, Fava's and Kelener's Symptom Questionnaire) (p. 52). The replication of this survey in the city of Sienna by Grassi et al., (1992) could show the same results. However, for both surveys, the absence of a correlation between these high scores of psychological well-being and occupational status has to be underlined. Also the review of general statistical data from Figà-Talamanca and Pagano (1987) confirms a higher presence of both subjective and objective health complaints for women.

2.2.3.3 *Education*

Sarchielli et al. (1991, p. 190) underlined that "educational path, gender, or residential area (...) have given rather limited explanations" for the understanding of the psychological costs faced by young unemployed persons. In general, the school variable has shown to act as a reinforcement of other factors – especially with regard to the availability of psychosocial resources: Young persons who have only few psychosocial resources available show a lower level of psychosocial well-being. This relation is reinforced in less educated young unemployed persons. At the same time, a successful school history seems to increase the psychological well-being of the affected person – however, only in cases where psychosocial resources are also available: "The school history alone does not modify GHQ results" (p. 179).

2.2.3.4 *Social class*

No data was found with regard to the link between unemployment, health, and social class.

2.2.3.5 *Length of unemployment*

Sarchielli et al. (1991, p. 189) reported that, within their research, no relation between length of unemployment and level of psychological well-being among young persons could be found.

2.2.4 *Moderators*

2.2.4.1 *Work orientation*

The hypothesis of a relation between work commitment and psychological well-being could be confirmed by Sarchielli et al. (1991, p. 131 and p. 167). In case of a condition of unemployment, a higher level of work commitment was linked to lower levels of psychological *well-being*. The researchers also found that this relation was different with regard to the age of the affected young persons, with the younger sample (17-19 years of age) showing an influence on the psychological well-being by their work commitment. This relation was not present in the older sample (22-24 years of age) of unemployed youth.

2.2.4.2 *Financial strain/stress*

In Italy, the available studies did not report any results on financial strain/stress.

2.2.4.3 *Social support*

Sarchielli et al. (1991) identified four aspects which they called "indicators for psycho-social resources". These indicators are a significant variable in predicting the capability of facing a situation of unemployment including the level of psychological well-being of the affected youth. Interestingly, results revealed that young persons pay lower psychological costs with regard to the condition of unemployment in case of

- a sustaining person giving support in moments of difficulties;
- a good family atmosphere according to their own definition of the young unemployed;
- a group of friends which, at least, exists in general;
- an absence of pressure both by parents and friends in finding a job.

3 Summary of results

From the empirical research in Italy on youth unemployment and health, the following conclusions can be drawn:

- the condition of unemployment in general seems to be clearly associated with worse conditions of health and with higher morbidity/mortality rates;
- some statistical data analyses show that this association is particularly evident among young people seeking their first job – especially when considering the result that, among this group of people, an excess of 50% death risk exists;
- therefore, it has to be stressed that questions about the nature and the direction of these correlations – that is, does unemployment cause a deterioration of health or is unemployment caused by ill health? – still remains unclarified.

The studies dealing with the target group of this research project have focussed more on the psychosocial effects of unemployment than on its objective health effects. As far as this issue is concerned it can be underlined that:

- even if not confirmed by all research studies, youth unemployment seems to be associated with a condition of psychosocial uneasiness; in particular, young unemployed persons show a clear discomfort in the perception of their own future, reporting more hopelessness leading to a passive adaptation towards a condition of exclusion;

- some variables, such as gender (females often report higher scores in tests on depression, loss of hope, and self-esteem; even if these findings are not correlated to the unemployment condition) and work involvement (unemployed young persons with high work commitment show lower levels of psychological well-being) influence this association; although education is an important aspect, the educational level alone does not affect the health of the unemployed young person; however, it tends to reinforce other factors;
- as it will be discussed afterwards, social support both from family and friends is an important factor in determining the capabilities and strategies of coping with the unemployment condition; and therefore, it strongly influences the psychological costs young people experience in this unfavourable situation.

Interestingly, the results on the state of uneasiness from the surveys carried out in the course of the research described in the summary table (see annex) showed a more important correlation with gender (greater presence of uneasiness indicators for women apart from the occupational status) or with the quality of work (low quality jobs, that are, particularly stressing, repetitive, or incongruent with the persons' expectations show a certain association with uneasiness indicators) rather than with the unemployment situation in itself. Many explanations have been give for a meaningful interpretation. Among these, especially the following four have to be looked at more closely:

1. The chronic depression of the economy (e.g., in some parts of the South) might cause "the condition that unemployment no longer represents (...) either a social stigma or a weakening factor of self-esteem" (Crepet et al., 1992, p. 52 f.).
2. The prolonged cohabitation of the young with the family in Italy as compared to the countries of Northern Europe might allow "to soften the negative effects of unemployment, both on the actual and self-esteem level" (ibid., p.53).
3. However, it has to be taken into consideration that youth uneasiness associated with unemployment might assume forms and expressions (extreme poverty, micro-criminality) not detectable through the research instruments used during these studies.
4. Finally, it is important to bear in mind that, despite the fact, that no great clarity on the effects of unemployment emerge from the respective research, the reason for this result might as well depend upon a simple and trivial reason: the age of the target group. Being young does not involve, by itself, relevant pathological risks, and it seems that only through following a young unemployed person for a long time could we understand and better evaluate the causes of the emerging symptomatology (Crepet, 1990, p. 144).

Therefore, it is relevant to consider that the event of unemployment in the investigated youth context is not a total catastrophe involving every aspect of the persons' life: There are areas of the individual life – such as the planning stage, serenity, family relationships – particularly affected by the negative effects of unemployment. But alongside these, there are life spaces – such as leisure time, physical health, friendships – which are not necessarily 'exposed' in the same way to these effects (see the conclusion of Sarchielli et al., 1991, p. 184 f.). In this regard, the studies on youth condition have shown (Buzzi, 1994,) that young people demonstrate a great dissatisfaction with those difficulties that make them prolong the juvenile phase, and it is not without importance that "the level of dissatisfaction among young people in the South and on the Islands

(23.1%) is therefore higher when compared to young people who live in the northern regions (9.9%)" (ibid., p. 58 f.). It has, moreover, been pointed out that, apart from diseases or a difficult situation in the family, "the youth depression does not seem to be disjointed from the difficulties to enter the labour market, the failures followed once entered, and the traumatic impact with the first job" (ibid., p.65). At the same time it has to be stressed that the proximity of the risk cannot automatically be associated with these factors due to the fact that they can be found across different social, cultural, and economic conditions of young people.

"The acceptability of the risk (...) assumes an eminently cultural value": according to this, behaviours which accept a high risk must not be considered so much as "an effect of individual pathology, but rather as the product of a recent evolution of youth condition." (ibid., p. 152). Taking into consideration such facets of the social environment, it is necessary to bear in mind Sarchielli's (1995) suggestion to a "differential approach". Such an approach means avoiding "inappropriate and mechanistic generalisations" on the correlation between unemployment and social marginality while, instead, singling out the different articulations of the risk through which such a correlation effectively realises itself within the different social groups which experience unemployment. It succeeds in focussing on aspects "in which personal and social conditions lead to the point of producing noticeable effects on the decay of capabilities, behaviours, and self-representation of people without work". Therefore, the orientation we intend to take on further studies on this subject is to widen the focus and to approach further articulations and peculiarities on the relation between youth unemployment and health.

Youth unemployment and health: Italian studies – an overview

Author	Sample	Instruments/ Methods	Population	Dependent variables	Results
Fraccaroli (1989)	N = 416	work involvement survey	– 17-19 years with compulsory school degree – 22-24 years with secondary school degree – 2 areas of Northern Italy	– ideology: relations of work involvement with the image of work or unemployment, and with different work and school experiences	– relation between work involvement and other representational factors such as the image of ideal work and the image of social-psychological effects of unemployment – leading to a representational interpretation of work involvement – different school experiences lead to variation in work orientation, whereas work history and labour market position do not appear to influence work orientation
Sarchielli, Depolo, Fraccaroli, Colasanto (1991)	N = 416, of which: urban population with large-scale industry (n = 320) rural population with small enterprises (n = 96)	Interview through semi-structured questionnaire and General Health Questionnaire	– 17-19 years with compulsory school degree – 22-24 years with secondary school degree – 2 areas of Northern Italy	– psychological state – cognitive and social strategies	– collocation of interviewees on the basis of the GHQ score in a position of low psychological well-being seems to confirm the general assumption about the problematic nature of their condition – experience of unemployment is not interpreted as a catastrophe – attitude of worry for the threatening aspect of such condition prevails; depending on the social and family situation this is articulated in a different way – importance of psychosocial resources in reducing some of the psychological costs of the lack of occupation becomes evident

Author	Sample	Instruments/ Methods	Population	Dependent variables	Results
Crepet, Vetrone, Piazzi, Costa, Lomardi (1992)	N = 379	semi-structured interview Beck Depression Scale GHQ – Goldberg Fava and Kellner Symptom Check List Rosenberg Self Esteem Scale Inni Bille-Brahe Social Support Scale Beck Hopelessness Scale	– 18-26 years – 204 females 175 males – secondary school degree – medium size town in Southern Italy – economically weak area	– psycho-physiological state of young people – relation between psychopathological parameters and occupational state	– diffuse psychological uneasiness among young age classes – moreover, the results partially disappointed the expectations, especially as to the correlation between occupation and depression: this may depend on the fact that Italian young people almost always continue to live with their parents, on whom they often depend economically – significant differences in all psychometric values considered between males and females; however the statistical value of data on females is lost when analysing for occupation according to occupational condition; the data may rather indicate a diffuse discomfort of female identity
Vetrone, Crepet, Costa, Piazzi, Di Tommaso, Ferrara, Petrangeli, Frighi (1992)	N = 400	semi-structured interview Beck Depression Scale GHQ – Goldberg Fava and Kellner Symptom Check List Rosenberg Self Esteem Scale Inni Bille-Brahe Social Support Scale Beck Hopelessness Scale	– 147 males 253 females – secondary school degree – medium sized town in the centre of Italy – economically strong area	– psycho-physiological state of young people – relation between psychopathological parameters and occupational status	such as previous study: – diffuse psychological uneasiness among young age groups – higher psychological uneasiness among women, strictly associated with the general problems of the female condition – occupational status instead does not appear as a factor determining psychological uneasiness, although more hopelessness was found among the unemployed

Author	Sample	Instruments/ Methods	Population	Dependent variables	Results
Grassi, Falzoni, Fasoli (1992)	N = 127 (selected from the beneficiaries of the National Health Service): metalworkers exposed to occupational mental health risks (n = 30) metal workers not exposed (n = 57) young unemployed (at least 6 months or seeking first job (n = 40)	questionnaire	– 20-29 – only males – small city in economically strong area – living with their family	– mental health in relation to different occupational positions and unemployment	– significant higher frequencies and averages only in the group of metalworkers exposed to mental health risks
Depolo, Fraccaroli, Sarchielli (1992)	N = 115; of the sample study Sarchielli et al (1991): interviewed 18 months after the first research, and now in a different occupational status	psychosocial resources self-collocation economic availability social relations; psychological well-being self-esteem GHQ 12	– 17-19 years + compulsory school degree – 22-24 years + secondary school degree – 2 areas of north Italy	– cognitive strategies of self-constitution – psychological well-being	– getting a job does not necessarily imply an improvement in psychological well-being (no improvement was found for subjects holding jobs not consistent with their expectations, and/or non permanent)

Youth Unemployment and Health in Spain

Louis Lemkow & Josep Espluga

1 Introduction to youth unemployment and health

1.1 National development of youth unemployment

1.1.1 Unemployment in general

In Spain, the past three decades have seen several periods of recession and economic recovery, and the strong influence of these recessions on the development of employment and unemployment as well as on the overall composition of the labour market are clearly visible.

Table SP-1: General unemployment rates (all ages) by gender (1970-1998)

	1970	1975	1980	1985	1990	1995	1998
Total	1.2	3.4	11.2	22.1	16.7	23.5	19.6
Men	1.3	3.4	10.6	20.8	12.5	18.7	14.9
Women	0.9	3.2	12.6	24.8	24.8	31.4	27.0

Source: EPA, first quarters and corrected series.

For most of the period between 1970-1977 the unemployment rate was fairly low, although in 1976 and 1977 it had already begun to increase notably. In the period from 1977 to 1985 there was a severe recession and large-scale job deterioration. At the same time, the active population continued to grow as a result of the arrival of the generations born during the 1960s baby boom to the labour market. These two developments resulted in a spectacular increase in unemployment. The deterioration of employment mainly affected permanent jobs which, despite the subsequent creation of employment in the following years, were never recovered as they were replaced with temporary and highly unstable jobs. The incorporation of women into the labour market was considerable during these years and, despite the fact that it is still not complete, would be a highly relevant phenomenon for interpreting the Spanish labour market. With all these changes the economic structure of Spain drifted progressively towards the tertiary or service sector.

In 1984 the Employees' Charter was reformed, thus allowing greater flexibility of the labour market and encouraging temporary contracts. As a result, an important change took place in the structure and composition of the labour force and the labour market itself, a change which is fundamental for understanding the subsequent instability for young people. Despite the economic recovery of the period 1985-1991, the growth was highly speculative, based mainly on very unstable service and finance sectors. Between 1991 and 1993 there was a considerable job deterioration which affected all groups and sectors of activity (especially industry). Employment fell and the creation of jobs slowed down. Since the active population continued to grow, this creation of employment did not reduce the unemployment rates. Again unemployment increased immensely – this time exceeding the historic figure of three million unemployed. In 1994 this deterioration of jobs slowed slightly with the increase in productive activity, although this was not sufficient to generate a net increase in employment. In 1994 the government promoted a reform of labour policies and introduced different forms of temporary hiring (different training contracts, temporary employment agencies, etc.) with the underlying argument of facilitating youth employment. With this reform, however, the likelihood of instability for the newly employed increased considerably. The dynamic of the labour market was linked to a process of segmentation of workers and hampered the entry of young people into employment.

From 1996 onwards there has been a recovery in economic activity in general, and the recession has begun to recede. The global figure for unemployment has fallen especially since 1997. However, as the active population has continued to increase, unemployment remains above 3,000,000. In 1997 a new reform of the labour legislation was approved which establishes measures for minimally stabilising employment.

1.1.2 Youth unemployment

Since 1974 youth unemployment has begun to reach worrying levels much higher than the general unemployment rates. The increase in unemployment for all ages and genders recorded on a global level was also reflected among the younger population with markedly higher initial unemployment rates among people of less than 25 years of age. During the period of recession (1977-1985), many young people with a minimum level of formal education attempted to enter the labour market for the first time and stumbled across enormous (and unexpected) difficulties of finding a job.

Table SP-2: Youth unemployment rates by age and gender (1970-1998)

Age and gender	1970	1975	1980	1985	1990	1995	1998
16-19: Men	3.6	10.1	30.7	56.7	32.3	46.6	41.2
16-19: Women	2.0	9.2	35.0	59.7	45.3	57.2	55.6
20-24: Men	1.5	6.0	22.3	42.4	25.5	35.5	28.2
20-24: Women	1.3	4.8	21.0	46.5	39.6	47.4	41.8
25-29: Men	1.0	3.5	12.5	26.1	16.5	25.4	20.1
25-29: Women	0.6	3.1	11.0	28.8	30.6	38.4	31.2

Source: EPA, first quarters.

Despite the sharp increase in employment in the next period (1985-1991), unemployment did not undergo a positive mass development. The reduction in unemployment rates took place in all groups of young people, but especially in those between 16-19 years of age, and was more notable for men than for women. Despite everything, the growth in employment was not sufficient to reduce unemployment drastically. The measures adopted by the social agents to improve this situation were not very energetic since it was assumed that these people (young people) have sufficient family aid and coverage to maintain themselves in the hope of better times. This supposition considerably hindered their access to the labour market since the dynamics of the world of employment gave priority to the entry of 'heads of families', thus creating further dependence among other members of the family (Miguélez & Martín, 1996).

From the second half of 1991 onwards, general unemployment rates have once again increased spectacularly. This increase especially affected young people with female rates being continuously higher than male unemployment rates. Since 1995 there has been a slight but sustained reduction in unemployment rates among young people. However, the 16-19 years of age group has maintained a level of greater than 50% with no downward trend being detected. Again, unemployment rates are higher among young women than young men.

1.1.3 Territorial differences with respect to unemployment

It should be pointed out that unemployment does not affect the different geographical areas of Spain in the same way. The autonomous communities where the general unemployment rates have increased the most are located in the South and West of Spain. These are precisely those areas where the agricultural sector is predominant (Andalusia, Extremadura, Galicia, Murcia, etc.). The autonomous communities where the increases have been the smallest are those where the service and industrial sectors predominate (Madrid, Catalonia, etc.) (Miguélez & Martín, 1996; Plaza, 1994). Nevertheless, there are indications that in the industrialised areas (Catalonia, Basque Country, etc.) unemployment fluctuates more than in rural areas (Andalusia, Extremadura, etc.) where despite being higher, the rates are more stable. Garrido and Toharia (1996) point out that the different unemployment situations in the different Spanish communities are not really comparable because subsidised jobs coexist with unemployment which is not accounted for.

1.2 Unemployment and health – some theoretical considerations

According to the bibliography obtained and the opinion of the experts consulted, the theoretical debate in Spain on the relationship between unemployment and health began in the mid-80s in the area of social psychology and health and, to a lesser extent, medicine. Some doctors and psychologists suspected that the vast increase in unemployment rates in Spain in the late 70s and early 80s must have had some kind of negative effect on the health of unemployed individuals and led to problems in public health in general. The development of the theoretical debate took place mainly in the second half of the 80s, a time when most of the empirical studies on the matter were carried out. In the early 90s, this debate stagnated and the relationship between unemployment and the health of young people became second-rated to new research objectives which appeared on the scene, such as questions of youth identity, the processes of transition from school to work, and unemployment among women, etc. Different factors led the attention of researchers on youth unemployment in the 80s. In Spain during those years, one of the subjects which was a cause for greatest concern in the mind of the public was the growing public perception of the dangers of drug use (the case of heroin being the most dramatic) and the heightened perception of civil insecurity – curiously enough, two problems built around the figure of 'youth'. In this context, unemployment was seen by public and political opinion as the variable which caused all these problems. Because of this, different academic and political institutions made youth unemployment a priority area of research, and many studies on this topic were financed. The impact of the Annual Youth Year encouraged public authorities to organise conferences, events, and meetings, with young people as protagonists in the debate (e.g., Torregrosa, Bergere & Alvaro, 1989). Nevertheless, aspects of youth unemployment related to health did not have a very strong presence in this research context, and the few studies carried out were merely descriptive (cross-sectional design). They were limited to tested hypotheses of studies performed in the English-speaking world and went into no detail when explaining the phenomena.

Generally speaking, it cannot be said that there has been much Spanish contribution to the international debate. In fact, even the most recent studies have imported theories, hypotheses, and research methodologies from the English-speaking bibliography. The studies and reflections of M. Jahoda, M.H. Brenner, P. Warr, R. Catalano, D. Dooley, K. A. Moser, M. H. Banks, and S. Platt are some of the most cited in the Spanish bibliography on unemployment and health in contemporary Spanish society. There are few empirical studies on the relationship between unemployment and health. J. L. Alvaro, J. del Llano, J. M. Blanch, J. R. Torregrossa, V. J. Buendia, A. Rodríguez, and J. M. Peiró are some of these Spanish authors who have carried out most of the research on this subject. There is also another group of authors who touch upon the subject from the perspective of the study of social inequalities (J. M. de Miguel, V. Jimeno, M. A. Durán, J. A. Rodríguez, L. Lemkow, F. J. Benavides, O. Ramis-Juan, etc.).

The basic points accepted in this debate (mainly used in the English-speaking theoretical area) are as follows:

- There is no doubt about the existence of some kind of relationship between unemployment and the deterioration of health, but all have agreed that the nature of this relationship is all but clear. It is considered that the different hypotheses which may provide an answer to this question are not mutually exclusive and that all are partly right.
- There is considered to be sufficient evidence providing support for the idea that unemployment leads to mental health problems. It is thought that among the unemployed there is a greater proportion of depression, psychiatric disorders, and psychosomatic disorders and a greater reduction in self-esteem than among the employed. This point, however, is relative at present since it is considered to be an aspect which is intimately linked with specific social values, and some change in the values scale might reduce (or maybe increase) these mental health problems.
- However, the relationship between unemployment and physical health is not so clearly demonstrated, especially in young people.
- There is a consensus that unemployment increases the probability of premature death and that the unemployed and their families have a higher morbidity, which may lead to greater use of health services. However, there is also evidence that this is not always the case.
- There is a consensus that unemployment leads to a loss of social relations, destructuring of time, changes in lifestyles, and reduced participation in public affairs.

In general, it is thought that the effects of unemployment today have to be understood within the framework of economic transformations which directly affect the labour market. Attitudes have changed from thinking of the labour crisis as a transitory situation to seeing unemployment as a structural problem, making it difficult to think of a near future with full employment. This introduces a cause for concern and a demand for more political attention to the health problems of the unemployed. Nevertheless, over time, this concern seems to have been redefined. The new situation on the labour market with a considerable increase in temporary employment and precariousness (in June 1998, 93 of every 100 new contracts were temporary) means that health problems need to be considered in a broader framework. Some studies have shown that the deterioration of mental health in people with unstable (temporary) employment is similar to that of the unemployed.

Most of the empirical studies carried out in Spain on this subject compare the health of unemployed people with that of employed people and analyse the significance of the correlation. These are normally studies on adults. Research on young people is scarce.

Many approximations in the Spanish literature on the unemployment/youth equation are through a thorough conceptualisation of 'work' – considering that in our society work is, on the one hand, a means of subsistence, a means of access to a series of goods, and, on the other hand, an element of social value, a channel of socialisation and personal realisation. Its consequences for health, therefore, will contain biophysical and psychosocial elements. There is, however, no Spanish author who proposes a single satisfactory model to describe the relationships between health and unemployment. In the Spanish works the functional explanatory model based on M. Jahoda predominates. In addition, the focus is also on studies and theorisation emphasising the interdependence between the individual and the social structure which explain the individual repercussions caused by a social fact (unemployment). Having work creates needs which cannot be satisfied when the individual is unemployed. The consequences of unemployment are interpreted, therefore, by analysing the functions provided by the fact of having work such as facilitating social relations, assigning roles, secondary socialisation, group affiliation, imposition of trans-individual goals, etc. (as well as the obvious functions of financial independence and access to consumption). Unemployment is conceptualised as a social situation and as an individual state. From this perspective, the main consequences of unemployment are psychological, which explains the greater presence of studies on the mental health of the unemployed.

Blanch (1990) warns that most studies emphasise the negative aspects of unemployment while presupposing the importance of the positive aspects of employment. Unemployment appears as the opposite to employment, without any other alternative. In the employment/unemployment system, the only alternative to one is the other. Moreover, this vicious circle inspires the political imperative to resolve the social problem of unemployment via the creation of employment alone.

In criticism of this situation it can be said that the most relevant point with regard to the theoretical debate on unemployment and health in Spain is the incorporation of the variable 'valuation of work', which is defined by the level of centrality work has in the value system of the individual. Some authors (Alvaro, 1989a; Blanch, 1986), inspired by the theories of Warr, indicate the need to add a complementary model which takes into consideration the differences of cognitive styles, values associated with work, and different conducts for dealing with situations, since by means of these elements, individuals can change the social environment in which they live and, therefore, eliminate, minimise or increase the negative consequences of unemployment for health. Other authors (De la Torre, 1989) add that the type of causal ascription which unemployed people make regarding their situation may have important implications which manifest themselves in the psychological effects they suffer.

For this reason, many psychosocial studies dedicate a large part of their efforts to studying the role played by work in people's lives – especially for young people since the moment of entering employment is considered to be a critical moment which can produce multiple psychosocial effects. When studying the unemployment–depression relationship, it can be seen that the prevalence of depression is greater among unemployed young people, but not in a uniform way. The level of depression suffered by certain types of unemployed people is not derived from their status as unemployed (a necessary but not sufficient condition), but from a socio-cognitive factor: the valuation they have learned to give to the importance of work (an intervening variable) with respect to one's personal and social development. Different researchers (Blanch, Alvaro) try to show that the extreme depression of some unemployed people is not so much due to the objective lack of employment, but due to the subjective identity crisis brought on by the perceived contradiction between a cultural end assumed in the process of socialisation (personal and social self-realisation as a working human being) and the social means established for achieving it (the structural deficit of jobs).

One line of research which has also been developed in Spain focusses on the description of the transition processes of young people such as those from school to employment versus to unemployment, etc. (Alvaro & Luque, 1990; Torregrosa et al., 1989; Casal, Masjuan & Planas, 1990; Peiró & Moret, 1987), and on evaluating the impact of different models of transition to active life on the psychological well-being of young people. These studies also include different tests for isolating aspects of health. Usually they have a longitudinal design which makes it possible to explain somewhat more than a simple comparison between employed and unemployed people. In general, the results show that among the unemployed, the level of psychological well-being tends to fall, whereas it tends to improve among the employed. However, it has to be considered that a) there is no homogeneity among young people in the model of transition to active life, b) it is difficult to designate the situations of young people because of the considerable blurring of borders between the situations of employment, inactivity, unemployment, and training, and c) there exist a number of personality variables which means that the same type of transition does not have the same psychological effects (Alvaro & Luque, 1990).

Young unemployed people, as a group, show less deterioration than unemployed people in middle age – a fact which is explained by the different environmental circumstances (financial availability, physical health, social position, etc.) However, it must also be remembered that many young people do not yet have work experiences. This fact suggests to some authors that unemployment among young people is more associated with an inhibition of the psychological development than with a psychological imbalance (García Rodríquez, 1993).

Epidemiological studies with secondary data on a population basis are scarce in Spain due to the lack of systematic, rigorous data. It is barely possible to obtain mortality rates specific to social stratification indicators; nor are the data on morbidity very useful in this matter (Ramis-Juan, 1984). Some interesting studies have been carried out based on data from health surveys (Spanish National Health Survey, Catalan Health Survey, etc.), but no monitoring has been done of systematic yearly series; these are rather cross-sectional, isolated studies with an individual basis (not aggregate).

The cross-sectional comparison between the categories 'unemployed' / 'employed' highlights the poorer quality of life among the unemployed. Contemporary transition towards unemployment is thought to lead to a drop in the general psychological well-being, whereas the transition to employment is often associated with a significant increase in this level. This, however, is influenced by a large number of variables including the duration and quality of the transition process (Blanch, 1990). To check these results it would be necessary to carry out studies with a longitudinal design, but in Spain, as far as we have been able to ascertain, only one study of this type exists.

The psychopathological symptoms detected among the unemployed in Spain are very similar to those described for the unemployed in other countries (Ramis-Juan, 1984). Unemployment is somehow related to immediate and long-term losses (loss of economic income, loss of working skills and of the social relations related to work, fear, isolation, anxiety, desperation, negative self-esteem, physical health problems, mental health problems (De la Torre, 1989), family problems, tension (relations between couples are affected, and tensions are also transferred to children and friends) (Càritas, 1985), breaking of the social temporal rhythm (Càritas, 1985) (work imposes a temporal structure) (Torregrosa, 1982), sense of privatisation of freedom (Càritas, 1985), learned states of attribution and defenselessness (García Rodríguez, 1993), changes in attitudes, interests and values, suicide, etc. Moreover, it has been found that the lack of economic resources may also hinder provision of the necessary food for the normal growth of the children. Undernourishment affects their performance at school (Càritas, 1985).

Although not yet satisfactorily resolved, in relation to these last aspects there is a question of debate among Spanish researchers whether unemployment is the effective cause of all these problems or whether it is a symptom of a more profound problem – *poverty*. Despite the fact that all researchers consider that the variables related to unemployment are complex and that it is not possible to establish direct causal relations, in the commentaries on the results of their research, a tendency can be seen to grant the situation of unemployment more importance than can be derived from the data. The situation of unemployment forms part of a vicious circle where it is difficult to order the different factors causally, and the pathological effects associated with this situation must be studied through multiple mediating and moderating variables including the poverty factor.

As regards the proposals for dealing with the unhealthy situations associated with youth unemployment, the usual course of action is to think of interventions by means of employment policies. However, if – as has been mentioned – it may be considered that the main disorders associated with unemployment are those of mental health, and these are a function of the type of values associated with work and the type of cognition regarding the real situation of unemployment, other measures seem to be needed. Since it is assumed that in the future it will not be possible to think of a society with full employment, in order to combat the negative effects associated with unemployment it will be necessary to do as much as possible to reduce the value placed on work as the main path for social integration. This will mean redefining the concepts of 'work', 'employment', and 'unemployment' in order to change the social image they currently enjoy and to offer a more optimistic vision of the world, susceptible to change.

With the generalisation of this idea, the theoretical debate on the relationships between unemployment and health, especially in the case of young people, has moved to a broader sphere based on the reconceptualisation of work and of the meaning of life for the individual in a complex, global, reflexive society which is constantly moving away from the parameters of traditional, industrial society.

1.2.1 Definition of young person, unemployment, and health

With regard to the concept of 'young person', the Spanish bibliography on youth contains a predominance of conceptions based on 'productive' parameters, that is, young people are defined according to their productive capacities and functions within the theoretical perspective of the 'social division of work'. The production crises which have occurred in the past two or three decades are essential elements for explaining the current definition of 'young person', since it is considered that these crises have abruptly transformed the functions assigned to each generation. As a result, certain generation groups have become displaced and lose the place they once had reserved within the social fabric (INJUVE, 1997). The groups with social integration problems are fundamentally 'young people' and the 'elderly'.

Most of the bibliography on youth unemployment assumes a functional conception oriented towards the value of work for organising society. It is assumed that in the past, labour integration was a passage that took place mainly through employment but that today, it is a process of transition in various forms codified as active life: employment, unemployment, and training. In the early 70s in Spain, integration in active life generally took place without any abrupt leaps and each person, according to the social capital obtained, achieved labour recognition without any great delay (Roquero, 1995, p. 9). Analyses of social integration in the 70s used an age interval to limit the different stages of a social process: Childhood was linked to school which, together with the family, formed the basic element of socialisation; youth, as a transition stage to adult life, identified the passage from dependency to autonomy. In these social identities, the biological process through the different ages tended to coincide with the established social temporalisations: The first socialising instances had effect until 14-16 years of age for most of the population, giving way to the autonomy of the adult state via labour integration from these ages (although the established stages also allowed for more or less heterogeneity by age groups due to other stratification elements such as social background, level of education, area of residence, etc.). The social function attributed to 'young people', understood as a time of passage towards adult autonomy, has moved increasingly further away from fixed limits established by age, as the difficulties involved in obtaining or maintaining a dwelling and a family are not exclusive to any age group. The fragility of employment has increased this age limit to the point where it now includes two groups traditionally considered to be adults.

The empirical studies on youth unemployment and health in Spain use different temporal limits for the category of 'youth'. Hence, Blanch (1986, 1990) and Alvaro (1989a) take the limits to be 16-25 years of age, whereas Blanch (1989) considers young people as being between 16 and 30 years of age. Other authors, such as Rodríguez and García (1989) and Alvaro and Garrido (1990) build their samples of young people using students who have just finished university or secondary education. This latter approach includes something more than mere age limits: A young person is a person in the transition stage.

In general, these authors tend to consider 'youth' as a homogeneous group when compared with adults. In practice, however, it is difficult to define a barrier which makes it possible to establish a clear difference between the two groups. Different studies clearly show that the category 'youth' does not represent a homogeneous group of people (Casal, Masjuan & Planas, 1990; Martín, 1998), but a group with a high level of heterogeneity, especially when taking into consideration the variable 'social class'. Furthermore, the paths of social integration themselves are changing the perception of the temporary nature linked to the category of youth. The diversity of options which currently exists between school and activity include education, unemployment, temporary work, vocational training courses, long-term unemployment, etc., and there is no determinable heterogeneity in either time or permanence of any of these instances or in the order of these instances for the entire group of young people. This questions the possibility of establishing an age limit for the time of passage towards acknowledgement of adult status, since the diversity of ages affected by this instability is not parallel to the situations defined by demographic or biological criteria.

Analysis of the passage from dependence to autonomy, although traditionally coinciding with age delimitation, has made use of these limits without taking the internal heterogeneity due to their class differences into consideration. To think that age produces a homogeneous group is a reductionistic concept since factors related to the position occupied within the social structure are more relevant (without falling into the trap of absolute determinism) than biological time (Roquero, 1995; Martín, 1998).

The concept of 'unemployment' also provides different possibilities in terms of conceptualisation in Spain. Beginning with the official definitions there is considerable disparity between the two main sources of secondary data on unemployment: the Employment Statistics, published monthly by the National Employment Institute (INEM), and the Active Population Survey (EPA), published quarterly by the National Institute of Statistics (INE).

The INEM prepares a monthly registered unemployment indicator based on the number of monthly job requests and placements and this is calculated according to the formula: registered unemployment = 'job requests pending' minus 'individuals of nonunemployed groups'. 'Job requests pending' are taken as those who, on the closing day for the statistics, have not found employment. From this figure the number of job seekers that are catalogued by the INEM as 'nonunemployed groups' are subtracted for statistical purposes. The criteria for deciding which groups fall under this heading of nonunemployed groups have changed over time and today include the following:

- employees affected by employment regulation (those who have lost their job due to the collapse of an enterprise, and therefore receiving benefits)
- students
- employees employed in community work
- retired people
- people seeking work at home
- people seeking interim employment
- people seeking part-time employment
- people seeking work abroad
- casual subsidised agricultural labourers
- people suffering from transitory disability
- military service
- those registered as a requisite for selection for a job
- subsidised individuals participating in social collaborations
- people with total disability pensions
- people with extreme disability pensions
- job seekers over 65 years of age who need to continue working due to insufficient years of social security contribution.

The exclusion of these groups from the definition of unemployment implies a restriction on those seeking employment who voluntarily register with the employment offices. Furthermore, since registration is voluntary, this indicator does not cover the 'discouraged', that is, those who are not motivated to register with the INEM, thus producing a greater underestimation of unemployment figures.

The Active Population Survey (EPA) is an ongoing survey which is published quarterly and which offers information on the basic characteristics of active and inactive people. The population covered by the survey includes people from 16 years of age upwards (from 14 before 1980) living in family homes. The size of the sample is 62,000 people and the area included is the entire Spanish territory. Over time, this survey has undergone considerable methodological changes, the most important of which, regarding unemployment, took place in the second quarter of 1987. From this date, the 'unemployed' are considered to be those individuals who, in the week in question (week of the survey), were without employment, seeking work with specific measures during the previous month, and available for work in the two weeks following the interview.

Explicit exclusion is maintained by those who classify themselves as unemployed but who are not seeking work. The innovation introduced by the EPA in 1987 offers qualifications regarding whether the search for work takes place before or during the month preceding the survey. This distinction serves to delimit the 'unemployed' from the 'discouraged' and to be able to consider everyone who has sought work in the previous month as unemployed, whereas those who have not done so are considered as inactive (such as retired people, students, the disabled, etc.). Considering those who are 'discouraged' with seeking work as part of the 'inactive population' poses serious doubts since it is probable that given a more favourable employment situation these people would suppress their 'discouragement' and put their potential for activity into action. Roquero (1995) states that these people include in their reasons for not seeking work the "belief that they won't find work", "not knowing where to look", "waiting for the results of previous applications", "being affected by regulation of employment", "waiting for the season of greater activity to start looking" and "waiting to recommence an activity on their own account that they cannot currently do due to lack of production resources" (p. 89). For this author, it is paradoxical, to say the least, that these reasons provide justification for the INEM for including these people among the inactive population. Furthermore, changes in the segmentation of the labour market have produced an increase in borderline situations between activity and inactivity, making them so complex that the EPA cannot account for them.

In summary, regarding the official definitions of unemployment, the EPA considers unemployed people to be those who do not have work and who state that they are seeking employment, whereas the employment statistics place more stock on the voluntary census of job seekers. Logically, because of the different concepts and procedures in obtaining data, the differences between one source and the other are considerable.

In the empirical studies found on youth unemployment and health, the following concepts appear:

Blanch (1986, 1989, 1990) uses highly restrictive definitions, searching for almost ideal types:

- *Unemployed*: "person who, whether or not previously employed, is unemployed, seeking employment and has been registered as a *job seeker* in an employment office of the INEM for at least six months";
- *Employed*: "person who, for at least six months, has been living off the income obtained for carrying out a professional activity full time, with a work contract and affiliated with the social security";
- *Student*: "person identifying themselves as such and remaining 'inactive' in terms of employment due to dedicating a considerable part of their time and effort to studying".

On the other hand, Alvaro, in order to include in the sample the discouraged, those who, due to the lack of employment, do not register with the INEM (Alvaro, 1989a), considers the unemployed to be "all those who do not have a job and who want to have one" (in the line of work of Jahoda). Other authors, such as Rodriguez and García (1989) and Alvaro and Garrido (1990) consider the unemployed in their studies to be young people with secondary or higher educational qualifications who have not yet taken up their first employment. Evidently, these authors carry out studies on the transitional aspects of young people from school to work activity or unemployment.

The concept of 'health' is one of the most difficult to define due to its social and cultural relativity, despite the fact that some objective and subjective indicators can be identified to construct it. In the studies presented here on youth unemployment and health, when health is talked about it refers almost exclusively to mental health, expressed as psychological well-being which can be measured subjectively by means of different scales and questionnaires. The most commonly used questionnaire seems to be the Goldberg General Health Questionnaire (GHQ). There is no reference to biophysical health disorders in these studies and almost none in the studies found on unemployment and health in general. Only del Llano (1990) makes some marginal reference to biophysical health indicators in his research.

2 Analysis of research on youth unemployment and health

2.1 Description of the available data (design and methods)

After reviewing different Spanish bibliographical sources on unemployment and health, it has been found that there are very few references to empirical studies devoted specifically to young people. To search for this information, the bibliographical databases of the Autonomous University of Barcelona, Pompeu Fabra University, the University of Barcelona, the National Centre of Labour Conditions, and the Department of Health and the Department of Labour of the Catalan Autonomous Government were used, as well as examining the contents of social science and medical journals (Revista Española de Investigaciones Sociológicas, Psicología del Trabajo y las Organizaciones, Revista de Sociología del Trabajo, Gaceta Sanitaria, etc.). Experts were also contacted from the Department of Sociology and the Department of Social Psychology and Health of the Autonomous University of Barcelona, the School of Social Studies of the University of Zaragoza, the School of Social Work of the University of Valencia, the National Institute of Safety and Hygiene in the Workplace, and the Municipal Health Institute of Barcelona.

In total, 17 empirical studies were found on unemployment and health, of which only six took people aged between the limits proposed in this paper (16-29 years of age) as their sample. Five of these studies have a cross-sectional design and the relationships between the variables are not causal in any of the cases. The six studies on youth unemployment and health can be classified and described as follows:

2.1.1 Cross-sectional studies

The study by Blanch (1986), a questionnaire with 93 items included questions on sociodemographic data and scales on cognitive styles and on the depressive syndrome. The sample was composed of 200 subjects between 16 and 25 years of age residing in the Barcelona metropolitan area, stratified by their employment situation in three categories: employed, unemployed, and students. The unemployed were divided into young people who lost their jobs and young people who have not yet been employed. The dependent variable was the level of depression of the individuals as measured by the CQ and BDI (Cognition Questionnaire and Beck Depression Inventory, respectively). It is a design which considers the possible reciprocal interaction of socio-economic circumstances, representational keys of an ideological nature, and cognitive-affective-motivational experiences in the production of the depressive effect. However, the author makes it quite clear that this relationship is not mechanistic. It is not possible to speak of a causal direction, but merely a correlation between variables. All in all, the study confirms the hypothesis regarding a significant difference between the different labour statuses with respect to the level of depression. The unemployed group is the most severely affected by depressive disorders, whereas the employed group is the least affected. However, the differentiation among the unemployed themselves is shown in accordance with the evaluational representation of work and employment. That is, the level of depression suffered by a given type of unemployed person does not derive so much from their situation as unemployed as from a socio-cognitive factor: the value they have learned to place on the importance of work with regard to one's personal and social development (and the consequent attraction they have come to experience towards professional self-realisation through employment). Thus, some unemployed people suffer excessive depression which does not derive so much from the objective lack of work, but from a subjective identity crisis caused by the perceived contradiction between an assumed cultural end in the process of socialisation (personal and social self-realisation as a working human being) and the socially established means for achieving it (structural deficit of jobs).

This study from Blanch (1989) was carried out in three phases. During the first phase, a three-hour meeting was held with 17 young unemployed people of both sexes living in the Barcelona metropolitan area. The first two hours were devoted to discussing the problems of unemployment, where the researcher handled the independent variables, 'discussion topic' and 'orientation of the debate'. Originally, the idea was to hold two more meetings, but due to problems in locating the people in the sample, only one meeting was held, which – according to the author – was a failed experiment though not totally useless as it provided ideas for the subsequent phases. In the second phase, a questionnaire was handed out to 150 individuals between 16 and 30 years of age, of both sexes, unemployed, and residing in the Barcelona metropolitan area. The main independent variable consisted of a 'text' which adopted two different ideological forms, one in favour of work and another against it. The questionnaire included questions that aimed at evaluating this text. Each subject was randomly given one form of the text. The dependent variable was 'ideology' (with respect to work, employment, and unemployment). There were also questions on 'reference group' (another independent variable), and the CQ, BDI, and Rathus questionnaires were included to evaluate the dependent variable 'emotional state' (assertiveness in Rathus depression in BDI and CQ, (1983). During the third phase, the part of the questionnaire referring to the independent variable 'type of text' and the dependent variable 'ideology' was handed out to another group of 250 young people of both sexes studying psychology and social work, subject to the same experimental conditions. The results of the study could show that unemployment as a socio-economic circumstance leads, in this place and at that time, to a significant deficit of quality of life in terms of basic depression. Furthermore, specific types of ideological messages which are present in daily life in the media and in public opinion have a reinforcing effect on the clichés of the work culture (centrality of productive activity, positive value of employment, stigma of unemployment, etc.) and lead to a particular deficit of psychological resources in the unemployed person.

In the study by Alvaro (1989a), questionnaires were given to 232 young people aged between 16-26 years, residing in Madrid. 105 persons were employed (59 women and 44 men) and 127 were unemployed (66 men and 61 women). The questionnaire included questions on socio-demographic variables, description of the activity carried out (the employed), personal involvement in work (centrality of work), and mental health (Goldberg GHQ-12). The unemployed people in the sample were stratified in four groups according to the duration of unemployment (1-3 months, 3-6 months, 6-12 months, and more than 12 months). 56% of the sample had been unemployed for more than 12 months and the author considered 'unemployed' to include all those who did not have a job but who would like to have one (independent of whether they are officially registered as unemployed or not). The dependent variable was the psychological well-being of the individual (mental health) as measured by the GHQ. The variables sex, level of education, employment situation of the head of the family, family income, duration of unemployment, and value or centrality attributed to work are also taken into account. All in all, the unemployed group obtained higher scores on the GHQ than the employed group. These differences were statistically significant. No significant differences, however, were observed by sex or level of education. Significant differences were observed according to the employment situation of the head of the family: young people in families where the head is unemployed showed poorer psychological well-being than those in families where the head is employed. The author attempts to explain this by arguing that the change in status and in the exercise of authority can lead to tensions within the family and affect the psychological well-being of its members. There is also a significant association between family income and psychological well-being: the better the family's economic situation, the better the young person's psychological well-being. However, it is also clear that young unemployed people present poorer psychological well-being than young employed people regardless of the level of family income. It was found that 33% of employed and 60% of unemployed young people are at risk of suffering mild (nonpsychotic) psychological disorders. Interestingly, the duration of unemployment did not significantly affect mental health. Finally, the more unemployed young people attributed centrality or a positive value to work, the greater their mental health deterioration was. However, among the unemployed young people, lower centrality of work did not correspond to a significant increase in psychological well-being.

In Rodríguez and García's (1989) study, a questionnaire was handed out to 438 individuals, stratified in the following manner: 208 men and 230 women; 293 young people with university degrees who had not yet taken up their first job and 145 employed professionals with secondary or higher education (as a control group). Age was not given, but it was assumed that the young university graduates were between the age of 21-29 years. The questionnaire included socio-demographic questions, a scale of attitudes on 14 values, an A and B personality questionnaire (Bortner), and the 12-item GHQ (Goldberg). The independent variables proposed were the values internalised by the individuals, the personality pattern (type A or B), and the expectations regarding obtaining employment. The dependent variables proposed were the behaviour of the young people in an unemployment situation and the mental health of the unemployed.

The GHQ was only carried out on a subsample of unemployed people (N= 73). Most notably, significant differences were detected for the effect of the employment situation, placing the employed closer to a type A personality. Contrary to what might be expected, it was also found that a given personality type is not associated with a specific level of expectation. On the other hand, unemployed people who expected to find employment within a year obtained significantly lower scores in the GHQ (and therefore have greater psychological adjustment) than the unemployed with low expectations (those who expect to take more than a year to find employment). That is, the unemployed with low expectations of being successful in finding work show a greater mental health deterioration than those with high expectations of finding work.

The study from Blanch (1990) had several phases. It attempted to unravel the relationships between a large number of variables which affect the mental health of young people in one way or another. A questionnaire was handed out to two samples of young people of both sexes, aged between 16-25 years, residing in Barcelona and the metropolitan area. The questionnaire included census (socio-demographic) variables, questions on the social representation of work, employment, and unemployment and two scales of depression: the BDI (Beck Depression Inventory) and the CQ (Cognition Questionnaire). The questionnaire was applied to two different samples by means of stratified random sampling. Sample A was composed of 771 individuals with the following stratification: 371 unemployed, 200 students, and 200 employed. Sample B was made up of 461 individuals, stratified in the unemployed and students. The dependent variable was depression in young people. The employed group was least affected by depressive disorders, whereas the unemployed group was the most affected. The differences between them were statistically significant. 25% of the employed, 31% of the students, and 40% of the unemployed presented a risk of suffering mild psychiatric disorders. The unemployed presented poorer quality of life than the employed (but it was not possible to say whether this imbalance reflected the negative effects of unemployment on the unemployed or the positive effects of employment on the employed). Among the employed, women displayed a higher level of depressive disorder than men. However, among the unemployed the situation was reversed: men presented a higher average level of depression than women. According to the author, the reason for this result is historically relative, and in the current context of socio-cultural change they are subject to debate and revision. Among the three categories of socio-occupational statuses (unemployed, employed, and students), a significant relationship was detected between the level of economic stress perceived and the level of depression measured. There was a clear differentiation with regard to the average levels of depression between the unemployed group receiving unemployment benefits and those who do not have access to this financial support. The latter suffered from a greater level of depression than the former. The problem derived from the lack of work could not be reduced to the lack of money (most people would not exchange a salary for unemployment benefits) and poverty explained only part of the pathological effects of unemployment. On the other hand, a vicious circle was generated between unemployment/lack of interest in politics/ depression. Only in the unemployed group was political apathy associated with depression. Therefore, it may be supposed that political apathy is an effect of unemployment. The hypothesis was confirmed that the more an unemployed person participates in the work-oriented world view (associating the value and dignity of the person with work and the development of professional roles), the more depressing is his or her experience of unemployment. Among the unemployed, those who attributed the fact of not finding work to personal deficiencies have had significantly higher average levels of depression than those who did not. Finally, two out of five unemployed people were fundamentally in agreement with the following item: 'an unemployed person gives the impression of being a parasite and being lazy'. Among the unemployed, having a negative stereotype of unemployed persons in general correlated positively with depression and negatively with assertiveness.

2.1.2 Longitudinal studies

The only study found with a longitudinal design was conducted by Alvaro and Garrido (1990). A questionnaire was handed out to a sample of people in two different occasions. The sample in T1 consisted of 318 young people of both sexes in the fifth year of vocational training (students) who lived in the city of Madrid. The same questionnaire was mailed to the same individuals 9 months later (T2) and was returned completed by 172 people who were classified in the following manner: 43 continued studying, 28 were unemployed, 66 were employed, and 35 were performing obligatory military service. The questionnaire included socio-demographic variables and the Goldberg GHQ. Variance analysis was the statistical test used. The dependent variable was psychological well-being. At T1 there were no significant differences in psychological well-being within the sample. At T2 the unemployed young people and those performing military service had a reduced psychological well-being, the employed young people showed an improvement, and those who continued studying experienced no significant change.

2.1.3 Aggregated studies

No study of this type was found.

2.1.4 Type of statistical analysis

In the studies reviewed on youth unemployment and health the most commonly used statistical analyses consisted of variance analysis to discover whether differences between parameters were significant or not, other descriptive measurements such as the comparison of means and the Chi Square.

2.2 Overview of present studies

2.2.1 Objective health indicators

The level of aggregation of data within the Spanish statistics does not allow for an analysis of this type of indicator for a population as specific as the one in question. It has barely been possible to find data of this type referring to unemployed young people. It was possible to obtain some information from the results of empirical studies on unemployment and health which, despite studying the population in general, do offer some data broken down by age (with the limitations that this extrapolation may involve from a methodological point of view).

2.2.1.1 Mortality rates

No data has been found referring to mortality rates related to youth unemployment.

2.2.1.2 Morbidity

No specific data on morbidity among young unemployed persons is available in Spain. In a cross-sectional study of a sample of 1,068 people (501 employed and 567 unemployed) from Madrid aged 16-65 years, del Llano (1987) made an inventory of chronic symptoms presented by the unemployed with the most frequency: greater percentages of high cholesterol levels, nervous problems and depression, high blood pressure, and heart problems. The inventory of symptoms shows a greater incidence of headaches, weight loss, and reduced sexual appetite. It should be remembered that these results are only generalisable to the overall sample and, therefore, it is impossible to know which symptoms are attributable specifically to young people.

2.2.1.3 Suicidal behaviour (suicides and parasuicides)

No data have been found on this variable and its relation to youth unemployment. However, there are some data on suicides and attempted suicides in general and in young age groups, but with no breakdown by occupational status.

Table SP-3: Suicides and attempted suicides

Age	1986	1987	1988	1989	1990	1991	1992	1993	1994	1995
All ages	2,060	2,118	2,431	2,161	2,299	2,599	2,372	2,412	2,344	2,711
13-19	106	115	123	113	105	120	104	95	89	138
20-29	264	298	392	343	350	430	327	410	366	463

Source: Spanish Statistical Yearbook 1996.

Over the period from 1986 to 1995, suicides and parasuicides increased considerably with the highest absolute values being detected in 1995. With regard to employment, almost half of the suicides in the age group 20-29 years are 'farmers, hunters, and forestry workers', and 'artisans and production workers'. In most of the other half, the data does not indicate the profession. Despite the fact that it is not possible to say how many of the suicides were committed by unemployed persons, it is striking that most of the young people who committed suicide (or attempted to do so) worked in the sectors with the highest registered unemployment (agriculture and industry).

2.2.1.4 Utilisation of health services

In a study based on data from the 1986 Barcelona Health Survey, Rodríguez (1994) showed that students (inactive population) pay a significantly higher number of visits to the medical services than employed people, and that among the active population (employed and unemployed), the use of health services increases with age. The study also indicates that women of all ages make more use of health services than men. This statement was also made by Benavides, Garcia, Sáez-Lloret & Librero, (1994) in a study on data from the 1987 Spanish National Health Survey and, furthermore, it was added that in Spain, the unemployed use the health services with greater frequency than the employed, independent of age, sex, and level of education. In his sample of employed and unemployed people in Madrid del Llano (1990) found that the groups most vulnerable to health disorders related to unemployment are those who use available social healthcare resources the least. This situation also appears in the qualitative study by del Llano, Aracil, Del Llano, González, Fernández, Romá & Esquivias, (1996) on the long-term unemployed (35-55 years of age, residents of the city of Madrid) who state that they rarely use social and health services. The relationship found by the author is that the fewer the resources and the greater the need, the less the services are used.

2.2.2 *Subjective health indicators*

2.2.2.1 *Psychosocial strains*

Rodríguez and García (1989) outlined that young unemployed people with a low expectation of successfully finding work display a greater deterioration in their health than young people with high expectations of finding work. Alvaro (1989a), when analysing a sample of young people, stated that 33% of those employed and 60% of those unemployed are at risk of suffering from mild (nonpsychotic) *psychological disorders*, and that the changes in role status within the family (such as the fact that the head of the family is unemployed) may generate tension and affect the psychological well-being of the family members. The author also detected that young people with an unemployed father have poorer psychological well-being than young people whose father is employed. Also worth mentioning is the psychological tension generated by the social representation of work in the sense that young people who share a world view centred on the value of work as the only path of social insertion suffer from excess *depression* (Blanch, 1990). This author also indicated that unemployed young people who attribute their inability to find work to their own personal deficiencies have significantly higher levels of depression than unemployed young people who do not. In Spain, regional differences also exist which affect the level of tension generated by unemployment. This phenomenon could be detected by Benavides et al. (1994) when analysing samples of employed and unemployed people from Andalusia, Catalonia, and the Basque Country. Despite having lower unemployment rates than Andalusia, the unemployed of Catalonia and the Basque Country have higher *stress and depression levels* than the unemployed of Andalusia. Unfortunately, this study does not make distinctions between age groups, and it is impossible to say whether the model can be directly extrapolated to young people. However, in a qualitative study of long-term unemployed (both sexes, aged 35-55 years), del Llano et al. (1996) found out that the situation of vital stress implied by unemployment is filtered by the capacity for adaptation of each person. This study also suggests another tension factor: requesting aid from parents tends to become a highly stressful factor in the long run. Alvaro (1989b) underlined the importance to structure time among the unemployed. The author found out that those who are able to structure their time have fewer *mental health disturbances* and less negative *self-esteem* than those with difficulties. (It has to be pointed out that this is a sample of people of working age (16-65 years). Therefore, the result cannot be extrapolated directly to young people).

2.2.2.2 *Subjective well-being*

The level of psychological well-being and depression is the most studied disorder among unemployed young people, and in all the studies the same result appears: The unemployed have significantly higher levels of *depression* or *psychological disturbance* than the employed. This result also appears in studies on unemployment for a population of all ages. Rodríguez (1994) showed that women (of all ages) assess their health status in a more negative way than men.

2.2.2.3 *Self-esteem*

According to Blanch (1990), two out of five unemployed young people agree that "unemployed people give a certain impression of being parasites and lazy" and that these attitudes correlate positively with depression. This author also detected that a group of unemployed young people attribute their failure to find work to personal deficiencies and that these individuals have significantly higher *depression* rates than young people who believe the contrary. On a more general level, de la Torre (1989) found that unemployed persons (of all ages) attribute their unemployment situation to external agents in a clear example of ego defensiveness, whereas the employed blame the unemployed people themselves for their situation (victimisation). Also Alvaro (1989b), in a study of 622 people (320 employed and 302 unemployed) aged 16-65 years, stated that unemployed people with a greater involvement in work (i.e., they consider work to be a central value in their lives) have higher levels of positive self-esteem. According to the author, this result may be interpreted in the way that unemployed people with a high work motivation maintain a positive image of themselves as a defense mechanism in an adverse situation.

2.2.2.4 Alienation (political orientations)

Some empirical studies have shown that unemployment affects the political attitudes of young people. Bergere (1989), using qualitative techniques in a sample of young people (age 16-28 years, both sexes, structured by socio-occupational status), detected a rejection of traditionally accepted institutions and values; they oppose politics as it is organised today and demand greater responsibility and participation in political life. However, according to the author, scepticism is the defining characteristic of their ideological-political attitudes. In this context, scepticism is not equated with de-ideologisation, but indicates a lack of interest in current, specific politics and suggests the need for another type of politics and ideology. Blanch (1990) found that there is considerable political apathy among unemployed young people. This apathy is not due to the depressive psychological state of the young people, but is rather an effect of the unemployment situation. According to the author, this is something which suggests that unemployment is not only a state of deficit in the quality of personal and social life, but that it is also an indicator of the fragility of a political system.

2.2.2.5 Social deviation (delinquency)

According to conversations held with experts (Blanch, Artázcoz), youth unemployment was fairly directly related to 'civil insecurity' and delinquency in the 80s in Spain. The *consumption and traffic of drugs* was the other variable involved in the social construction of a problem which occupied a large part of the political debate in Spain in the last decade. Today, however, this argument has been deconstructed and there does not seem to be any relevant empirical relationship between youth unemployment and delinquency.

2.2.2.6 Health behaviour

None of the empirical studies found on young people deals with this indicator, although other more general studies do have something to say about it. Rodríguez (1994), while analysing the data of the 1986 Barcelona Health Survey, tried to prove the hypothesis that unemployment can lead to psychological disorders which, in turn, can lead to unhealthy behaviour. However, his study finds no evidence that the unemployed have a more unhealthy behaviour than other occupational groups. He even notes that unemployed people tend to sleep 30 minutes more per day than the employed which can be beneficial to their health.

2.2.3 *Mediators (demographic variables)*

2.2.3.1 *Age*

The empirical studies available on young people do not make distinctions by age subgroups. Thus age is not analysed as it is a substantial characteristic of the sample itself. The other studies found on unemployment and health at the level of the entire working population (16-65 years of age) refer to the importance of age. Deniel, Bosch, Culi & Olmeda, (1996), in a study of a sample of 378 people (189 unemployed and 189 employed, aged 16-64 years, residents of a rural area), states that by age groups there is a significant relationship between unemployment and mental health problems only in the 30-36 year age group. By analysing the 1994 Catalan Health Survey, Cortés (1997) found out that, among unemployed men, the lower prevalence of *mental disorders* is in the 16-25 year age group, whereas the highest is in the 46-55 year age group. In order to analyse the importance of age in the relationships between unemployment and psychological well-being, Alvaro (1989b) divided the subsample of unemployed people into three age groups: young people (16-29 years), intermediate (30-50 years) and older people (over 50 years). He performed a variance analysis and tested the differences between the mean scores for each group. Significant differences were detected between the group of young people and the intermediate age group with the latter showing poorer *mental health* and a higher level of *depression.*

2.2.3.2 *Gender*

Blanch (1990) states that among employed young people, women have a higher incidence of *depressive disorders* than men, but that among unemployed young people, the situation is reversed: Men have a higher average level of depression than women. Nevertheless, this author warns that this is a phenomenon which is historically relative and which depends on the socio-cultural context. Alvaro (1989a), on the other hand, does not observe significant differences for gender in a study on psychological well-being with a sample of 232 young people (105 employed and 127 unemployed). With regard to the description of results from studies on the working population, in an analysis of the 1986 Barcelona Health Survey Rodríguez (1994) found out that women (of all ages) have a poorer *perception of their state of health* than men, women who describe themselves as housewives have poorer *levels of health* than the group of employed people, and women – independent of the occupational group they belong to – show a higher prevalence of *depression.* Benavides et al. (1994), in analysing the 1987 Spanish National Health Survey, found that there is a significant interaction between unemployment and gender with regard to the perceived poor state of health, *drug consumption (medication*), and frequency of *medical visits.* However, in the analysis of 1994 Catalan Health Survey, Cortés (1997) found that the prevalence of *mental disorders* is higher among the unemployed population than among the employed population. In the case of the unemployed no gender differences occur with regard to this prevalence, whereas, in the case of the employed, women have higher values than men. In this sense, in their study of a sample of unemployed and employed people in a rural area, Deniel et al. (1996) found that the relationship between sex and mental health problems is not significant. Also, Alvaro (1989b) found that in comparison with employed persons, both unemployed men and women present poorer *psychological well-being* (GHQ), more *depressive symptoms* (BDI), a more negative *self-image,* and less *satisfaction* with their current lifestyle. Thus, gender differences are not that clear within the Spanish literature.

2.2.3.3 Education

In Spain the official status of an unemployed person is incompatible with that of a student. Therefore, in a formal sense it is only possible to speak of young unemployed people when they are not students. However, in reality, many young people are students precisely because they are looking for work and cannot find it, and meanwhile, they remain in the academic world. From this perspective, a young person with a high level of education may be both someone who wants to study, and someone who wants to work but has not found work for a long time. It can be assumed that the situation regarding the health of young people in these two situations is very different. Alvaro (1989b) stated that in his study, no significant differences were observed with regard to *psychological well-being* according to level of education among the young people in his sample (232 young people, aged 16-26 years, employed and unemployed, of both sexes, residents of the city of Madrid). The studies examining the unemployment/health relationship in the working population show something different. In his analysis of the 1986 Barcelona Health Survey, Rodríguez (1994) observed that the level of education is inversely associated with *depression* meaning that the higher the level of education, the lower the level of depression. Del Llano (1990) also reached similar conclusions and observed that the individuals most vulnerable to *health problems* related to unemployment are those with poor professional qualifications.

2.2.3.4 Social class (social milieu)

Some authors detected a significant association between family income and the *mental health* of young people in the sense that the better the economic situation of the family, the better the mental health of the young person. However, Alvaro (1989a) observed that unemployed young people present poorer *psychological well-being* than employed young people regardless of the family's social milieu. Similarly, this author states that in families where the father is unemployed, the young people show poorer well-being than in families where the father is employed. Studies on other age groups also contribute data to the relationship between social class, unemployment, and health. Del Llano (1990) noted that, according to his research, the individuals who belong to lower social classes are more vulnerable to health problems related to unemployment. In another study, del Llano et al. (1996) observed that the effects of unemployment are more harmful if the social and economic conditions of the families were already unfavourable before the unemployment situation occurred, and pointed out that people living in lower socio-economic areas display more health problems. Rodríguez (1994), on the other hand, notes that social class is not so relevant for suffering psychological disorders but, despite everything, that coming from upper social classes helps to have better mental and physical health. Blanch (1990) talks of unemployment as a symptom of a more profound problem, namely poverty. Unemployment tends to affect employed people in companies in sectors hit by crisis, whose living and working conditions are already deficient before becoming unemployed. On the other hand, unemployment for those who cannot find or maintain their first job tends to affect people with few personal resources – physical, psychological, social, professional – often associated with or derived from prior deficits in the family social situations.

2.2.3.5 Length of unemployment

Only one of the available studies on young people deals with this topic. Alvaro (1989a) stated that in his cross-sectional study with young people (16-26 years of age) – employed and unemployed – the duration of unemployment does not significantly affect the psychological well-being of the individuals studied. The other empirical studies found on young people do not deal with this variable. On the other hand, this variable is included in some studies on the population of working age (16-64 years): Del Llano et al. (1996) noted that forced maintenance of unemployment over time aggravates the *psychological health and the family situation.* Garrido, Castillo, Benavides and Ruíz (1994) pointed out an increased *psychological morbidity* in the unemployed over time, with 2 years as a crucial time when the highest stress scores appear. From this moment on, the magnitude of the association diminishes to almost half, although it continues to be very strong. The authors explain the phenomenon by the capacity of the unemployed person to adapt to their situation (but they have doubts due to a selection bias: The unemployed people were recruited from the records of the INEM and it could be that only the most psychologically resistant continue going to the INEM offices after 2 years of unemployment). Cortés (1997), in his analysis of the Catalan Health Survey, observed that the relationship between *mental disorders* and unemployment is greater among those who have been unemployed for longer (this association is strongest among men). Nevertheless, there is room for all kinds of reservations since these results are only generalisable to the sample group and not to the group of young people.

2.2.4 Moderators (psychological variables)

2.2.4.1 Work and job orientation

In many Spanish unemployment and health studies the most relevant question is the presence of the variable 'centrality of work'. There are a number of stereotypes surrounding work (centrality of productive activity, positive value of employment, stigmatisation of unemployment, etc.) which have circulated in the media and public opinion have led to greater levels of *mental disorders* in unemployed people. Alvaro (1989a) observed that the greater the centrality or positive value attributed to work is, the greater the deterioration in the mental health of unemployed young people. However, among employed young people, greater centrality given to work does not correspond with a significant increase in psychological well-being. Blanch (1986) showed that the level of *depression* suffered by a determined group of unemployed people does not derive so much from their unemployment status, as from a socio-cognitive factor: the value they have learned to place on the importance of work with regard to one's personal and social development. From this perspective the situation of unemployment is a necessary though insufficient condition, since most unemployed people studied exhibit as little depression as the healthiest of the employed. This hypothesis has been confirmed in different studies on youth unemployment and health (Blanch, 1986, 1989, 1990; Alvaro, 1989a) – a fact which suggests that, to solve the health problems related to unemployment, it is necessary to act on or modify the social representation of work. Interestingly, this aspect has only been formulated and dealt with extensively in studies on young people.

2.2.4.2 Financial strain/stress

The better the family economic situation, the better the psychological well-being of the young people (Alvaro, 1989a). Among the three categories of socio-occupational statuses (unemployed, employed, and students) established by Blanch (1990) in his research, a significant relationship was detected between the level of economic stress perceived and the level of *depression* measured – with those with fewer economic resources having a higher level of depression. Furthermore, there is a clear differentiation between the mean levels of depression of the group of unemployed people who collect unemployment benefits and those who do not have access to this financial support. The latter show worse mental health. The author also observed that in all socio-occupational statuses there is a significant relationship between the level of economic stress perceived and the level of depression. On another level, the studies on unemployment and health carried out on the entire working population (16-65 years) also mention this variable. Del Llano (1990) observed that economic stress is the factor which best explains the transition from a situation of unemployment to a situation of ill health. Rodríguez (1994) found that the most important factor for mitigating the negative impact of unemployment on health is the availability of unemployment benefits – even after controlling for the individual and social factors and total family income. In his study, it can be seen that unemployed people who receive benefits have health levels no different from those of the employed, and that unemployed people who do not receive benefits have worse health levels. In the same sense, Cortés (1997) observed that the relationship between mental disorders and unemployment is greater among unemployed people who do not receive benefits (especially among men). Alvaro (1989b) distinguished three different groups in his research: those who stated that they never or almost never had financial problems; those who stated they had financial problems with some frequency; and those who stated they were always or almost always worried by economic problems. The groups which stated that they experienced financial problems with the greatest frequency were the ones with the most marked *psychological deterioration*, the greatest sense of *depression*, least *satisfaction with their current lives,* and a relevant drop in *self-esteem.*

2.2.4.3 Social support

Alvaro (1989b) stated that unemployed young people who live in families without tensions have the best level of *psychological well-being*. In general, there are some references in this regard for the set of all economically active age groups: Del Llano (1990) notes in his study that the role of family support in Spain acts as a kind of buffer and alleviates the possible effects of unemployment on health. In another study (Del Llano et al., 1996) the same author observed that having children between the ages of 12 and 18 at the time of becoming unemployed predisposes the unemployed person to reduced family support, and that women over 45 years of age with family responsibilities and being unemployed have more *psychosomatic problems* than men. Alvaro (1989b) also took into account the variable 'social support' in his study. Unemployed who state that they feel barely or not at all cushioned by family and/or friends score significantly higher in the GHQ than those who say they feel cushioned. That is, a greater deterioration is observed in the well-being of those with less social support. Benavides et al. (1994) stated that unemployment in Andalusia (an area with very little industrialisation in Southern Spain) is less stressful because it is a common situation and moreover people have strong social support (family, neighbours, friends, etc.), contrary to the situation in Catalonia and the Basque Country (industrialised areas in Northern Spain).

3 Summary of results

The Spanish research on unemployment and health has adopted a large part of the English-speaking literature. It is accepted that unemployment is related to the appearance of health problems, especially psychological problems. The vast majority of empirical studies carried out in Spain on unemployment and health deals with mental health disorders. Spanish publications are predominated by theories which emphasise the interdependence between the individual and the social structure and which assume that work fulfills an important function in the integration of the individual into society. The most relevant theoretical aspect has been the inclusion of the variable 'social representation of work' to explain the high level of deterioration in mental health in certain profiles of unemployed people (those who are socialised with the centrality of work). This theorisation leads, according to some authors, to the need to tackle the problems of unemployment not only through employment policies but also through a reconceptualisation of work, employment, and unemployment. In the specific case of young people, there is a line of research which centres on the description of the processes of transition of young people (from school to employment, to unemployment; from unemployment to employment, etc.), and which sometimes takes into consideration the psychological impact of the different models of transition to active life. Empirical studies containing secondary data with a populational basis are scarce in Spain due to the lack of systematic, rigorous data.

There are few Spanish studies on youth unemployment and health and almost all of them have a cross-sectional design which makes them merely descriptive, without the possibility of an in-depth explanation of the phenomena. In general, the cross-sectional comparison between the unemployed and the employed highlights the poorer quality of life among the unemployed, but it must be remembered that this is influenced by a large number of variables. The following paragraphs summarise the findings outlined in the previous chapters.

Among objective health indicators no data could be found on *mortality rates* referring to unemployed young people. The data on *morbidity* refer to young people between 16-24 years of age, but does not distinguish between occupational statuses. Young people are the age group which presents the least damage to health, and most of their medical visits are for general medical purposes. It has to be noted that visits to psychiatrists are very frequent among this age group (compared with other age groups). A study on the most common disorders among unemployed people of all ages indicates that mental health problems and coronary problems are those which appear most in this population. The number of *suicides* has increased throughout the entire period, but there are notable differences according to age. Thus the number of suicides and parasuicides has increased more among the 20-29 years age group than among the population as a whole. Paradoxically, the trend in suicides and parasuicides appears to follow a pattern inverse to unemployment: the number fell in 1992 and increased again considerably in 1995 – just the opposite of unemployment. It should also be mentioned that the proportions of male suicides are three times as high as female suicides. Although no distinction is made specifically by socio-occupational status, from the available data it can be seen that the level of *utilisation of health services* among the active population (employed and unemployed) increases with age, thus leading to the conclusion that there is a low level of use among young people. For all ages, utilisation by women is higher than by men. It is also known that, independent of age, the unemployed make more use of these services than the employed. Unfortunately, no specific data have been found on young unemployed people in Spain.

The subjective health indicators may be described based on the results of the different studies. Nevertheless, not all the required indicators appear in studies devoted to young people and accordingly results have been used from studies on unemployment and health carried out on the entire population of working age. With regard to *psychosocial strain* among the unemployed, young people with poor expectations of finding work show a greater deterioration in their health than young people with higher expectations. It has also been demonstrated that young unemployed people with the head of the family being unemployed suffer from poorer mental health. Similarly, young people who conceive work as the principal route of social integration suffer from higher levels of tension. A situation appears among the unemployed of all ages which generates certain psychosocial tensions: requesting money from parents for long periods of time. It should also be pointed out that in the nonindustrialised areas of Southern Spain (Andalusia, Extremadura, etc.) which are characterised by high and permanent levels of unemployment, the unemployed exhibit lower levels of stress and depression than the unemployed in industrialised areas with lower levels of unemployment. The variable *subjective well-being* shows that the unemployed have significantly higher levels of depression or psychological disturbance than the employed. Furthermore, young unemployed women have a worse perception of their state of mental health than men in the same situation. Regarding *self-esteem* it can be said that some studies determined that those unemployed young people who attribute their failure to find work to personal deficiencies have significantly higher depression scores than their peers. However, some authors state that unemployed people with a greater involvement in work have higher levels of positive self-esteem. In this regard the ability to structure their time also seems to be an important dimension. Among unemployed young people there is considerable political apathy (*political alienation*) not due to their depressive psychological state, but rather due to an effect of the unemployment situation. Among unemployed young people a rejection of traditionally accepted institutions and values was detected. Scepticism is the defining characteristic of their ideological-political attitudes. With regard to *social deviation* it has to be stressed that today there seems to be no relevant relationship to unemployment. Despite the fact that no studies on *health behaviour* could be found referring to young unemployed people, several studies outlined that no evidence exists that the unemployed show more unhealthy behaviour than the other occupational groups. However, it should be pointed out that in Spain, the most problematic periods for the use and traffic of drugs have always coincided with periods of recession and excessive unemployment.

For the different mediators it can be said that belonging to one *age* group or another is important when establishing relationships between health and unemployment. The unemployed with most health problems are the intermediate group (30-50 years of age). From age 30 on more health problems appear, especially mental health problems. However, there is a possibility that many of these individuals have suffered from periods of unemployment before this age. Thus, although the age group which is the object of this study (16-29 years of age) is less affected by health problems related to unemployment, it accumulates an important potential for the later life of the individuals. *Gender* differences are highly relativised in the Spanish literature. On one hand studies could show that women in general have higher levels of depressive disorders than men, but among unemployed young people the situation is reversed (Blanch, 1990). Some authors, however, did not observe significant differences for gender, especially in the case of unemployed. The available studies on young people could not detect any significant differences with regard to mental health according to *level of education*. On the other hand, such a difference was found in the population of working age as a whole: The level of education is inversely associated with the level of depression. Regardless of the *social class* of the family, unemployed young people present poorer psychological well-being than employed young people. Studies on other age groups also contribute data to the relationship between unemployment and health and social class: The effects of unemployment are more harmful if the social and economic conditions of the families were already unfavourable before the unemployment situation occurred. However, unemployment for those who cannot find or maintain their first job tends to affect people with few personal resources (often associated with or derived from prior deficits in the family social situation). There is evidence that in the population of working age, *long-term unemployment* leads to a greater deterioration of mental health – with two years of uninterrupted unemployment being the moment of maximum association (it has been shown that from this moment on the magnitude of the association decreases). However, a study has been found (Alvaro 1989a) on unemployed young people according to which the length of unemployment has no significant effect on the psychological well-being of the young people. Hence caution is advised when evaluating the influence of this variable.

The moderator variable *work and job orientation* seems to be a central issue of debate in Spain which can be seen by the high presence of the variable 'centrality of work' within the studies on unemployment and health. There are a number of stereotypes surrounding the work culture (centrality of productive activity, positive value of employment, stigma of unemployment, etc.) which circulate in the media and public opinion and which lead to a greater level of mental disorders in unemployed people. Several Spanish studies show that the level of depression suffered by a determined group of unemployed people does not derive so much from their unemployment status as from a socio-cognitive factor: the value they have learned to place on the importance of work with regard to one's personal and social development. From this perspective, the situation of unemployment is a necessary though insufficient condition since most unemployed people studied have as little depression as the healthiest of the employed. Nevertheless, it is possible that a socio-cultural change is taking place among young people which is displacing these social representations of primary socialisation.

Financial stress is one of the main factors in the relationship between unemployment and health. Young people with fewer economic resources have higher levels of depression. The different studies available indicate that there is a clear differentiation between the mean levels of depression of the group of unemployed people who receive some kind of economic unemployment benefits and those who do not. The latter suffer from poorer mental health. In general, a significant relationship has been found in young people of all the different socio-occupational statuses between the level of perceived economic stress and the level of depression. Other studies on the unemployed of all ages also have observed that the relationship between mental disorders and unemployment is greater among the unemployed who do not receive any economic benefits, especially in the case of men. The importance of the variable *social support* is reflected in the fact that young people who live in families without tensions have the highest levels of psychological well-being. In general, the role of the family is highly valued in the Spanish literature, and it is considered to help support high rates of unemployment without generating relevant social conflicts. Furthermore, it has been observed that in regions where the situation of mass unemployment is common (poorly industrialised regions such as Southern Spain), the unemployed have wide social support networks (family, neighbours, friends, etc.) and a much stronger level of support than in industrialised areas with less unemployment and, therefore, they have better health.

Youth unemployment and health: Spanish studies – an overview-

Author		Instruments/ Methodes	Population	Dependent variables	Results
Blanch (1986)	N = 200 young people; stratified sample according to occupational status, with the following categories: – unemployed – students – employed	cross-sectional design questionnaire with 93 items	– 16-25 years – resident in the city of Barcelona and the metropolitan area	– level of depression	– unemployed group most heavily affected by depression; employed group least affected – level of depression suffered by a specific type of unemployed person not derived from their occupational state (unemployed), but from a socio-cognitive factor: value the person has learned to place on the importance of work with regard to one's personal and social development – situation of unemployment is a necessary but not a sufficient condition, since many of the unemployed people studied show as little depression as the healthiest of the employed
Blanch (1989)	1. N = 17 people 2. N = 150 people 3. N = 250 people	cross-sectional design 1. sample: 3-hour meeting (2 hours discussion + 1 hour completion of questionnaire) 2. sample: self-applied questionnaire 3. sample: questionnaire with items referring to ideology	1.+2. sample: – 16-30 years 3. sample: – 18-25 years – students of psychology and social work) all samples: – resident in the Barcelona and metropolitan area	– "emotional state" (depression, measured in BDI and CQ, and assertiveness in Rathus) – "ideology" (with respect to work, employment and unemployment)	– 1. study: provided ideas for subsequent phases – unemployment leads to a deficit in quality of life which frequently includes a significant level of basic depression – specific types of ideological messages, frequent in daily life, have a reinforcing effect on specific clichés of the work culture (such as centrality of productive activity, positive value of employment, stigma of unemployment, etc.) and lead to an increased depressive deficit in the unemployed person

Author	Sample	Instruments/ Methodes	Population	Dependent variables	Results
Rodríguez & García (1989)	N = 438 people stratified in the following manner: – unemployed qualified young people who have never worked (n = 293) – employed professionals with secondary-education or higher qualifications (n = 145)	cross-sectional design attitudes regarding values A and B personality questionnaire (Bortner) 12-item GHQ (Goldberg)	– 208 men 230 women – 20-29 years (young unemployed people) – no age recorded for employed professionals	– behaviour and level of mental health of the young unemployed people	– individuals with low expectation of success in gaining employment experience greater deterioration in mental health than individuals with higher expectations
Alvaro (1989)	N = 232 young people; of which: – 105 employed – 127 unemployed separated in 4 categories according to duration of unemployment: a) 1-3 months b) 3-6 months c) 6-12 months d)>12 months	cross-sectional design socio-demographic variables description of activity carried out (by the employed) 6-item: level of work involvement (Warr), 12-item GHQ (Goldberg)	– 16-26 years of age – resident in the city of Madrid.	– psychological well-being.	– unemployed higher scores on GHQ than employed group – no significant differences with regard to gender or level of education – significant differences with regard to employment situation of father: young people with unemployed fathers display poorer psychological well-being than young people with employed fathers – significant association between family income and psychological well-being – 33% of employed and 60% of unemployed are at risk of suffering mild (non-psychotic) disorders – duration of unemployment does not significantly affect mental health. – the greater the centrality or positive value attributed to work, the greater the deterioration in the mental health of the unemployed.

Author	Sample	Instruments	Population	Dependent variables	Results
Blanch (1990)	N1= 771 – unemployed: n = 371 – students: n = 200 – employed: n = 200 2. N2= 461 – students – unemployed	cross-sectional design census variables questions on the social representation of work, employment and unemployment 2 scales on depression (BDI and CQ)	– 16-25 years – resident in the city of Barcelona and metropolitan area.	– depression	– employed group least affected by depressive disorders; unemployed group most affected – 25% of employed, 31% of students and 40% of the unemployed present a risk of mild psychiatric disorders – unemployed have a poorer quality of life than the employed. – among the employed, women have the highest level of depressive disorder; the situation is reversed among the unemployed persons – unemployed who collect unemployment benefits have lower levels of depression than unemployed who do not (this is an unemployment-apoliticism-depression relationship) – the more an unemployed person participates in a world view centred on work, the more depressing his or her unemployment experience – negative self-stereotype is positively correlated with level of depression and negatively correlated with assertiveness
Alvaro & Garrido (1990)	1. N = 318 (at T1) 2. N = 172 (at T2) – study (n = 43) – unemployed (n = 28) – employed (n = 66) – military service (n = 35)	longitudinal design socio-demographic variables Goldberg GHQ	T1: 19-25 years studying 5th year vocational training resident in the city of Madrid T2: same sample nine years later	– psychological well-being	– T1: no significant differences in the psychological well-being of the sample – T2: young people doing military service show a fall in psychological well-being; the employed young people showed an improvement and those who continued to study did not show any significant change

References

Accornero, A. & Carmignani, F. (1986). *I paradossi della disoccupazione.* [The Unemployment Paradoxes]. Bologna: Il Mulino.

Aelvoet, W., Capet, F., & Vanoverloop, J. (Eds.). (1998). *Gezondheidsindicatoren 1996.* [Health Indicators 1996]. Brussel: Ministerie van de Vlaamse Gemeenschap, Departement Welzijn, Volksgezondheid en Cultuur.

Alaluf, M., Desmarez, P., & Domb, I. (1982). *Les chômeurs et leur culture: Analyse des modes de vie des jeunes chômeurs peu scolarisés: Le cas de la région de Charleroi.* [Unemployed Persons and their Culture: Analysis of the Way of Life of Young Unemployed Persons with few Qualifications: The Case of the Region of Charleroi]. Bruxelles: Comité pour l'étude des problèmes de l'emploi et du chômage.

Albrecht, H.-J. (1988). Kriminell weil arbeitslos? Arbeitslos weil kriminell? Der Stand der Forschung zum Zusammenhang von Kriminalität und Arbeitslosigkeit. [Criminality as a result of unemployment? Unemployment as a result of criminality? The development of research on the correlation between crime and unemployment]. *Bewährungshilfe, 2*, 133-147.

Alheit, P. & Glaß, Ch. (1986). *Beschädigtes Leben. Soziale Biographien arbeitsloser Jugendlicher. Ein soziologischer Versuch über die "Entdeckung" neuer Fragestellungen.* [Damaged life. Social Biographies of Unemployed Young Persons. A Sociological Essay on the 'Discovery of New Formulations of Questions']. Frankfurt a.M.: Campus.

Alvaro, J.L. (1989a). Desempleo juvenil y salud mental. In J.R. Torregrosa, J. Bergere, & J.L. Alvaro (Eds.), *Juventud, trabajo y desempleo: un análisis psicosociológico.* [Youth Unemployment and Mental Health] (pp. 305-319). Madrid: Ministerio de Trabajo y Seguridad Social.

Alvaro, J.L. (1989b). *Desempleo y bienestar psicológico.* [Unemployment and Psychological Well-Being]. Madrid: Universidad Complutense de Madrid.

Alvaro, J.L. & Garrido, A. (1990). Modelos de transición tras la FP-2 y cambio psicológico: Un estudio longitudinal. [Models of transition after FP-2 (secondary education) and psychological change: A longitudinal study]. *Psicología del Trabajo y de las Organizaciones, 16*, 74-78.

Ambeni, D., Davoli, M., & Faggiano, F. (1994). Le differenze sociali nella frequenza di tossicodipendenza e Aids. [Social differences in the frequency of drug addiction and AIDS]. In G. Costa & F. Faggiano (Eds.), *L'equità nella salute in Italia. Rapporto sulle diseguaglianza sociali in sanità.* [Equality in Health in Italy. Report on Social and Health Inequalities]. Milano: Angeli.

ANBA (1997). *Die Entwicklung des Arbeitsmarktes im November 1997.* [The Development of the Labour Market in November 1997]. No. 12. Nürnberg: Bundesanstalt für Arbeit.

Antonovsky, A. (1981). *Health, Stress and Coping.* San Francisco: Jossey Bass.

Arbeitskammer des Saarlandes (1980). *Ursachen und Folgen der Jugendarbeitslosigkeit im Saarland.* [Causes and Consequences of Youth Unemployment in the Saarland]. Eine empirisch-soziologische Studie des ISO-Institutes für Sozialforschung und Sozialwirtschaft e.V.. Saarbrücken: Arbeitskammer des Saarlandes.

Athanasouli, T., Koletsi-Kounari, H., Mamai-Homata, H., & Panagopoulos, H. (1990). Oral health status of adult population in Athens, Greece. *Community Dental Oral Epidemiology Review, 17,* 82-84.

Axerio, M. (1994). *Il bere a Milano.* [The Question of Drinking in Milan]. Milano: Unicopli.

Backlund, A. (1973). *Företagsnedläggningars konsekvenser för personalen. Läget för de anställda ca ett år efter nedläggningen.* [The Effects of Company Closures on their Personnel. Conditions for the Employees about a Year after Closure]. Stockholm: Delrapport 5. Specialstudie av de långtidsarbetslösa. Rapport från PA-rådet, 0052.

Bagnasco, A. (1977). *Tre Italie. La problematica territoriale dello sviluppo economico italiano.* [Three Italys. The Territorial Issue of the Italian Economic Development]. Bologna: Il Mulino.

Bagnasco, A. (1996). *L'Italia in tempi di cambiamento politico.* [Italy in Times of Political Changes]. Bologna: Il Mulino.

Baldacci, E., Gazzelloni, S., & Inglese, L. (1997). Italy. In Istat (Ed.), *A Statistical Portrait of Youth Exclusion. A Siena Group Monitoring Report* (pp. 117-142). Roma: Istat.

Banks, M.H. & Jackson, P.R. (1982). Unemployment and risk of minor psychiatric disorder in young people. *Psychological Medicine, 12,* 789-798.

Banks, M.H. & Ullah, P. (1988). *Youth Unemployment in the 1980s: Its Psychological Effects.* Beckenham: Croom Helm.

Barbieri, P. (1997). Cambiamenti del modello occupazionale italiano e problemi di regolamentazione. Uno sguardo d'insieme. [Changes in the Italian employment model and regulation problems. An overall view]. *L'Assistenza Sociale, 3,* 9-34.

Baumann, U., Becker, U., Gerstenmaier, J., Schickle, O., & Tippelt, R. (1979). *Handlungsperspektiven und politische Einstellungen arbeitsloser Jugendlicher.* [Prospects for Action and Political Views of Unemployed Young Persons]. Frankfurt: Campus.

Beales, A.D. & Lambert, R.S. (1934). *Memoirs of the Unemployed.* London: Collanz.

Becattini, G. (Ed.). (1987). *Mercato e forze locali: Il distretto industriale.* [Market and Local Forces: The Industrial District]. Bologna: Il Mulino.

Bellens, W. (1996). De arbeidsmarkt van de jongeren. [The labour market and the young]. *Arbeidsblad, 24,* 19-27.

Benavides, F.G., García, A.M., Sáez-Lloret, I., & Librero, J. (1994). Unemployment and health in Spain. The influence of socio-economic environment. *European Journal of Public Health, 4,* 103-107.

Bergere, J. (1989). Las actitudes ideológico-políticas de los jóvenes madrileños en situación de desempleo: Un análisis cualitativo. In J.R. Torregrosa, J. Bergere, & J.L. Alvaro (Eds.), *Juventud, trabajo y desempleo: un análisis psicosociológico.* [The Ideological-Political Attitudes of the Unemployed Youth from Madrid: A Qualitative Analysis] (pp. 25-55). Madrid: Ministerio de Trabajo y Seguridad Social.

Berkman, L.F. & Syme, L.S. (1979). Social networks, host resistance and mortality: A nine-year follow-up study of Alameda County residents. *American Journal of Epidemiology, 109*(2), 186-204.

Bezze, M. (1998). Analisi quantitativa e qualitativa della disoccupazione giovanile. [Quantitative and qualitative analysis of youth unemployment]. In Caritas Italiana – Fondazione Zancan (Ed.), *Gli ultimi della fila. Rapporto 1997 sui bisogni dimenticati.* [The Last of the Row – Report 1997 on the Forgotten Needs] (pp. 97-117). Milano: Feltrinelli.

Bille-Brahe, U. & Crepet, P. (1992). Trend in the frequency of suicide in Denmark and in Italy. A comparison study. In P. Crepet, G. Ferrari, S. Platt, & M. Bellini (Eds.), *Suicidal Behaviour in Europe* (pp. 55-61). London: John Libbey.

Blanch, J.M. (1986). *Desempleo juvenil y salud psicosocial.* [Youth Unemployment and Psychosocial Health]. Barcelona: Universitat Autònoma de Barcelona.

Blanch, J.M. (1989). Valoración del trabajo y patología en el paro. In J.R. Torregrosa, J. Bergere, & J.L. Alvaro (Eds.), *Juventud, trabajo y desempleo: Un análisis psicosociológico.* [Valuation of Work and Pathology in Unemployment] (pp. 365-392). Madrid: Ministerio de Trabajo y Seguridad Social.

Blanch, J. M. (1990). *Del viejo al nuevo paro. Un análisis psicológico y social.* [From the Old to the New Unemployment. A Psychological and Social Analysis]. Barcelona: Promociones y Publicaciones Universitarias.

Borghi, V. & La Rosa, M. (Eds.). (1995). *Tempo di lavoro, tempo di vita.* [Working Time, Time for Life]. Milano: Angeli.

Bormann, C. (1992). Arbeitslosigkeit und Gesundheit. Empirische Analyse auf der Basis der Daten aus dem 1. Nationalen Gesundheitssurvey der Bundesrepublik Deutschland aus den Jahren 1984 bis 1986. [Unemployment and health. Empirical analysis on the basis of the data acquired during the first National Health Survey in the Federal Republic of Germany from 1984 to 1986]. *Sozialer Fortschritt, 3*, 63-66.

Born, M. & Gavray, C. (s.d.). Differential psychosocial precariousness of men and women. In M. T. Neuilly (Ed.), *Gestion de crise: Crises technologiques et crises sociales* (Cahiers de l'Ipsa n°19). S.l.: l'Harmattan.

Born, M. & Gavray, C. (1995). Differential psychosocial precariousness of men and women. In M.T. Neuilly (Ed.), *Gestion de crise: Crises technologiques et crises sociales* (Cahiers de l'Ipsa n°19). S.l.: l'Harmattan.

Born, M., Gavray, C., & Cattelino, E. (1998). *Relation between adolescent and young adult psychosocial well-being.* (Poster presented at the EARA-conference, June 1998). Budapest: EARA.

Borrell, C. (1996). *Les desigualtats socials en la salut.* [Social Inequalities in Health]. Barcelona: Institut Municipal de la Salut.

Brenner, M.H. (1980). *Estimating the social costs of youth unemployment problems 1947-1976.* Waltham: Brandeis University, Center for Public Service, The Vice President's Task Force on youth unemployment.

Brenner, M.H. (1987). Economic change, alcohol consumption and heart disease in nine industrialised countries. *Social Science & Medicine, 25*(2), 119-132.

Brenner, M.H. & Mooney, A. (1983). Unemployment and health in the context of economic change. *Social Science & Medicine, 17*(2), 1125-1138.

Brenner, S.O., Petterson, I.L., Levi, L., & Arnetz, B. (1988). *Stressreaktioner på hot om arbetslöshet och upplevd arbetslöshet.* [Stress reactions, Threats of Unemployment and Experiences of Unemployment]. Stockholm: Stressforskningsrapporter nr 210. Statens Institut för Psykosocial Miljömedicin.

Briante, G. (1991). *Non lavorare stanca.* [If you don't work you get tired]. Torino: Tirrenia Stampatori.

Briar, K.H. (1977). The effect of long-term unemployment on workers and their families. *Dissertation Abstract International, 37* (9-A), 6062.

Broomhall, H.S. & Winefield, A.H. (1990). A comparison of the affective well-being of young and middle-aged unemployed men matched for length of unemployment. *British Journal of Medical Psychology, 63*, 43-52.

Brusco, S. (1982). The Emilian Model: Productive Decentralization and Social Integration. *Cambridge Journal of Economics*, 2.

Bruzzone, E. (Ed.). (1991). *Cassintegrati e disagio psichico.* [Redundancy Fund Recipients and Psychic Uneasiness]. Torino: Sagep.

Burger, A. & Seidenspinner, G. (1977). *Jugend unter dem Druck der Arbeitslosigkeit.* [Young Persons under the Pressure of Unemployment]. München: Juventa.

Buzzi, C. (1994). *La salute del futuro. Indagine Iard sui giovani e la salute.* [The Health of the Future. Iard Survey on Youth and Health]. Bologna: Il Mulino.

Buzzi, C., Cavalli, A., & de Lillo, A. (Eds.). (1997). *Giovani verso il Duemila. Quarto rapporto Iard sulla condizione giovanile in Italia.* [Youth towards 2000. Fourth Iard Report on Youth Condition in Italy]. Bologna: Il Mulino.

Càritas (1985). *La cara amagada de l'atur.* [The Hidden Face of Unemployment]. Barcelona: Cáritas Diocesanas de Barcelona.

Caritas Italiana – Fondazione Zancan (1997). *I bisogni dimenticati. Rapporto 1996 su emarginazione ed esclusione sociale.* [The Last of the Row – Report 1996 on Alienation and Social Exclusion]. Milano: Feltrinelli.

Caritas Italiana – Fondazione Zancan (1998). *Gli ultimi della fila. Rapporto 1997 sui bisogni dimenticati.* [The Last of the Row-Report 1997 on the forgotten Needs]. Milano: Feltrinelli.

Casal, J., Masjuan, J. M., & Planas, J. (1990). La inserción social de los jóvenes. [The social insertion of young people]. *Revista de Educación, 293*, 109-122.

Celata, C., Cirri, M., & Zanon, L. (Eds.). (1997). *Il mondo dell'adolescenza: Pensieri, enigmi, provocazioni. Indagine OMS sui giovani e la salute a Milano.* [The World of Adolescence: Thoughts, Enigmas, Provocations. OMS Survey on Youth and Health in Milan]. Milano: Angeli.

Christe, G. (1989). Aspekte der Lebenswelt arbeitsloser Jugendlicher in einer ländlichen Region. [Life aspects of unemployed young persons in rural regions]. *Zeitschrift für Sozialisationsforschung und Erziehungssoziologie, 9*(1), 41-58.

Cortés, I. (1997). *Relació entre l'atur i la salut mental d'una mostra de la població activa catalana entrevistada en l'Enquesta de Salut de Catalunya 1994.* [Relationship Between Unemployment and Mental Health in a Sample of the Active Population Interviewed in the 1994 Catalan Health Survey]. Barcelona: Institut Municipal de la Salut.

Costa, G. & Faggiano, F. (Eds.). (1994). *L'equità nella salute in Italia. Rapporto sulle diseguaglianza sociali in sanità.* [Equity in Health in Italy. Report on Social and Sanitary Inequalities]. Milano: Angeli.

Costa, G. & Segnan, N. (1988). Mortalità e condizione professionale nello studio longitudinale torinese. [Mortality and professional condition in the Turin longitudinal study]. *Epidemiologia e prevenzione, 36*, 48-57.

Costa, G., Faggiano, F., Cadum, E., Lagorio, S., Arcà, M., Farchi G., Demaria, M., & Pagnanelli, F. (1994). Le differenze sociali nella mortalità in Italia. [Social differences in the mortality in Italy]. In G. Costa & F. Faggiano (Eds.), *L'equità nella salute in Italia. Rapporto sulle diseguaglianza sociali in sanità.* [Equality in Health in Italy. Report on Social and Sanitary Inequalities]. Milano: Angeli.

Crepet, P. (1989). Effetti psicopatologici della disoccupazione. Analisi della letteratura internazionale. [Psychopathological effects of unemployment. Analysis of the international literature]. *Rivista Sperimentale di Freniatria, 6,* 1169-1192.

Crepet, P. (1990). *Le malattie della disoccupazione.* [The unemployment diseases]. Roma: Edizioni Lavoro.

Crepet, P. (1991). Stress e condizioni di non lavoro. Teorie interpretative, metodologia della ricerca, strumenti di valutazione ed evidenze empiriche dell'impatto psicosociale della perdita di lavoro. [Stress and unemployment conditions. Interpretative theories, methodology of research, evaluation instruments and empirical evidences of the psychosocial impact of the job loss]. In M. La Rosa (Ed.), *Stress e lavoro.* [Stress and work]. Milano: Angeli.

Crepet, P., Baldasseroni, A., Zoppi, O., & Carnevale, F. (1994). Indagine psicosociale in un gruppo di giovani apprendisti. [Psychosocial survey in a group of young apprentices]. *Salute e Territorio, 93*, 60-63.

Crepet, P., Vetrone, G., Piazzi, A., Costa, M., & Lombardi, V. (1992). Aspetti psicologici della disoccupazione giovanile nella città di Foggia. Studio trasversale. [Psychological aspects of youth unemployment in the town of Foggia. Transversal study]. *Difesa Sociale, 2*, 39-54.

Crepet, P., Caracciolo, S., Cappi, S., Tugnoli, S., Cielo, M., & Simonato, L. (1995). Mortalità per suicidio ed omicidio in età giovanile. [Mortality for suicide and murder during youth age]. In M. Geddes (Ed.), *Rapporto sulla salute in Italia.* [Report on Health in Italy] (pp. 57-70). Roma: Ediesse.

D'Avanzo, B. (1995). Suicidi in Italia. Andamenti temporali della mortalità tra il 1955 e il 1990. [Suicides in Italy. Temporal trends of mortality between 1955 and 1990]. *Prospettive Sociali e Sanitarie, 17*, 16-19.

Daniel, W.W. (1974). A national survey of the unemployed. *Broadsheet, 40*, 546.

Davidsson, U. (1997). *Välfärd och ojämlikhet i 20-årsperspektiv 1975-1995.* [Living Conditions and Inequality in Sweden – a 20-Year Perspective 1975-1995]. Stockholm: Statistics of Sweden.

Degimbe, N. (1996). *De dreiging van de werkloosheid: een recente historische analyse van de rotatie binnen de werkloosheid van korte duur.* [The Threat of Unemployment: A Recent Historical Analysis of the Rotation within Short-term Unemployment]. Brussel: Ministerie van Tewerkstelling en Arbeid, Directie van de studie der arbeidsproblemen, Administratie van de werkgelegenheid.

De la Torre, A. (1989). Aproximación al desempleo desde las atribuciones de trabajadores y desempleados. [Approach to the attributes of unemployed persons and workers]. *Psicología del Trabajo y de las Organizaciones, 12*, 27-37.

Deliens, L. (1989). Jongeren tussen zorgzame samenleving en verzorgingsstaat: Een empirisch onderzoek over de invloed van werkloosheid op de inkomenspositie van laaggeschoolde jongeren. [Youngsters between careful society and welfare state: An empirical research on the influence of unemployment on the income position of youngsters with low school qualifications]. *Tijdschrift voor Sociologie, 10*(3-4), 547.

Deliens, L., Bosman, E., & Louckx, F. (1988). *Crisisjongeren in Wonderland: Een surveyonderzoek over de invloed van werkloosheid en sociale omgeving op het sociaal-economisch gedrag van crisisjongeren en hun gezin.* [Crisis Youngsters in Wonderland: A Survey Research on the Influence of Unemployment and Social Environment on Socio-Economic Behaviour of Crisis Youngsters and their Family]. Brussel: Ministerie van de Vlaamse Gemeenschap, Administratie voor Gezin en Maatschappelijk Welzijn, Centrum voor Bevolkingsen gezinsstudiën.

Del Llano, J. (1987). Los efectos de la situación de desempleo sobre el estado de la salud. [The Effects of the Unemployment Situation on the State of Health]. In *Actas del Primer Congreso Nacional de Medicina del Trabajo.* Madrid: INSALUD.

Del Llano, J. (1990). *Desempleo y salud: Relación existente entre la situación de desempleo y el estado de salud en población en edad de trabajar del municipio de Madrid.* [Unemployment and Health: Relationship between Unemployment and Health Among Working Age People from Madrid]. Madrid: Universidad Complutense de Madrid.

Del Llano, J. & Del Llano, J. (1989). Desempleo: Valoración y estrategias desde la salud comunitaria. [Unemployment: Valuation and Strategies for Community Health]. *Gaceta Sanitaria, 12*(3), 437-439.

Del Llano, J., San Martín, R., Espinosa, L., Del Llano, J., Costa, M., & Ruíz, M. (1993). Desempleo y salud. Revisión de la literatura y análisis crítico de los diferentes diseños de investigación utilizados. [Unemployment and Health. Revision of the Literature and Critical Analysis of Different Research Designs]. *Revisiones de Salud Pública, 3*, 215-242.

Del Llano, J., Aracil, E., Del Llano, M., González, J.L., Fernández, F., Román, B., & Esquivias, M. (1996). Una enfermedad llamada paro: La trastienda del desempleo de larga duración. [An Illness Called Unemployment: The Background of Long-term Unemploment]. *Gaceta Sanitaria, 10*, 73-80.

Deniel, J., Bosch, M., Culf, N., & Olmeda, C. (1996). Influencia del paro sobre los problemas de salud mental. [Influence of Unemployment on the Mental Health Problems]. *Atención Primaria, 18*(7), 379-382.

De Pauw, M. (1985). Studie werkloosheid en geestelijke gezondheidszorg. [Study of unemployment and mental health care]. *Sociaal, 6*(4), 23-24.

De Pauw, M. (1988). Weerslag van de ekonomische krisis, en in het bijzonder werkloosheid, op de geestelijke gezondheidszorg. [Effects of the economic crisis, especially unemployment, on mental health care]. In Nationale Vereniging voor Geestelijke Gezondheidszorg v.z.w. *Werkloosheid en Geestelijke gezondheidszorg* (Report of a Seminar) (pp. 23-133). Gent: Nationale Vereniging voor Geestelijke Gezondheidszorg.

Depolo, M. & Sarchielli, G. (1987). *Psicologia della disoccupazione.* [Psychology of unemployment] (pp. 31-37). Bologna: Il Mulino.

Depolo, M., Fraccaroli, F., & Sarchielli, G. (1992). Tipi di inserimento lavorativo e benessere psicologico: Uno studio longitudinale. [Types of work insertion and psychological well-being: A longitudinal study]. *Difesa Sociale, 5.*

De Witte, H. (1986). Werkloosheidsbeleving bij jongeren. [Experience of unemployment among youngsters]. *Welzijnwerk-kroniek, 10*(94), 23-27.

De Witte, H. (1989). Liever moe dan lui: Werkloosheid en tewerkstelling van jongeren in Vlaanderen. [Rather tired than idle: Employment and unemployment of youngsters in Flanders]. *Tijdschrift voor Sociologie, 10*(3-4), 509-545.

De Witte, H. (1992a). Unemployment, political attitudes and voting behaviour. *Politics and the Individual, 2*(1), 29-41.

De Witte, H. (1992b). *Tussen optimisten en teruggetrokkenen: een empirisch onderzoek naar het psycho-sociaal profiel van langdurig werklozen en deelnemers aan de Weer-Werkactie in Vlaanderen.* [Between Optimists and Withdrawn Persons: An Empirical Research on the Psychosocial Profile of Long-term Unemployment and Participants in the 'Work Again'-Action in Flanders]. Leuven: Katholieke Universiteit Leuven, Hoger Instituut voor de Arbeid.

De Witte, H. (1993). Gevolgen van langdurige werkloosheid voor het psychisch welzijn: Overzicht van de onderzoeksliteratuur. [Consequences of long-term unemployment on the psychological well-being: Overview of the research literature]. *Psychologica Belgica, 33*(1), 1-35.

De Witte, H. (1994). ('t Is geen) leven zonder werk: Een overzicht van recente literatuur over de psychische gevolgen van werkloosheid. [(No) life without a job: An overview of the recent literature on the psychological consequences of unemployment]. *Welzijnsgids-Noden, werken, 12*, 1-23.

De Witte, H. & Hooge, J. (1995). Een vergelijking van typologieën van kort- en langdurig werklozen: wetenschappelijke en beleidsmatige implicaties. [A comparison of typologies of short- and long-term unemployed persons: scientific and policy implications]. In Van der Hallen (Ed.), *De arbeidsmarktonderzoekersdag 1995: Verslagboek* (Dossier nr 12) (pp. 127-142). Leuven: Steunpunt Werkgelegenheid, Arbeid en Vorming.

De Witte, H. & Hooge, J. (1997). Aanpassing aan werkloosheid? Een cross-sectionele vergelijking van kort- en langdurig werklozen. [Adaptation to unemployment? A cross-sectional comparison of short- and long-term unemployed persons]. *Gedrag & Gezondheid, 25*(3), 145-155.

De Witte, H. & Wets, J. (1993). Over de (heterogeniteit in de) werkloosheidsbeleving van jonge, langdurig werkloze vrouwen. [On the (heterogeneity in) the experience of unemployment among young, long-term unemployed women]. In A. Goethals & J. Groothoff (Eds.), *Gezondheid en hulpverlening in sociaal-cultureel perspectief* (SISWO-publikatie 365) (pp. 35-60). Amsterdam: SISWO.

De Witte, H. & Wets, J. (1996). On the heterogeneity of the experience of long-term unemployment among young women. In M. De Goede, P. De Klaver, J. Van Ophem, C. Verhaar, &

A. De Vries (Eds.), *Youth: Unemployment, Identity and Policy*. (pp. 65-85). Aldershot: Avebury.
Diezinger, A., Marquardt, R., Bilden, H., & Dahlke, K. (1983). *Zukunft mit beschränkten Möglichkeiten. Entwicklungsprozesse arbeitsloser Mädchen. Band 1: Aktuelle Belastungen und berufliche Konsequenzen.* [A Future of Limited Possibilities. Developmental Processes of Unemployed Girls. Volume 1: Relevant Burdens and Effects on Working Life]. München: Verlag Deutsches Jugendinstitut (DJI).
Dooley, D. & Prause, J. (1995). Effect of unemployment on school-leavers' self-esteem. *Journal of Occupational and Organizational Psychology, 68*, 177-192.
Dooley, D. & Prause, J. (1997). Effect of students' self-esteem on later employment status: Interactions of self-esteem with gender and race. *Applied Psychology: An International Review, 46*(2), 175-198.
Dubos, R. (1984). Mirage of Health. In N. Black et al. (Eds.), *Health & Disease – A Reader.* Milton Keynes, England: Open University Press.
Eales, M. J. (1989). Shame among unemployed men. *Social Science and Medicine, 28*(8), 783-789.
Elchardus, M. & Glorieux, I. (1995). *Niet aan de arbeid voorbij: De werkloosheidservaring als reflectie over arbeid, solidariteit en sociale cohesie.* [Not beyound Work: The Experience of Unemployment as a Reflection on Labour, Solidarity and Social Cohesion]. Brussel: VUBPRESS.
Elkeles, T. & Seifert, W. (1992). *Arbeitslose und ihre Gesundheit. Empirische Langzeitanalysen.* [The Unemployed and their Health. Empirical Longitudinal Analyses]. Veröffentlichungsreihe der Forschungsgruppe Gesundheitsrisiken und Präventionspolitik. Berlin: Wissenschaftszentrum Berlin für Sozialforschung.
ENSE 1995 (1996). *Encuesta Nacional de Salud de España 1995.* [Spanish National Health Survey]. Madrid: Ministerio de Sanidad y Consumo.
EPA (several years). *Encuesta de Población Activa.* [Active Population Survey]. Madrid: Instituto Nacional de Estadística.
ESCA 1994 (1996). *Enquesta de Salut de Catalunya 1994.* [Catalan Health Survey]. Barcelona: Servei Català de la Salut.
European Commission (1997). *Employment in Europe*. Bruxelles: Author.
European Commission (1998). Employment Guidelines. DG for Employment, Industrial Relations and Social Affairs. Luxemburg: Office for Official Publications of the European Communities.
European Monitoring Centre for Drugs and Drug Addiction (1997). *Annual Report on the State of the Drugs Problem in the E.U.* Lisbon: EMCDDA.
Eurostat (1985-1996). *Labour Force Surveys.* Bruxelles: Author.
Eurostat (1995). *Demographic Statistics*. Bruxelles: Author.
Eurostat (1996). Eurostat Jahrbuch '96. (Eurostat Yearbook '96). Brüssel: Amt für Veröffentlichung der Europäischen Gemeinschaften.
Eurostat (1997). *Youth in the European Union. From Education to Working Life*. Bruxelles: Author.
Eurostat (1998). *News release*, no. 32, 1998, *Seasonally adjusted unemployment rates*. http://www. lex.unict.it/eurolabor/diritto-sociale/eurostat/febbraio.htm.
Eurostat (1998). *Unemployment*, no. 3.
Eurostat (1998). *Basic Statistics of the Community*. Bruxelles: Author.
Ezzy, D. (1993). Unemployment and Mental Health. A critical review. *Social Science and Medicine, 37*(1), 41-52.
Fagin, L. & Little, M. (1984). *The Forsaken Families: The Effects of Unemployment on Family Life.* England: Penguin Books Ltd.
Feather, N.T. (1990). *The Psychological Impact of Unemployment*. New York: Springer.
Feather, N.T. & O'Brien, G.E. (1986a). A longitudinal analysis of the effects of employment and unemployment on school-leavers. *British Journal of Psychology, 77*, 459-479.

Feather, N.T. & O'Brien, G.E. (1986b). A longitudinal study of the effects of employment and unemployment on school-leavers. *Journal of Occupational Psychology, 59*, 121-144.

Federaal Ministerie van Tewerkstelling en Arbeid (1997). *Werkloosheid in België: Statistische Reeksen.* [Unemployment in Belgium: Statistical series]. Brussel: Federaal Ministerie van Tewerkstelling en Arbeid, Directie van de studie der arbeidsproblemen, Administratie van de werkgelegenheid.

Feldman, J.M. (1973a). Race, employment and the evaluation of work. *Journal of Applied Psychology, 58*(1), 10-15.

Feldman, J.M. (1973b). Race, economic class and perceived outcomes of work and unemployment. *Journal of Applied Psychology, 58*(1), 16-22.

Fergusson, D.M., Horwood, L.J., & Lynskey, M.T. (1997). The effects of unemployment on psychiatric illness during young adulthood. *Psychological Medicine, 27*(2), 371-381.

Ferrera, M. (1996). The "Southern Model" of welfare in social Europe. *European Social Policy, 6*(1).

Figà-Talamanca, I. & Pagano, R. (1987). Disoccupazione e salute: che cosa dicono le statistiche italiane. [Unemployment and health: What the Italian statistics say]. *Epidemiologia e prevenzione, 34*, 50-53.

Fineman, S. (Ed.). (1987). *Unemployment: Personal and Social Consequences.* London: Tavistock.

Fraccaroli, F. (1989). Work involvement, immagine del lavoro e della disoccupazione in un gruppo di giovani disoccupati. [Work involvement, image of work and unemployment in a group of young unemployed]. *Giornale italiano di psicologia, 4*, 651-666.

Fredlund, P. & Tomth, J.-E. (1985). *Sociala följdverkningar av ungdomsarbetslöshet.* [Social Consequences of Youth Unemployment]. Stockholm: Stad. Utrednings- och statistikkontoret.

Freund, P. (1990). The Expressive Body: A common ground for the sociology of emotions and health and illness. *Sociology of Health and Illness, 12*, 452-477.

Fryer, D. (1986). Employment deprivation and personal agency during unemployment – A critical discussion of Jahoda's explanation of the psychological effetcs of unemployment. *Social Behaviour, 1*(2), 3-23

Fryer, D. (1997). International perspectives on youth unemployment and mental health: Some central issues. *Journal of Adolescence, 20*(3), 333-342.

Fryer, D. & Ullah, P. (Eds.). (1987). *Unemployed People: Social and Psychological Perspectives.* Philadelphia: Milton Keynes.

Gallie, D. (1994). Are the unemployed an underclass? Some evidence from the social change and economic life initiative. *Sociology, 28*(2), 737-757

García Rodríguez, Y. (1992). *Desempleo: Alteraciones psicológicas.* [Unemployment: Psychological Impact]. Valencia: Promolibro.

García Rodríguez, Y. (1993). Conclusiones sobre los efectos psicológicos del desempleo en la juventud. [Conclusions about the psychological effects of unemployment among young people]. *Psicología del Trabajo y las Organizaciones, 24*, 51-62.

Garcia Rodriguez, Y. (1997). Learned helplessness or expectancy-value? A psychological model for describing the experiences of different categories of unemployed people. *Journal of Adolescence, 20*(3), 321-332.

Garrido, P., Castillo, I., Benavides, F.G., & Ruíz, I. (1994). Situación laboral y salud mental. Resultados de un estudio transversal. [Working state and mental health. Outcomes of a cross-sectional study]. *Gaceta Sanitaria, 8*, 128-132.

Garrido, L.J. & Toharia, L. (1996). Paro y desigualdad. [Unemployment and Inequality]. In M. Aguilar, C. García, L.J. Garrido, M. Laparra, M.A. Malo, A. Mora, V. Renes, L. Toharia, C. Valiente (Eds.), *Pobreza, necesidad y marginación.* [Poverty, Need and Discimination] (pp. 9-63). Madrid: Fundación Argentaria.

Gavray, C. (1996). *Résultats du panel démographique et socio-économique belge, trajectoire d'emploi et précarité d'emplo.* [Results of the Belgian demographic and socio-economic panel study, employment passages and precarity of employment]. (Paper presented at the 3èmes journées d'étude Céreq-Cérétim-Lasmas IdL, 23 et 24 may 1996). Rennes: 3èmes journées d'étude Céreq-Cérétim-Lasmas IdL.

Gavray, C. (1997). Trajectoire déviante à la lisière entre adolescence et âge adulte. [Deviant passages at the transition from adolescence to adulthood]. *Déviance et Société, 21*(3), 273-288.

Giannelli, G., Orientale Caputo, G., & Pugliese, E. (1996). La disoccupazione giovanile in Europa. [Youth unemployment in Europe]. In E. Pugliese (Ed.), *Una disoccupazione mediterranea. Giovani e mercato del lavoro nel Mezzogiorno e a Napoli.* [Mediterranean Unemployment. Youth and Labour Market in the South]. Napoli: Libreria Dante & Descartes.

Ginsborg, P. (1989). *Storia d'Italia dal dopoguerra a oggi. Società e politica.* [History of Italy from the End of Second World War until now].Torino: Einaudi.

Giullari, B. & La Rosa, M. (1995). *Disoccupazione: Perché. Scienze sociali a confronto.* [Unemployment: Why. Social Sciences in Comparison]. Milano: Angeli.

Glorieux, I. (1995). *Arbeid als zingever: een onderzoek naar de betekenis van arbeid in het leven van mannen en vrouwen.* [Labour as a Source of Significance: A Research on the Significance of Labour in the Life of Men and Women]. Brussel: VUBPRESS.

Gore, S. (1978). The effects of social support in moderating the health consequences of unemployment. *Journal of Health and Social Behavior, 19*, 157-165.

Grassi, A., Falzoni, M.C., & Fasol, R. (1992). Indagine di popolazione sulle condizioni psichiche di giovani operai metalmeccanici e di giovani disoccupati. [Population survey on the psychic conditions of young metalworkers and young unemployed]. *Difesa Sociale, 4*, 143-152.

Greek Monitoring Centre for Drugs and Drug Addiction (1997). *Greek Annual Report on Drugs.* (Kokkevi, Stefanis et al.). Athens: University Mental Health Research Institute.

Grieswelle, D. (1977). *Jugendliche Arbeitslose und Jungarbeiter. Berufsbezogene Einstellungen und Verhaltensweisen berufsschulpflichtiger Jugendlicher in sogenannten Jungarbeiterklassen im Saarland.* [Unemployed Young Persons and Young Workers. Profession-related Views and Behaviour of Young Persons Required to Attend Vocational School in Classrooms for Young Workers in the Saarland]. Saarbrücken: Wirtschaftsvereinigung der CDU Saar.

Gurney, R.M. (1980a). Does unemployment affect the self-esteem of school leavers? *Australian Journal of Psychology, 32*, 175-182.

Gurney, R.M. (1980b). The effects of unemployment on the psychosocial development of school leavers. *Journal of Occupational Psychology, 53*, 205-213.

Gurney, R.M. (1981). Leaving school, facing unemployment, and making attributions about the causes of unemployment. *Journal of Vocational Behavior, 18*, 79-91.

Häfner, H. (1988). Macht Arbeitslosigkeit krank? Ein Überblick über den Wissensstand zu den Zusammenhängen zwischen Erwerbslosigkeit, körperlichen und seelischen Gesundheitsrisiken. [Does unemployment result in sickness? An overview of the latest information on the correlation between unemployment, physical and psychological health risks]. *Fortschritte der Neurologie und Psychiatrie, 56*, 326-343.

Hagquist, C. (in print). Youth unemployment, economic deprivation and suicide. *Scandinavian Journal of Social Welfare.*

Hagquist, C. & Starrin, B. (1996). Youth unemployment and mental health – gender differences and economic stress. *Scandinavian Journal of Social Welfare, 5*, 215-228.

Hahn, T. (1996). Jugendliche Arbeitslose. Zwischen sozialer Ausgrenzung und individuellen Integrationsbemühungen. [Unemployed young persons. Between social exclusion and individual efforts at integration]. In J. Mansel & A. Klocke (Ed.), *Die Jugend von heute.* [The Youth of Today] (pp. 174-192). Weinheim: Juventa.

Hahn, T. & Schön, G. (1996). *Arbeitslos – chancenlos? Verläufe von Arbeitslosigkeit in Ostdeutschland.* [Without Work – Without Prospects? Development of Unemployment in East-Germany]. Opladen: Leske+Budrich.

Hamilton, S.F. (1987). Work and maturity: Occupational socialization of non-college youth in the United States and West Germany. *Research in the Sociology of Education and Socialization, 7*, 283-312.

Hammarström, A. (1986). *Ungdomsarbetslöshet och ohälsa.* [Youth Unemployment and Ill Health]. Stockholm: Karolinska Institute (Doctoral thesis.).

Hammarström, A. (1991). Ungdomsarbetslöshet försämrar hälsan och ökar missbruk. [Youth unemployment causes poorer health and increases substance abuse]. *Läkartidningen, 88*, 36.

Hammarström, A. (1994). Health consequences of youth unemployment – Review from a gender perspective. *Social Sciences Medicine, 5*, 699-709.

Hammarström, A. (1996) *Arbetslöshet och ohälsa – om ungdomars livsvillkor.* [Unemloyment and Ill Health – On Vital Conditions of Youth]. Lund: Studentlitteratur.

Hammarström, A. & Janlert, U. (1994). Unemployment and change of tobacco habits. A study of young people from 16 to 21 years of age. *British Journal of Addiction, 89*, 1691-1696.

Hammarström, A. & Janlert, U. (1997). Nervous and depressive symptoms in a longitudinal study of youth unemployment – Selection or exposure. *Journal of Adolescence, 20*(3), 293-305.

Hammarström, A. & Olofsson, B.-L. (1997). Hälsa och missbruk – samband med arbetslöshet och marginalisering. [Health and substance abuse – relationship between unemployment and marginalisation]. In J. Carle & I. Julkunen (Eds.), *Arbetslöshetens villkor – Om ungdom, arbetslöshet och marginalisering i 90-talets Norden.* [Unemployment Conditions – On Young Persons, Unemployment and Marginalisation in the Nordic Countries in the 1990s]. Köpenhamn.

Hannan, D.F., Oriain, S., & Whelan C.T. (1997). Youth unemployment and psychological distress in the Republic of Ireland. *Journal of Adolescence, 20*(3), 307-320.

Hawton, K. & Morgan, G. (1994). Implications for research and clinical audit. In R. Jenkins, S. Griffiths, I. Wylie, K. Hawton, G. Morgan, & A. Tylee (Eds.), *The Prevention of Suicide.* London: HMSO, Department of Health.

Hawton, K. & Rose, N. (1986). Unemployment and attempted suicide among men in Oxford. *Health Trends, 18*, 29-32.

Hawton, K., Fagg, J., Platt, S., & Hawkins, M. (1993). Factors associated with suicide after parasuicide in young people. *British Medical Journal, 306*(19), 1641-1644.

Hawton, K., O'Grady, J., Osborn, M., & Cole, D. (1982). Adolescents who take overdoses: their characteristics, problems and contacts with helping agencies. *British Journal of Psychiatry, 140*, 118-123.

Hayes, J. & Nutman, P. (1981). *Understanding the Unemployed.* London: Tavistock.

Heinemann, K. (1978). *Arbeitslose Jugendliche: Ursachen und individuelle Bewältigung eines sozialen Problems. Eine empirische Untersuchung.* [Unemployed Young Persons: Causes and Individual Coping with a Social Problem. An Empirical Survey]. Darmstadt, Neuwied: Luchterhand.

Heitmeyer, W., Buhse, H., Liebe-Freund, J., Möller, K., Müller, J., Ritz, H., Siller, G., & Vossen, J. (1993). *Die Bielefelder Rechtsextremismus-Studie. Erste Langzeituntersuchung zur politischen Sozialisation männlicher Jugendlicher.* [The Bielefeld Study of Right-Wing Extremism. The first Longitudinal Survey of the Political Socialisation of Male Youth]. Weinheim: Juventa.

Hill, Z. (1978). The psychological impact of unemployment. *New Society, 19 January*, 118-120.

HIVA-stuurgroep (1986). *Met een stempel door het leven? Werkloosheid en Tewerkstelling van jongeren: Beschrijving, gevolgen en perspectieven.* [Marked for life? Unemployment and Employment of Youngsters: Description, Consequences and Perspectives]. Leuven: Katholieke Universiteit Leuven, Hoger instituut voor de arbeid.

Hjelmeland, H. & Bjerke, T. (1996). Parasuicide in the county of Sor-Trondelag, Norway. General epidemiology and psychological factors. *Social Psychiatry Psychiatric Epidemiology, 31*(5), 272-283.

Hoger Instituut voor de Arbeid – Werkgroep jeugdwerkloosheid (1988). *En de jongeren, zij stempelden voort? Recente evolutie in de jeugdwerkloosheid en een beschrijving en evaluatie van opleidings- en tewerkstellingsinitiatieven voor jongeren.* [And the Young, are they still on the Dole? Recent Evolution in Youth Unemployment and a Description and Evaluation of Employment Initiatives for Youngsters]. Leuven: Katholieke Universiteit Leuven, Hoger Instituut voor de Arbeid.

Holzhüter, H., Hickel, R., & Kieselbach, T. (Eds.). (1997). *Arbeit und Arbeitslosigkeit: Die gesellschaftliche Herausforderung unserer Zeit.* [Employment and Unemployment. The Societal Challenge of our Times]. Bremen: Kooperation Universität – Arbeiterkammer Bremen.

Hooge, J. (1995). *Wie neemt deel aan het Individueel Begeleidingsplan? Psycho-sociaal profiel en opvolging van de deelnemers.* [Who participates in the Individual Counselling Plan? Psychosocial Profile and Follow-Up of the Participants]. Leuven: Katholieke Universiteit Leuven, Hoger Instituut voor de Arbeid.

Hormuth, S.E. (1997). Auswirkungen des Transformationsprozesses in Ostdeutschland auf individuelle Entwicklung, Bildung und Berufsverläufe. [Effects of transformational processes in East Germany on individual development]. *Berliner Journal für Soziologie, 4*, 561-568.

Horwitz, A. (1984). The Economy and Social Pathology. *Annual Revue of Sociology, 10*, 95-119.

Hurrelmann, K. (1988). *Sozialisation und Gesundheit. Somatische, psychische und soziale Risikofaktoren im Lebenslauf.* [Socialisation and Health. Somatic, Psychological, and Social Risk Factors in Biographies]. Weinheim, München: Juventa.

INJUVE (1997). *Informe Juventud en España 1996.* (IJE 1996) [Report on Spanish Young People]. Madrid: Instituto de la Juventud, Ministerio de Trabajo y Asuntos Sociales.

Institut d'Estudis de la Salut (Ed.). (1984). *Atur i salut.* [Unemployment and Health]. Barcelona: Generalitat de Catalunya.

Ioannidi, E. & Mestheneos, E. (1999). *Cocooned or Trapped? Greek National Report.* SOSTRIS Working Paper 5, Social Strategies in Risk Societies. University of East London: Department of Sociology.

Ioannidi, E. & Mestheneos, E. (2000). *Unqualified Unemployed Youth. Greek National Report.* SOSTRISS Working Paper 7, Social Strategies in Risk Societies. University of East London: Department of Sociology.

Istat (1988,1996). *Statistiche giudiziarie penali.* [Judicial and Criminal Statistics]. Roma: Istat.

Istat (1996). *Indagine sulle forze di lavoro.* [Survey on Labour Forces]. Roma: Istat.

Istat (1996). *Stili di vita e condizioni di salute. Indagini multiscopo sulle famiglie 1993-1994.* [Life Styles and Health Conditions. Multipurpose Surveys on Families]. Roma: Istat.

Istat (1997). *Rapporto sull'Italia.* [Report on Italy]. Bologna: Il Mulino.

Istat (1997). *A Statistical portrait of Youth Exclusion. A Siena Group Monitoring Report.* Roma: Istat.

Jackson, P.R. & Walsh, S. (1987). Unemployment and the family. In D. Fryer & P. Ullah (Eds.), *Unemployed People: Social and Psychological Perspectives* (pp. 194-216). Milton Keynes: Open University Press.

Jackson, P.R. & Warr, P.B. (1984). Unemployment and psychological ill health: The moderating role of duration and age. *Psychological Medicine, 14*, 605-614.

Jackson, P.R., Stafford, E.M., Banks, M.H., & Warr, P.B. (1983). Unemployment and psychological distress in young people: The moderating role of employment commitment. *Journal of Applied Psychology, 68*(3), 525-535.

Jahoda, M. (1982). *Employment and Unemployment. A Social-Psychological Analysis.* Cambridge: Cambridge University Press.

Jahoda, M., Lazarsfeld, P.F., & Zeisel, H. (1933). *Marienthal. The Sociography of an Unemployed Community.* London: Tavistock.

Jahoda, M., Lazarsfeld, P.F., & Zeisel, H. (1975). *Die Arbeitslosen von Marienthal. Ein soziographischer Versuch über die Wirkungen langandauernder Arbeitslosigkeit.* [The Unemployed of Marienthal. A Sociographic Essay on the Effects of Long-term Unemployment]. Frankfurt a. M.: Suhrkamp.

Janlert, U. (1981). Arbetslöshet och ohälsa. [Unemployment and ill health]. In SOU (Official Government Report Series), *Hälsorisker.* [Health Risks] (pp. 109-140). Stockholm: Socialstyrelsen.

Janlert, U. (1985). Unemployment and health. In G. Westcott, P.-G. Svensson, & H.-F.-K. Zöllner (Eds.), *Health Policy Implications of Unemployment* (pp. 7-26). World Health Organisation: Copenhagen.

Janlert, U. (1991). *Work Deprivation and Health.* Stockholm: Karolinska Institutet.

Janlert, U. (1992). Arbetslöshet som folkhälsoproblem. [Unemployment as a public health issue]. Folkhälsogruppen, Rapport nr 17. Stockholm.

Janlert, U. & Hammarström, A. (1992). Alcohol consumption among unemployed youths: Results from a prospective study. *British Journal of Addiction, 87*, 703-714.

Jenkins, R. (1978). Doing a double. *New Society, (20 April)*, 121.

Jeuris, W. (1984). *Sociaal-ekonomische analyse van de diensten voor geestelijke gezondheidszorg in Vlaanderen.* [Socio-Economic Analysis of the Mental Health Care Centres in Flanders]. (unpublished licenciate dissertation). Antwerpen: Universiteit Antwerpen, Faculteit Toegepaste Ekonomische Wetenschappen.

Jones, S.C., Forster, D.P., & Hassanyeh, F. (1991). The role of unemployment in parasuicide. *Psychological Medicine, 21*, 169-176.

Jordan, B. (1996). *A Theory of Poverty and Social Exclusion.* Cambridge: Polity Press.

Jugendwerk der Deutschen Shell (Ed.). (1997). *Jugend '97: Zukunftsperspektiven, gesellschaftliches Engagement, politische Orientierungen.* [Youth '97. Future Perspectives, Societal Commitment, Political Orientation]. Opladen: Leske+Budrich.

Kannas, L. & Hietarharju, M. (1979). Työttömista nourista sairaita keski-ikaisiä. Sosiaa-linen Aikakauskirja, *1*, 37-45 (quoted from Janlert, 1985).

Karasek, R. & Theorell, T. (1990). *Healthy Work – Stress, Productivity and the Reconstruction of Working Life.* New York: Basic Books.

Katsanopoulou, M. (1998). *H anergia vlaptei kai thn ygeia mas!* [Unemployment also damages our health!]. Newspaper "TA NEA", *24*(2), 5.

Kaufman, G. (1993). *The Psychology of Shame – Theory and Treatment of Shame-Based Syndroms.* London: Routledge & Kegan Paul.

Kelvin, P. & Jarrett, J.E. (1985). *Unemployment: Its Social Psychological Effects.* Cambridge: University Press.

KEPE (1990). *H anaptiksi tis Elladas; Parelthon – Paron – Protasis Politikis.* [The Development of Greece; Past – Present – Policy Suggestions]. Athens: Author.

Kieselbach, T. (1985). Jugend – ein Risikofaktor? Gesundheits- und sozialpolitische Konsequenzen aus der Forschung zur Jugendarbeitslosigkeit. [Youth. A risk factor? Health and sociopolitical consequences drawn from research on youth unemployment]. *Psychosozial, 8*(27), 47-69.

Kieselbach, T. (1988). El desempleo juvenil: Consecuencias en la salud y recomendaciones para las intervenciones psico sociales. [Youth unemployment – health consequences and recommendations for psychological interventions]. In J.R. Torregrosa, J. Bergere Dezahpi, & J.C. Alvaro Estramiana (Eds.), *Juventud, trabajo y desempleo: Un análisis psicosociológico.* [Youth, Work, and Unemployment: A Psycho-sociological Analysis] (pp. 523-555). Madrid: Ministerio de Trabajo y Seguridad Social.

Kieselbach, T. (1988). Youth unemployment and health effects. *The International Journal of Social Psychiatry, 34*(2), 83-96.

Kieselbach, T. (1998). Arbeitslosigkeit. [Unemployment]. In Statistisches Bundesamt (Ed.), *Gesundheitsbericht für Deutschland.* [Health Report for Germany] (pp. 116-121). Stuttgart: Metzler-Poeschl.

Kieselbach, T. & Svensson, P.-G. (1988). Health and social policy responses to unemployment in Europe. *Journal of Social Issues, 44*(4), 173-191.

Kieselbach, T. & Wacker, A. (Eds.). (1985). *Individuelle und gesellschaftliche Kosten der Massenarbeitslosigkeit – Psychologische Theorie und Praxis.* [The Society's and the Individual's Costs of Mass Unemployment – Psychological Theory and Practice]. Weinheim: Deutscher Studien Verlag.

Kieselbach, T. & Wacker, A. (1991). *Bewältigung von Arbeitslosigkeit im sozialen Kontext. Programme, Initiativen, Evaluationen.* [Coping with Unemployment in the Social Context. Programs, Initiatives, Evaluations]. Weinheim: Deutscher Studien Verlag.

Klink, F. & Kieselbach, T. (1990). Jugendarbeitslosigkeit als gesundheitlicher Risikofaktor. [Youth unemployment as a health risk factor]. *Bremer Beiträge zur Psychologie, Nr. 91.*

Kouveli, A., Armenakis, A., & Sakellaropoulos, K. (1997). *Stegastiko provlima ton sismoplikton Aigiou.* [The Housing Problem of the Earthquake Victims in Aigion]. Athens: EKKE.

Kouveli, A., Tsakiris, E., & Sakellaropoulous, K. (1998). *Consumption Behaviour, Consumption Models and Way of Living in the Greek Rural Regions.* National Centre of Social Studies: EKKE (forthcoming).

Krieger, I. & Schläfke, B. (1987). Die Lebenslage junger arbeitsloser Sozialhilfeempfänger. [The situation of young unemployed welfare recipients]. *Neue Praxis, 17*(4), 299-312.

Krupinski, J., Tiller, J.W., Burrows, G.D., & Hallenstein, H. (1994). Youth suicide in Victoria: a retrospective study. *Medical Journal of Australia, 160*, 113-116.

Kurella, S. (1992). *Arbeitslosigkeit und Gesundheit. Literaturstudie für die Jahre 1985-1991.* [Unemployment and Health. Literature Survey of the Years 1985-1991]. Veröffentlichungsreihe der Forschungsgruppe Gesundheitsrisiken und Präventionspolitik. Berlin: Wissenschaftszentrum Berlin für Sozialforschung.

Lagasse, R., Humblet, P., Lenaerts, A., Godin, I., & Moens, G. (1990). Health and social inequities in Belgium. *Social Science in Medicine, 31*(3), 237-248.

Lagrou, L. (1982). Werkloosheid en psychisch welzijn. [Work and psychological well-being]. *Kultuurleven, 49*(10), 880-888.

La Rosa, M. (Ed.). (1991). *Stress e lavoro.* [Stress and Work]. Milano: Angeli.

La Rosa, M. & Borghi, V. (1998a). Work and New Weak Groups. Monographic Section. *International Review of Sociology, 1*, 51-154.

La Rosa, M. & Borghi, V. (1998b). Il lavoro fra nuove opportunità e nuove precarietà. [Work between new opportunities and new precariousness]. In Dip. di Sociologia – Università di Bologna (Ed.), *Parabole sociali tra certezze e incertezze. Dove va la società italiana.* [Social Paths between Certainties and Uncertainties. Where is Italian Society going]. Milano: Angeli.

Leenaars, A.A. & Lester, D. (1995). The changing suicide pattern in Canadian adolescents and youth, compared to their American counterparts. *Adolescence, 30*(119), 539-547.

Lemkow, L. (1987). The subterranian economy as a survival strategy: The Spanish case. In D. Schwefel, P.-G. Svensson, & H.-F.-K. Zöllner (Eds.), *Unemployment, Social Vulnerability and Health in Europe* (143-150*)*. Heidelberg: Springer-Verlag.

Lemkow, L. (1987). The employed unemployed: The subterranean economy in Spain. *Social Science and Medicine, 25*(2), 111-113.

Lemkow, L. (1989). Equity: The state of the art. *Health Promotion, 4*(2), 103-108.

Lester, D. (1991). Social correlates of youth suicide rates in the United States. *Adolescence, 26*, 55-58.

Linos, A. (1998). *Cervical and Breast Screening Projects. University of Athens Medical School.* (Unpublished).

Ludevid, M. (1985). *Els joves obrers i el seu treball.* [*Young Workers and their Jobs*]. Barcelona: Generalitat de Catalunya.

Mackenbach, J. & Looman, C. (1994). Living standards and mortality in the European Community. *Journal of Epidemiology and Community Health, 48*, 140-145.

Makela, P. (1996). Alcohol consumption and suicide mortality by age among Finnish men, 1950-1991. *Addiction, 91*(1), 101-112.

Maley, B., *Youth Suicide and Youth Unemployment.* http://www.exhibit.com.au/nicholls/nichvol6/vol167.yo.htm.

Mann, J. & Arango, V. (1992). Integration of neurobiology and psychopathology in a unified model of suicidal behaviour. *Journal of Clinical Psychopharmacology, 12*, 2-7.

Marsden, D. & Duff, E. (1975). *Workless.* Harmondsworth: Pelican Books.

Martín, E. (1998). *Producir la juventud.* [Producing Young People] Madrid: Itsmo.

Masschelein, R. & De Witte, H. (1997). Preventieve gezondheidszorg in de arbeidssfeer. [Preventive health care for the labour market]. In *Vlaams Preventiecongres 1997.* (pp. 585-603). Diegem: Kluwer Editorial.

Mean Patterson, L.J. (1997). Long-term unemployment amongst adolescents: A longitudinal study. *Journal of Adolescence, 20*(3), 261-280.

Metha, A., Chen, E., Mulvenon, S., & Dode, I. (1998). A theoretical model of adolescent suicide risk. *Archives of Suicide Research, 4*, 115-133.

Miguélez, F. & Martín, A. (1996). *Paro juvenil y economia sumergida.* [Youth Unemployment and Submerged Economy]. Bellaterra: UAB.

Mingione, E. (1991). Le figure dei disoccupati nel contesto economico-sociale. [The profiles of unemployed in socio-economic system]. In G. Altieri (Ed.), *Tra Nord e Sud.* [Between North and South]. Roma: Ediesse.

Mingione, E. & Pugliese, E. (1995). Modelli occupazionali e disoccupazione giovanile di massa nel Mezzogiorno. [Occupational model and mass youth unemployment in the Southern part of Italy]. In B. Giullari & M. La Rosa (Eds.), *Disoccupazione: perché. Scienze sociali a confronto.* [Unemployment: Why. Social Sciences in Comparison]. Milano: Angeli.

Ministerie (1995). *Het federaal werkgelegenheisbeleid: Evaluatierapport 1995.* [The Federal Employment Policy: Evaluation Report 1995]. Brussel: Ministerie van Tewerkstelling en Arbeid.

Ministerium für Arbeit, Gesundheit und Soziales des Landes Nordrhein-Westfalen (Ed.). (1998). *Landessozialbericht Nordrhein-Westfalen: Arbeitslose, Langzeitarbeitslose und ihre Familie, Bd. 8.* [The Unemployed, the Long-term Unemployed, and their Families]. Bergheim: Druckpunkt Offset.

Moens, G., Haenen, W., & Van de Voorde, H. (1988). Epidemiological aspects of suicide among the young in selected European countries. *Journal of Epidemiology and Community Health, 42*(3), 279-285.

Moesler, T., Pontzen, W., & Rummler, W. (1990). The relationship between suicidal acts and unemployment. In G. Ferrari, M. Bellini, & P. Crepet (Eds.), *Suicidal Behaviour and Risk Factors* (pp. 189-194). Bologna: Monduzzi Editore.

Morrell, S.L., Taylor, R.J., & Kerr, C.B. (1998). Jobless. Unemployment and young people's health. *Medical Journal of Australia,168*(5), 236-240.

Morrell, S., Taylor, R., Quine, S., & Kerr, C. (1993). Suicide and unemployment in Australia 1907-1990. *Social Science & Medicine, 36*(6), 749-756.

Moser, K.A., Goldblatt, P., Fox, J., & Jones, I. (1990). Unemployment and mortality. In P. Goldblatt (Ed.), *Longitudinal Study and Social Organization* (pp. 81-97). London: H.M.S.O.

Mousourou, L. (1985). *Ginekia Ikiaki Apashlisi stin Ellada kai Allou.* [Female Occupation and Family in Greece and Elsewhere]. Athens: Estia, Kollarou et al. Ltd.

Mouzelis, N. (1978). *Modern Greek Society: Sights of underdevelopment* (2nd ed). Athens: Exantas.

Mruck, K. & Mey, G. (1992). *Jugendarbeitslosigkeit und lokale Identität. Ergebnisse einer Befragung Jugendlicher und junger Erwachsener aus den Berliner Bezirken Kreuzberg und Tiergarten.* [Young Persons' Unemployment and Local Identity. Results of a Survey of Adolescents and Young Adults from the Districts Kreuzberg and Tiergarten in Berlin]. Berlin: Technische Universität Berlin.

Nationaal Instituut voor de Statistiek (1997). *Sociale statistieken: Enquête naar de beroepsbevolking 1997.* [Social statistics: Questionnaire Among the Active Population]. Brussel: Nationaal Instituut voor de Statistiek.

O'Brien, G.E. (1986). *Psychology of Work and Unemployment.* Chichester: John Wiley & Sons Ltd.

O'Brien, G.E. & Feather, N.T. (1990). The relative effects of unemployment and quality of employment on the affect, work values and personal control of adolescents. *Journal of Occupational Psychology, 63*, 151-165.

OECD (1994). *The Oecd Job Studies.* Paris: Oecd.

Olaffson, O. & Svensson, P.-G. (1986). Unemployment-related lifestyle changes and health disturbances in adolescents and children in the Western countries. *Social Science and Medicine, 22*(11), 1105-1113.

Opaschowski, H.W. (1976). *Soziale Arbeit mit arbeitslosen Jugendlichen. Street work und Aktionsforschung im Wohnbereich.* [Social Work with Unemployed Young Persons. Street Work and Action Research in the Residential Area]. Opladen: Leske.

Opvoeding en Vrijetijdsbesteding der Jongeren – MJA (Ed.). (s.d.). *Jeugdwerkloosheid: Impakt op de welzijns- en gezondheidstoestand van de jongeren.* [Youth Unemployment: Impact on the Well-Being and Health State of Youngsters]. Brussel: Bulens.

Paci, M. (1996). Disuguaglianza, esclusione e nuova domanda di welfare state. Alcune riflessioni. [Inequality, exclusion and new welfare demand. Some relfections]. In E. Bartocci (Ed.), *Disuguaglianza e stato sociale. Riflessioni sulla crisi del welfare italiano.* [Inequality and Welfare State. Reflections on the Welfare State Crisis in Italy]. Roma: Donzelli.

Papanoutsos, E. (1992). *H krish tou politismou mas* (15th ed.). [The Crisis of our Civilization]. Athens: Fillipoth Editions.

Patton, W. & Noller, P. (1984). Unemployment and youth: A longitudinal study. *Australian Journal of Psychology, 36*, 399-413.

Patton, W. & Noller, P. (1990). Adolescent self-concept: Effects of being employed, unemployed or returning to school. *Australian Journal of Psychology, 42*, 247-259.

Pearlin, L.I. & Lieberman, M.A. (1979). Social sources of emotional distress. In R.-G. Simmons (Ed.), *Research in Community and Mental Health* (pp. 217-248). Greenwich: JAI Press.

Peiró, J.M. & Moret, D. (Eds.). (1987). *Socialización laboral y desempleo juvenil: la transición de la escuela al trabajo.* [Working Socialisation and Youth Unemployment: The Transition from the School to Work]. Valencia: Nau.

Petmesidou, M. (1996). Social protection in Greece: A brief glimpse of a welfare state. *Social Policy and Administration, 30*(4), 200-208.

Pihl, A. & Starrin, B. (1998). Ekonomiska påfrestningar, socialt stöd och ohälsa – En prövning av ekonomi–sociala band modellen. [Financial hardship, social support and ill health – A test of financial-social bond model]. *Socialmedicinsk tidskrift, 75*(6) 297-304.

Pilgrim Trust (1938). *Men without Work.* Cambridge: University Press.

Pissart, F., Poncelet, M., & Voisin, M. (1990). Vivre en chômage: L'installation des jeunes sans emploi dans la vie adulte. [To be unemployed: Integration of young unemployed persons into adulthood]. *Revue française de sociologie, 31*, 573-590.

Platt, S. (1986). Parasuicide and unemployment. *British Journal of Psychiatry, 149*, 401-405.

Platt, S. & Kreitman, N. (1985). Parasuicide and unemployment among men in Edinburgh 1968-1982. *Psychological Medicine, 15*, 113-123.

Platt, S., Micciolo, R., & Tansella, M. (1992). Suicide and unemployment in Italy: A replication study. In P. Crepet, G. Ferrari, S. Platt, & M. Bellini (Eds.), *Suicidal Behaviour in Europe.* London: John Libbey.

Platt, S., Hawton, K., Kreitman, N., Fagg, J., & Foster, J. (1988). Recent clinical and epidemiological trends in parasuicide in Edinburgh and Oxford: A tale of two cities. *Psychological Medicine, 18*, 405-418.

Plaza, R. (1994). *Desempleo y salarios en España.* [Unemployment and Wages in Spain].

Polus, C. & Louckx, F. (1991). Sociale ongelijkheid en gezondheid. [Social inequality and health]. *Tijdschrift voor Sociologie, 12*(3-4), 469-511.

Ponti, A. & Faggiano, F. (1994). La distribuzione sociale dei fattori di rischio di malattia: Il caso del fumo di tabacco. [The social distribution of the illness risk factors: The case of tobacco smoking]. In G. Costa & F. Faggiano (Eds.), *L'equità nella salute in Italia. Rapporto sulle diseguaglianza sociali in sanità.* [Equality in Health in Italy. Report on Social and Sanitary Inequalities]. Milano: Angeli.

Prause, J. & Dooley, D. (1997). Effects of underemployment on school-leavers' self-esteem. *Journal of Adolescence, 20*(3), 243-260.

Pugliese, E. (1993). *Sociologia della disoccupazione.* [Sociology of Unemployment]. Bologna: Il Mulino.

Pugliese, E. (Ed.). (1996). *Una disoccupazione Mediterranea. Giovani e Mercato del Lavoro nel Mezzogiorno e a Napoli.* [A Mediterranean Unemployment. Youth and Labour market in the Southern Part of Italy and in Naples]. Napoli: Libreria Dante & Descartes.

Pritchard, C. (1992). Is there a link between suicide in young men and unemployment? A comparison of the UK with other European Community Countries. *British Journal of Psychiatry, 160*, 750-756.

Pyke, F., Becattini, G., & Sengenberger, W. (Eds.). (1991). *Distretti industriali e cooperazione fra imprese in Italia.* [Industrial Districts and Co-operation Among Enterprises in Italy]. Firenze: Studi e Informazioni – Quaderni 34.

Raes, V., Kerkhofs, E., & Louckx, F. (Eds.). (1993). *Sociale ongelijkheid en verschillen in gezondheid.* [Social Inequality and Differences in the State Health]. Brussel: VUBPRESS.

Ramis-Juan, O. (1984). Desigualtats, pobresa, atur i les implicacions en la salut: Evidència i problemes metodològics a Catalunya. [Inequalities, poverty, unemployment and their health implications: Evidence and methodological problems in Catalonia]. In Institut d'Estudis de la Salut (Ed.), *Atur i salut.* Barcelona: Generalitat de Catalunya.

Rantakeisu, U., Starrin, B., & Hagquist, C. (1997). Unemployment, shame and ill health – an exploratory study. *Scandinavian Journal of Social Welfare, 6*, 13-23.

Rantakeisu, U, Starrin, B., & Hagquist, C. (1999). Financial hardship and shame: a tentative model to understand the social and health effects of unemployment. *British Journal of Social Work, 29*, 877-901.

Regidor, E., De Mateo, S., Gutiérrez-Fisac, J.L., & Rodríguez, C. (1996). Diferencias socioeconómicas en mortalidad en ocho provincias españolas. [Socioeconomic differences in the mortality rates in eight Spanish provinces]. *Medicina Clinica, 106*, 285-289.

Reich, R. (1991). *The Work of the Nations. Preparing Ourselves to the 21th Century Capitalism.* New York: Random House.

Reyneri, E. (1996). *Sociologia del mercato del lavoro.* [Sociology of the Labour Market]. Bologna: Il Mulino.

Reyneri, E. (1997). *Occupati e disoccupati in Italia.* [Employed and Unemployed in Italy]. Bologna: Il Mulino.

Rijksdienst voor Arbeidsvoorziening (1997). *Maandelijks Bulletin december 1997.* Brussel: Rijksdienst voor Arbeidsvoorziening (RVA).

Rijksdienst voor Arbeidsvoorziening (1998). *Maandelijks Bulletin februari 1997.* Brussel: Rijksdienst voor Arbeidsvoorziening (RVA).

Roberts, K. (1984). Problems and initiatives in youth unemployment. *Journal of Community Care, 62*(8), 320-326.

Robinson, A.D. & Duffy, J.C.A. (1989). A comparison of self-injury and self-poisoning from the Regional Poisoning Treatment Centre, Edinburgh. *Acta Psychiatrica Scandinavica, 80*, 272-279.

Rodríguez, E. (1994). Health consequences of unemployment in Barcelona. *European Journal of Public Health, 4*, 245-251.

Rodríguez, A. & García, J.M.A. (1989). Personalidad, valores y expectativas en jóvenes titulados en paro. [Personality, values and expectations in young university degree holders]. In J.R. Torregrosa, J. Bergere, & J.L. Alvaro (Eds.), *Juventud, trabajo y desempleo: Un análisis psicosociológico* (pp. 191-204). Madrid: Ministerio de Trabajo y Seguridad Social.

Roquero, E. (1995). *La inserción a la vida activa.* [The Insertion into Active Life]. Granada: Universidad de Granada.

Rosseel, E. (1988). Werkloosheid, krisis en veranderende arbeidsopvattingen bij jongeren: Een sociaal-psychologische analyse. [Unemployment, crisis and changing thoughts about work among youngsters: A socio-psychological analysis]. In Nationale Vereniging voor Geestelijke Gezondheidszorg v.z.w. Werkloosheid en Geestelijke gezondheidszorg (Report of a Seminar). Gent: Nationale Vereniging voor Geestelijke Gezondheidszorg v.z.w..

Rowley, K.M. & Feather, N.T. (1987). The impact of unemployment in relation to age and length of unemployment. *Journal of Occupational Psychology, 60*, 323-332.

Runeson, B.S. (1992). Youth suicides unknown to psychiatric care providers. *Suicide Life Threat Behaviour, 22*(4), 494-453.

Sand, E., Verhaegen, L., & Meyer, J. (1989). Symptomes dépressifs chez l'adolescent: Prévalence – Recours. [Depressive symptoms among adolescents: Prevalence – Solutions]. *Arch Belg., 47*(1-4), 29-33.

Sarchielli, G. (1995). Approcci psicologici allo studio della disoccupazione. [Sociological approaches to the study of unemployment]. In B. Giullari & M. La Rosa (Eds.), *Disoccupazione: Perché. Scienze sociali a confronto.* [Unemployment: Why. Social Sciences in Comparison]. Milano: Angeli.

Sarchielli, G., Depolo, M. Fraccaroli, F., & Colasanto, M. (1991). *Senza lavoro. Vincoli, strategie e risorse per la costruzione sociale della occupabilità.* [Without work. Ties, Strategies and Resources for the Social Building of Employment]. Bologna: Il Mulino.

Schaufeli, W.B. (1997). Youth unemployment and mental health: Some Dutch findings. *Journal of Adolescence, 20*(3); 281-292.

Scheff, T.J. (1990). Microsociology. Discourse, Emotion, and Social Structure. Chicago: The University of Chicago Press.

Scheff, T.J. (1992). Emotion and Illness: Anger, bypassed shame and heart disease. *Perspectives on Social Problems, 3*, 117-134.

Schelsky, H. (1952). *Arbeitslosigkeit und Berufsnot der Jugend (2 Bd.).* [Unemployment and Job Needs of the Youth]. Köln: Bund-Verlag.

Schindler, H., Wacker, A., & Wetzels, P. (Ed.). (1990). *Familienleben in der Arbeitslosigkeit.* [Family Life During Unemployment]. Heidelberg: Asanger.

Schmidtke, A., Bille-Brahe, U., De Leo, D., Kerkhof, A., Bjerke, T., Crepet, P., Haring, C., Hawton, K., Lonnqvist, J., Michel, K., Pommereau, X., Querejeta, I., Phillipe, I., Salander-Renberg, E., Temesvary, B., Wasserman, D., Fricke, S., Weinacker, B., & Sampaio-Faria, J. G. (1996). Attempted suicide in Europe: Rates, trends and sociodemographic characteristics of suicide attempters during the period 1989-1992. Results from the WHO/EURO Study on Parasuicide. *Acta Psychiatrica Scandinavica, 93,* 327-338.

Schober, K. (1978). Arbeitslose Jugendliche: Belastungen und Reaktionen der Betroffenen. [Unemployed young persons. Burdens and reactions of the affected]. *Mitteilungen aus der Arbeitsmarkt- und Berufsforschung*, 2, 198-215.

Schober, K. (1987). Die soziale und psychische Lage arbeitsloser Jugendlicher. [The social and psychological situation of unemployed young persons]. *Mitteilungen aus der Arbeitsmarkt- und Berufsforschung, 4,* 453-478.

Schwefel, D. (1986). Unemployment, health, and health services in German-speaking countries. *Social Science & Medicine*, 22(4), 409-430.

Seva-Díaz, A. (1982). *Salud mental y desempleo. Aproximación psicopatológica al paro agrícola.* [Mental Health and Unemployment. Psychopathological Approach to Agricultural Unemployment]. Zaragoza: Universidad de Zaragoza.

Shepherd, J. P, Robinson, L., & Levers, B. G. (1990). Roots of urban violence. *Injury, 21*, 139-141.

Siebers, R. & Vonderach, G. (1991). Unterschiedliche lebensgeschichtliche Bewältigungsmuster junger Menschen gegenüber langandauernder Arbeitslosigkeit. [Different biographical patterns of coping of young persons facing long-term unemployment]. *Mitteilungen aus der Arbeitsmarkt- und Berufsforschung, 1*, 193-205.

SINUS (1983). *Die verunsicherte Generation. Jugend und Wertewandel.* [The Uncertain Generation. Adolescents and the Change in Values]. Opladen: Leske+Budrich.

Sissouras, A., Deligianni, Y., Kalomenidis, K., Karokis, A., & Mitropoulos, G. (1995). *Report on the Health Level and the Use of Health Services in the City of Patras.* University of Patras.

Sissouras, A., Kalokairinos, T., Kalomenidis, K., Karokis, A., & Mitropoulos, G. (1997). *H Taftotita Igias tis Patras.* [Health Identity of the City of Patras]. Typorama: Municipality of Patras.

Snyder, M. L. (1992). Unemployment and suicide in Northern Ireland. *Psychological Reports, 70*, 1116-1118.

Social Rapport 1997 (1997). [Social Report 1997]. Stockholm: Socialstyrelsen.

Sokou, K. (1987). Unemployment in a developing country: The case of Greece. In D. Schwefel, P.-G. Svensson, & H. F. K. Zöllner (Eds.), *Unemployment, Social Vulnerability and Health* (pp. 118-128). Springer-Verlag.

Sokou, K. (1988). Gineka ke Igia: H epidrasi tis ergasias, ikiakis apasholisis ke anergias stin igia tis ginekas. [Women and Health: The impact of work, domestic occupation and unemployment on women's health]. *Kinoniki ergasia, 9 & 10*, 13-19.

Sokou, K. (1989). Careers in Chronic Unemployment in Greece: Selected case studies. In B. Starrin, P.-G. Svensson, & H. Wintersberger (Eds.), *Unemployment, Poverty and Quality of Working Life* (pp. 115-134). Sigma Edition (WHO).

SOU 1994:3 (1994). *Ungdomars välfärd och värderingar.* [The Welfare and Values of the Youths]. Stockholm: Rapport till Barn- och ungdomsdelegationen och Generationsutredningen.

Spicker, P. (1984). *Stigma and Social Welfare.* London. Canberra: Croom Helm.

Spruit, I. P. (1983). *Unemployment, Employment and Health.* Leiden: Rijksuniversteit te Leiden Instituut voor Sociale Geneeskunde.

Spruit, I. P. & Svensson, P.-G. (1987). Young and unemployed: Special problems. In D. Schwefel & P.-G. Svensson, (Eds.), *Unemployment, Social Vulnerability, and Health in Europe* (pp. 196-210). Springer: Berlin.

Stack, S. (1991). The effect of religiosity on suicide in Sweden. *Journal of Scientific Study Religion, 30*(4), 462-468.

Ståhl, R. (1986). *Att vara rustad och att bli drabbad.* [Being Armed and Being Defeated]. Örebro: Högskolan i Örebro.

Starrin, B. & Jönsson, L.R. (1998). Ekonomisk påfrestning, skamgörande erfarenheter och ohälsa under arbetslöshet – En prövning av ekonomi-skam modellen. [Financial hardship, shaming experiences and ill health – A test of finances–shame model]. *Arbetsmarknad & Arbetsliv, 4*(2), 91-107.

Starrin, B., Rantakeisu, U., & Hagquist, C. (1996). Om arbetslöshetens ekonomi och skam. [Finances and shame during unemployment]. *Socialvetenskaplig Tidskrift, 1-2*, 91-114.

Stronks, K., van de Mheen, D., & Mackenbach, J. (1993). Achtergronden van sociaal-economische gezondheidsverschillen. Een overzicht van de literatuur en een onderzoeksmodel. [Backgrounds for socio-economic health differences. An overview of the literature and a research model]. In V. Raes, E. Kerkhofs, & F. Louckx (Eds.), *Sociale ongelijkheid en verschillen in gezondheid.* Brussel: VUBPRESS.

Stuurgroep Strategisch Arbeidsmarkt Onderzoek & Steunpunt Werkgelegenheid Arbeid en Vorming (1997). *De arbeidsmarkt in Vlaanderen: Jaarboek* 1997. [The Labour Market in Flanders: Yearbook 1997]. Leuven: Acco.

Svensson, P.-G., Westcott, G., & Zöllner, H.F.K. (Eds.). (1985). *Health Policy Implications of Unemployment.* Denmark: World Health Organization.

Tasco, C., Forastiere, F., Dell'Orco, V., Brancato, G., & Perucci, C.A. (1994). Le differenze sociali nella mortalità a Roma. [The social differences in the mortality in Rome]. In G. Costa & F.

Faggiano (Eds.), *L'equità nella salute in Italia. Rapporto sulle diseguaglianza sociali in sanità.* [Equality in Health in Italy. Report on Social and Sanitary Inequalities]. Milano: Angeli.
Tegenbos, G. (1998). Wie in Wallonië werk wil, moet er zelf voor zorgen. [Everyone who wants work in Wallonia, has to do it himself]. *Het Nieuwsblad, 24-8-1998*, 1.
Therborn, G. (1986). *Why Some People are more Unemployed than Others.* New York: Verso.
Tiggemann, M. & Winefield, A.H. (1984). The effects of employment on the mood, self-esteem, locus of control and depressive affect of school-leavers. *Journal of Occupational Psychology, 57*, 33-42.
Traisnel, V. (1997). *Werkloosheid bij jongeren.* [Unemployment among Youngsters]. (niet-gepubliceerde licenciaatsverhandeling). Brussel: Economische Hogeschool Sint-Aloysius.
Triandis, H.C., Feldman, J.M., Weldon, D.E., & Harvey, W.M. (1975). Ecosystem distrust and the hard to employ. *Journal of Applied Psychology, 60*(1), 44-56
Trigilia, C. (1992). *Sviluppo senza autonomia.* [Development without Autonomy]. Bologna: Il Mulino.
Torregrosa, J. R. (1982). Prólogo. In M. Jahoda (Ed.), *Empleo y desempleo: un análisis psicosociológico.* [Employment and Unemployment: A Psycho-sociological Analysis]. Madrid: Morata.
Torregrosa, J.R., Bergere, J., & Alvaro J.L. (Eds.). (1989). *Juventud, trabajo y desempleo: un análisis psicosociológico.* [Youth, Work and Unemploment: A Psycho-sociological Analysis]. Madrid: Ministerio de Trabajo y Seguridad Social.
Trovato, F. A. (1992). Durkheimian analysis of youth suicide: Canada, 1971 and 1981. *Suicide Life Threat Behaviour,* 22(4), 413-427.
Tselepis, C. & Agrafiotis, D. (1997). Sexoualikotita ke kinonikes anaparastasis. H periptosi ton neon anergon. [Sexuality and social representations. The case of young unemployed]. *Arheia Aids, 5*(2), 61-65.
Ullah, P., Banks, M.H., & Warr, P.B. (1985). Social support, social pressures and psychological distress during unemployment. *Psychological Medicine, 15*, 283-295.
Underlid K. (1992). *Arbeidslaus.* [Unemployment]. Oslo: Det Norske Samlaget.
Ungdomsstyrelsen (1996). *Krokig väg till vuxwn*, del 1. [The Winding Road to Adulthood, Part 1]. Stockholm: The Swedish National Board of Youth Affairs.
Van Heeringen, K. (1993). *Epidemiological Aspects of Attempted Suicide* (doctoral thesis). Gent: University Hospital Gent, Department of Psychiatry.
Van Heeringen, K. & Jannes, C. (1993). The association between employment status and attempted suicide: A case-control study in Gent. *Archives of Public Health, 51*, 303-316.
Vanheerswynghels, A. (Ed.). (s.d.). *Chômage des jeunes, délinquance juvenile, environnement urbain: Belgique.* [Youth Unemployment, Juvenile Offending and Urban Environment: Belgium]. Bruxelles: Comité pour l'étude des problèmes de l'Emploi et du Chômage (C.E.P.E.C.).
Van Loon, F., Pauwels, K., & Van Humskerke, H. (1982). *Werkloosheid en Gezin: Een onderzoek naar de gevolgen van werkloosheid.* [Unemployment and the Family: A Research on the Consequences of Unemployment]. Antwerpen/Amsterdam: De Sikkel-De Nederlandsche Boekhandel.
Van Oyen, H. & Tafforeau, J. (1993). Een gezondheidsenquête in België: een noodzakelijkheid ? [A health questionnaire in Belgium: a necessity?]. In V. Raes, E. Kerkhofs, & F. Louckx (Eds.), *Sociale ongelijkheid en verschillen in gezondheid.* Brussel: VUBPRESS.
Verhaegen, L., Deykin, E., & Sand, E. (1994). Depressive symptoms and employment status among Belgian adolescents. *Revue Epidémiologique et Santé Publique, 42*, 119-127.
Vetrone, G., Crepet, P., Costa, M., Piazzi, A., Di Tommaso, L., Ferrara, R., Petrangeli L., & Frighi, L. (1992). Aspetti psicologici della disoccupazione giovanile nella provincia di Siena. Studio trasversale. [Psychological aspects of youth unemployment in the province of Siena. A transversal study]. *Difesa Sociale, 5*, 71-82.
Vettenburg, N., Walgrave, L., & Van Kerckvoorde, J. (1984). *Jeugdwerkloosheid, delinquentie en maatschappelijke kwetsbaarheid: Een theoretisch en empirisch onderzoek naar de veron-*

derstelde band tussen werkloosheid en delinquentie bij 17-19 jarigen. [Youth Unemployment, Delinquence and Social Vulnerability]. Antwerpen: Kluwer.

Vilrokx, J. (1983). Werkloosheid als sociaal fenomeen. [Unemployment as a social phenomenon]. In E. Scholliers & P. Scholliers (Eds.), *Werktijd en werktijdverkorting* (pp. 154-162). Brussel: Vrije Universiteit Brussel.

Viney, L. (1983). Psychological reactions of young people to unemployment. *Youth and Society, 14*(4), 457-474.

Vonderach, G., Siebers, R., & Barr, U. (1992). *Arbeitslosigkeit und Lebensgeschichte: Eine empirische Untersuchung unter jungen Langzeitarbeitslosen.* [Unemployment and Biography. An Empirical Survey of Long-term Unemployed Young Persons]. Opladen: Leske + Budrich.

Vranken, J., Geldof, D., & Van Menxel, G. (1997). *Armoede en Socaile uitsluiting: Jaarboek 1997* [Poverty and Social Exclusion: Yearbook 1997]. Leuven: Acco.

Vuylsteek, K. (1984). Sociale ongelijkheid tegenover ziekte en dood. [Social inequality concerning disease and death]. *Tijdschrift voor Geneeskunde, 40*(5), 291-299.

Wacker, A. (1979). Jugendarbeitslosigkeit und Aggression. [Youth unemployment and aggression]. In M. Furian (Ed.), *"Du tust mir weh ...". Aggressionen im Leben der Kinder und Jugendlichen.* ['You are hurting me ...'. Aggressions in the Lives of Children and Adolescents] (pp. 163-179). Stuttgart: Bonz.

Wacker, A. (1983). Differentielle Verarbeitungsformen von Arbeitslosigkeit – Anmerkungen zur aktuellen Diskussion in der Arbeitslosenforschung. [Differential forms of coping with unemployment – Remarks on the recent discussion on research on unemployment]. *Prokla, 53*, 77-88.

Wacker, A. (1985). Ansätze, Probleme und Perspektiven der psychologischen Arbeitslosenforschung. [Approaches, problems, and perspectives of psychological unemployment research]. In T. Kieselbach & A. Wacker (Eds.), *Individuelle und gesellschaftliche Kosten der Massenarbeitslosigkeit – Psychologische Theorie und Praxis.* [The Society's and the Individual's Costs of Mass Unemployment – Psychological Theory and Practice] (pp. 23-39). Weinheim: Deutscher Studien Verlag.

Wadel, C. (1973). *Now, Whose Fault Is That! – The Struggle for Self-Esteem In the Face of Chronic Unemployment.* Memorial University of Newfoundland. Institute of Social and Economic Research, University of Toronto Press.

Warr, P.B. (1984). Job loss, unemployment and psychological well-being. In V. Allen & E. Vliert (Eds.), *Role Transitions* (pp. 263-286). New York: Plenum.

Warr, P.B. (1987). *Work, Unemployment and Mental Health.* Oxford: Oxford University Press.

Warr, P.B., Banks, M.H., & Ullah, P. (1985). The experience of unemployment among black and white urban teenagers. *British Journal of Psychology, 76*, 75-87.

Wets, J. & De Witte, H. (1997). *Van onsuccesvolle zoeker naar succesvolle vinder? Een onderzoek naar het psycho-sociaal profiel van de werklozen in de Duitstalige Gemeenschap.* [From Unsuccessful Searcher to Successful Finder? A Research on the Psychosocial Profile of Unemployed Persons in the German-Speaking Community]. Leuven: Katholieke Universiteit Leuven, Hoger Instituut voor de Arbeid.

Wilhelm-Reiss, M. (1980). *Psychische Veränderungen bei Jugendlichen ohne Arbeit. Eine empirische Studie zu den Folgewirkungen der Arbeitslosigkeit.* [Psychological Changes in Adolescents Without Work. An Empirical Survey of the Consequences of Unemployment]. Weinheim: Beltz.

Willis, P. (1986). Unemployment: The final inequality. *British Journal of Sociology and Education, 7*(2), 155-169.

Winefield, A.H. (1995). Unemployment: Its psychological costs. In C.L. Cooper & I. Robertson (Eds.), *International Review of Industrial and Organizational Psychology* (pp. 169-212). London: Wiley.

Winefield, A.H. (1997). Introduction to the psychological effects of youth unemployment. International perspectives. *Journal of Adolescence, 20*(3), 237-241.

Winefield, A.H. & Tiggemann, M. (1985). Psychological correlates of employment and unemployment: Effects, predisposing factors and sex differences. *Journal of Occupational Psychology, 58*, 229-242.
Winefield, A.H., Tiggemann, M., & Goldney, R.D. (1988). Psychological concomitants of satisfactory employment and unemployment in young people. *Social Psychiatry and Psychiatric Epidemiology, 23*, 149-157.
Winefield, A.H., Tiggemann, M., Winefield, H.R., & Goldney, R.D. (1993). *Growing up with Unemployment. A Longitudinal Study of its Psychological Impact.* London: Routledge.
Wolfinger, C. (1997). Jugendarbeitslosigkeit an den Übergängen zwischen Bildungs- und Beschäftigungssystem. [Youth unemployment at the transition between educational and employment system]. In G. Klein & H. Strasser (Ed.), *Schwer vermittelbar – Zur Theorie und Empirie der Langzeitarbeitslosigkeit.* [Difficult to Place – About the Theory and Empiricism of Long-term Unemployment] (pp. 149-178). Opladen: Westdeutscher Verlag.

About the authors

Baltiérrez, Josep (1946), is a sociologist and is currently a researcher of the Department of Sociology of the Autonomous University of Barcelona. He has been involved in research with several social movements. He has also worked as a sociologist in unions and political parties.

Bayetakou, Demetra (1971), is a social scientist trained in unemployment research. She has worked as an assistant in European projects related to school health promotion in the Health Promoting Schools Sector at the Institute of Child Health. She is an active member of the Greek Network of Health Promoting Schools.

Beelmann, Gert (1971), is a social scientist (received his degree in 1996) and a doctoral student in Psychology at the Institute for Psychology of Work, Unemployment and Health (IPG) at the University of Bremen. His main area of research is health psychology and unemployment. *Publications:* Beelmann, G. & Kieselbach, T. (1997). Subjektive Theorien von Gesundheit und Krankheit bei Jugendlichen im Stadt-Land-Vergleich. [Subjective theories on health and illness among adolescents: An urban-rural comparison]. *Zeitschrift für Gesundheitspsychologie*, *5*(4), 258-271; Kieselbach, T. & Beelmann, G. (1999). Jugendarbeitslosigkeit. [Youth unemployment]. In G. Wenninger (Hrsg.), *Lexikon der Psychologie.* [Encyclopedia of Psychology]. Stuttgart: Spektrum der Wissenschaft; Wacker, A., Beelmann, G., & Beyer, O. (1999). *Erhebungsinstrumente in der empirischen Arbeitslosenforschung. Ein Fragen- und Skalenhandbuch.* [Survey instruments in empirical unemployment research. A handbook of questionnaires and scales]. Institute for Psychology of Hanover University.

Borghi, Vando (1965), is a social scientist and researcher at the Department of Sociology, University of Bologna and a member of the International Centre for Documentation and Sociological Studies on Labour Issues (C.I.Do.S.Pe.L.). He is also editorial secretary of the journal "Sociologia del Lavoro" [Sociology of Labour]. His main interests focus on transformations of work and organization, labour market changes, and on broader economic sociology issues. Recently, he co-edited (with Michele La Rosa) a monographic section of the "International Review of Sociology" on *Weak bands and the labour market* (1998). *Publications:* Borghi, V. (1998). *Il lavoro tra economia e* *società* [Labour between Economy and Society]. Milano: Angeli; Borghi, V. (1998). *Progettazione come impresa sociale.* [Planning as Social Enterprise]. Milano: Angeli.

Christofi, Katerina (1970), is a social scientist specialised in social exclusion. She has worked as a research assistant in projects of the Greek National Centre of Social Research.

Erdwien, Birgitt (1968), is a psychologist (received her degree in 1998), and she worked at the Institute for Psychology of Work, Unemployment and Health (IPG), University of Bremen, as a trainee during the first phase of the YUSEDER project. Her diploma thesis was a pre-study to Workpackage 2 of YUSEDER in which the interview schedule for the qualitative interviews with unemployed youths was tested.

Espluga, Josep (1964), has a degree in both sociology and industrial relations. He is currently teaching at the Department of Sociology of the Autonomous University of Barcelona. His maininvolvement is in the area of Sociology of Health and Environment, with a special focus on occupational health issues and the social perception of risk. He also has been working on sociolinguistic topics. *Publications*: Espluga, J. & Capdevila, A. (1995). *Franja, frontera i llengua. Conflictes d'identitat en els pobles d'Aragó de parla catalana.* [Fringe, Frontier and Language. Identity conflicts among the Catalan-speaking People from Aragon]. Lleida, Pagès; Espluga, J. (1996). *Actos inseguros en el trabajo. Guía de intervención.* [Unsafe Acts at Workplace. Intervention Guide]. NTP 415. Barcelona, Instituto Nacional de Seguridad e Higiene en el Trabajo; Thompson, A., Espluga, J., & Alonso, M. (1999). *Participació ciutadana en la provisió de serveis de salut.* [Citizen Participation in the Provision of Health Services]. Barcelona, Servei Català de la Salut;

Forsberg, Erik (1941), is a trained social worker and lecturer at the Centre for Public Health Research, Karlstad University, Sweden. His main research area is the living conditions of disadvantaged groups. His actual research focus includes topics of social allowance and unemployment, health and social exclusion. *Publications:* Forsberg, E. (1992). The long-term mentally ill. In P.-G. Svensson & B. Starrin (Eds.), *Health policy development for disadvantaged groups.* Oslo: Scandinavian University Press; Forsberg, E. & Starrin, B. (1993). Deinstitutionalization and the 'long-term mentally ill' - a Swedish case study. *European Journal of Public Health, 3*(2), 137-140; Forsberg, E. (1993). Ill Health and Social Conditions amongst Migrants and Refugees - the Case of Sweden. *Innovation in Social Sciences Research, 6*(1), 75-83.

Kalander-Blomqvist, Marina (1956), has a degree in sociology and working life science. She is research assistant at the Centre for Public Health Research, Karlstad University, Sweden. Her research interest lies in the area of social allowance and unemployment, health and social exclusion.

Kieselbach, Thomas (1944), responsible for the international coordination and the project management of the YUSEDER research project, is a psychologist and head of the Institute for Psychology of Work, Unemployment and Health (IPG) at the University of Bremen. His focus is in the area of work psychology and health psychology. From 1993-1998 he was a professor for health psychology at the University of Hannover. His research areas are unemployment and health, evaluation of interventions, community psychology, and organizational responsibility in employee dismissals. During the 1980´s he served as an adviser for the WHO/EURO'S programme „Social

Equity and Health". He participates in several international research projects (EU-DGXII, DG V). He has published 150 articles and edited 15 books and is editor of the book series „Psychology of Social Inequality. *Publications:* Kieselbach, T. & Wacker, A. (Eds.). (1991, 2nd ed. 1995). *Bewältigung von Arbeitslosigkeit im sozialen Kontext - Programme, Initiativen, Evaluationen.* [Coping With Unemployment in a Social Context - Programmes, Initiatives, Evaluations] (Psychology of Social Inequality, Vol. 2). Weinheim: Deutscher Studien Verlag; Kieselbach, T. & Voigt, P. (Eds.). (1992, 2nd ed. 1993). *Systemumbruch, Arbeitslosigkeit und individuelle Bewältigung in der Ex-DDR.* [System Transformation, Unemployment, and Individual Coping in the Ex-GDR]. (Psychology of Social Inequality, Vol. 4). Weinheim: Deutscher Studien Verlag; Kieselbach, T. (Ed.). (1997). Job loss, unemployment, and social injustices [Special issue]. *Social Justice Research, 10*(2), 111-265.

La Rosa, Michele (1937), national coordinator of the Italian YUSEDER research group, is a professor of work and industrial sociology at the Faculty of Political Sciences and chairman of the Department of Sociology at Bologna University. He is also chairman of the "International Centre for Documentation and Sociological Studies on Labour Issues" (C.I.Do.S.Pe.L.). Over the past years his research has focussed on transformations of work, working time and quality of work, unemployment (special focus on young people), precariousness, and socially weak groups on the labour market (in regard to social exclusion). He is the founding director of the journal "Sociologia del Lavoro". Currently he is conducting a national research project on "Weak bands and work policies" and an international research project on "Health, Safety, and Quality of Work" in cooperation with the Universities of Valencia, Lisbon, and Paris. *Publications:* La Rosa, M. & Kieselbach, T. (Eds.). (1999). *Disoccupazione giovanile ed esclusione sociale.* [Youth Unemployment and Social Exclusion]. Milano: Angeli; La Rosa, M. & Stanzani, F. (Eds.). (1999). *Sicurezza, prevenzione e qualità del lavoro.* [Safety, Prevention, and Quality of Work]. Milano: Angeli.

Lemkow, Louis (1947), national coordinator of the Spanish YUSEDER research group, is a sociologist, professor of sociology and Vice-Rector of the Autonomous University of Barcelona. His research areas are social inequity and health, submerged economy, social exclusion, and social policies, with a special focus on environmental and technological risk perception and sociology of health. He has cooperated closely with the Regional Office of WHO/Europe for research in the area of inequalities and health. *Publications:* Lemkow, L. & Miguelez, F. (1990). The Submerged Economy, Precarious Employment and Flexibilization. In A. Enander, B. Gustavsson, J. Ch. Karlsson, & B. Starrin (Eds.), *Work and Welfare.* Karlstad: University of Karlstad; Lemkow, L. (1995). Identification and assessment of occupational health and safety strategies in Spain. In European Foundation for the Improvement of Living and Working Conditions (Ed.), *Dublin. Working Paper Series.* Dublin: Author; Lemkow, L. (1996). Spain. In D. Walters (Ed.), *The identification and assessment of occupational health and safety strategies in Europe.* Dublin: European Foundation for the Improvement of Living and Working Conditions.

Papantoniou, Valentine (1971), is a social scientist specialised in European social policy. She has participated as an assistant and evaluator in projects related to social exclusion and social policy and has cooperated with a Greek weekly economic journal.

Publications: Papantoniou, V. (1998a). Immigrants speak for their working conditions. *Oikonomikos Tahydromos Magazine*, Issue 25 (2302); Papantoniou, V. (1998b). The future of labour and clandestine immigrants. *Oikonomikos Tahydromos Magazine*, Issue 24 (2301).

Rantakeisu, Ulla (1966), is a Ph.D. student in social work at the University of Gothenburg and lecturer at the Centre for Public Health Research, Karlstad University, Sweden. Her main area of research is the living conditions of disadvantaged groups with a particular focus on the social and health consequences of unemployment. She has also conducted research on the phenomenon of violence aimed at ethnic minorities and immigrants. *Publications:* Rantakeisu, U., Starrin, B., & Hagquist, C. (1997). Unemployment, shaming and ill health. *Scandinavian Journal of Social Welfare*, *6*, 13-23; Rantakeisu, U., Starrin, B., & Hagquist, C. (1997). Unemployment – A double burden and a public issue. *Social Justice Research*, *10*(2), 153-173; Rantakeisu, U., Starrin, B., & Hagquist, C. (1999). Financial hardship and shame – A tentative model to understand the social and health effects of unemployment. *British Journal of Social Work*, *29*, 877-901.

Sokou, Katerina (1947), national coordinator of the Greek YUSEDER research group, is a health sociologist and director of the Health Promoting School Sector at the Institute of Child Health in Athens as well as the president of the Greek Network of Health Promoting Schools. Since 1974 she has been working as a researcher and project coordinator at the Institute of Child Health. She teaches health sociology at the National School of Public Health, Harokopeios School of Home Economics, and at the Medical School of Crete. She is a member of Ministerial Committees on Health Issues. Since 1983, she has been an advisor to the WHO/EURO participating in projects on health inequalities, unemployment, and health promotion. Since 1992, she has been the national coordinator of the European Network of Health Promoting Schools. In addition, since 1990, K. Sokou has coordinated and participated in several European projects dealing with the health of young people, substance abuse, school health promotion, mental health of young people, unemployment, social exclusion, and violence. *Publications:* Sokou, K. (1987). Unemployment in a Developing Country: The Case of Greece. In D. Schwefel, P.-G. Svensson, & H. Zoellner (Eds.), *Unemployment, Social Vulnerability, and Health in Europe.* (pp. 118-128) Springer; Sokou, K. (1989). Careers in Chronic Unemployment in Greece: Selected Case Studies. In B. Starrin, P.-G. Svensson, & H. Wintersberger (Eds.), *Unemployment, Poverty and Quality of Working Life. Some European Experiences* (pp. 115-134) Edition Sigma; Sokou, K. (1994). *A Guide for Health Education and Health Promotion.* Ellinika: Grammata Publ.

Starrin, Bengt (1947), national coordinator of the Swedish YUSEDER research group, is a professor of social work at Karlstad University, Centre for Public Health Research, Sweden. His main areas of research include economic stress, unemployment, qualitative methods, and social mobilisation. In the 1980's he was strongly involved in the WHO programme on unemployment and health. *Publications:* Starrin, B. & Svensson, P.-G. (1992): Gesundheit und soziale Ungleichheit – über Klasse, Armut und Krankheit. [Health and Social Inequality - About class, poverty, and illness] *Kölner Zeitschrift für Soziologie und Sozialpsychologie*, *32*, 403-420; Starrin, B., Rantakeisu, U., & Hagquist, C. (1997). In the wake of the recession – economic hardship, shame, and social erosion.

Scandinavian Journal of Work and Environment, 23, 47-54; Starrin, B. & Svensson, R. (Eds.). (1998) *Sverige efter välfärdskrisen - mellan hot och hopp.* [Sweden after the welfare crisis - between threats and hopes]. Umeå: Borea.

Stitzel, Andrea (1968), is a psychologist (she received her degree in 1997) and was project manager of YUSEDER until September 1999. Her main interest has been workplace health promotion. As a technical advisor for the World Health Organization (WHO), she was responsible for the development of a WHO project on Health and Work. *Publications:* Stitzel, A. & Järvisalo, J. (1997). Jakarta Summary on Healthy Workplaces. *Euronews, V*(3), 7-9; Stitzel, A. (1997). *WHO's global Healthy Work Approach.* Geneva: World Health Organization; Stitzel, A., Michel, A., & Röhrle, B. (1999). "Psychological Sense of Community" – Zur Entwicklung eines deutschsprachigen Meßinstruments. ["The Psychological Sense of Community" – development of a German measurement instrument]. *Gemeindepsychologischer Rundbrief*, 1/99.

Vanderplasschen, Wouter (1974), is an assistant at the University of Gent, Department of Orthopedagogics; before this he was at the Unit for Suicide Research at the same university where he worked in the field of suicide research and substance abuse treatment in the region of Gent *Publications:* Van Heeringen, K. & Vanderplasschen, W. (1999). Unemployment and suicidal behaviour in perspective. *International Archives of Occupational and Environmental Health, 72* (Suppl), 43-45; Broekaert, E., Vanderplasschen, W. & Soyez, V. (Eds.). (1999). *Proceedings of the International Symposium on Substance Abuse Treatment and Special Target Groups: Community as a Method.* Gent: University of Gent, Department of Orthopedagogics; Vanderplasschen, W. (1999). Substance abusing Parents, their Children and the Therapeutic Community. In Broekaert, E., Vanderplasschen, W., & Soyez, V. (Eds.), *Proceedings of the International Symposium on Substance Abuse Treatment and Special Target Groups: Community as a method.* Gent: University of Gent, Department of Orthopedagogics.

Van Heeringen, Kees (1955), national coordinator of the Belgian YUSEDER research group, is a professor of psychiatry, Chef de Clinique of the Department of Psychiatry - University Hospital Gent, and director of the Unit for Suicide Research at the University of Gent. His main interests are in the area of emergency psychiatry, training and teaching, and research on the epidemiology of psychological and biological causes of suicidal behaviour. He has been involved in several research programmes at national and international levels, including the European Commission and WHO, and has been involved in the development of a project for suicide prevention measures in secondary schools. He has also been involved in a suicide prevention programme entitled "Reaching Young Europe". He is a member of the board of several public health and mental health organisations and has published over 70 papers and chapters in books and is the editor of four books. *Publications*: Van Heeringen K., Buylaert, W., Jannes, C., Henderick, H., De Bacquer, D., & Van Remoortel, J. (1995). The management of non-compliance with outpatient aftercare in attempted suicide patients: a controlled intervention study. *Psychological Medicine, 25*, 963-970; Hawton, K. & Van Heeringen, K. (in print). *The International Handbook of Suicide and Attempted Suicide.* Chichester: Wiley (to be published in February 2000); Van Heeringen, K. & De Volder, V. (in print). *Trends in attempted suicide in adolescents and young adults in Gent, 1986-1995.* Archives of Suicide Research.

GPSR Compliance

The European Union's (EU) General Product Safety Regulation (GPSR) is a set of rules that requires consumer products to be safe and our obligations to ensure this.

If you have any concerns about our products, you can contact us on ProductSafety@springernature.com

In case Publisher is established outside the EU, the EU authorized representative is:

Springer Nature Customer Service Center GmbH
Europaplatz 3
69115 Heidelberg, Germany

Batch number: 10726298

Printed by Printforce, the Netherlands